Electronic Design Interchange Format

Notice

EIA Engineering Standards and Publications are designed to serve the public interest through eliminating misunderstanding between manufacturers and purchasers, facilitating interchangeability and improvements of products, and assisting the purchaser in selecting and obtaining with minimum delay the proper product for his particular need. Existence of such Standards and Publications shall not in any respect preclude any member or non-member of EIA from manufacturing or selling products not conforming to such Standards and Publications, nor shall the existence of such Standards and Publications preclude their voluntary use by those other than EIA members, whether the standard is to be used either domestically or internationally.

Recommended Standards and Publications are adopted by EIA without regard to whether or not their adoption may involve patents on articles, materials, or processes. By such action, EIA does not assume any liability to any patent owner, nor does it assume any obligation whatever to parties adopting the Recommended Standard or Publication.

This EIA Standard is considered to have International Standardization implication, but the International Electrotechnical Commission activity has not progressed to the point where a valid comparison between the EIA Standard and the IEC document can be made.

This standard does not purport to address all safety problems associated with its use or all applicable regulatory requirements. It is the responsibility of the user of this Standard to establish appropriate safety and health practices and to determine the applicability of regulatory limitations before its use.

The Electronic Industries Association (EIA) and the EDIF Committee do not possess full access to the data concerning the uses and applications for which someone may use the information contained within this document. Therefore, no responsibility is assumed by the EIA or EDIF Committee for the application of any design, nor for any infringements of patents or rights of others which may result from the use of this document. A user of EDIF assumes the risk that EDIF may be unsuitable for the user's purposes. The EIA and EDIF Committee reserve the right to change or amend this document at any time.

EDIF

Electronic Design

Interchange Format

Version 2 0 0

Edited by

Paul Stanford and Paul Mancuso

1989
Electronic Industries Association
EDIF Steering Committee

Published by
ELECTRONIC INDUSTRIES ASSOCIATION
Engineering Department
2001 Pennsylvania Ave., N.W.
Washington, D.C. 20006

Principal Editor: Paul Stanford
Assistant Editor: Paul Mancuso

ISBN: 0-7908-0000-4

Library of Congress Catalog Number: 87-81322

Price: $60.00 (student price: $40.00)

Second Edition 1990

Preface to the Second Edition

This edition of the EDIF Reference Manual incorporates various editorial corrections to the document but does not represent any change to the format itself.

Most of the corrections and clarifications are the result of Technical Committee replies to user questions. Many are of a simple typographical nature within the text or examples of the reference section. An appendix has also been added which summarizes the restrictions on *interface* and *contents* for each view type.

The following corrections and additions have been made since the first edition. Times are non-negative in *after, cycle,* and *loadDelay*. The expansion of arcs in *cornerType* and *endType* is explained. The temporary nature of *figureGroupOverride* is explained. Global port references in *globalPortRef* and *joined* are clarified. References within *instanceGroup* must be within the same view. Symbolic constants may not be aliased in *keywordAlias* and *keywordNameRef*. The contextual restrictions on *logicOneof* within *logicInput* and *logicWaveform* have been specified. Array sizes must match in *logicOneof* and *match*. Clarification of tree structure restrictions for *mustJoin, nonPermutable, permutable,* and *weakJoined* are given. The nature of object grouping taken together in *netGroup* and *portGroup* is given. The restrictions on *keywordDisplay* for *protectionFrame* and *symbol* are given. Clarification for the EDIF level restrictions within *parameterAssign* and *valueRef* are given.

There are also corrections to examples in *after, designator, difference, figure, follow, instanceMap, netMap, nonPermutable, parameterAssign, portGroup, portMap, string, userData, viewList, visible* and *when*.

Rewording for clarity has been done in *cell, enclosureDistance, figureGroupNameDef, intraFigureGroupSpacing, overhangDistance, portNameDef* and *transform*.

Typographical errors have been removed in *cellType, contents, cornerType, edif, follow, interface, iterate, joined, name, nameDef, netBackAnnotate, offPageConnector, portImplementation, property, protectionFrame, then, variable* and *viewType*.

Dallas, 1989   *Paul Stanford*

Foreward

This document is the authoritative reference document for EDIF Version 2 0 0. It defines the syntax and semantic content of every EDIF construct. It should be taken as correct when conflict or contradiction is found elsewhere. While great care has been taken to ensure accuracy and internal consistency, errors or ambiguous interpretations are always possible; if any such problems are noted the user is urged to contact the EDIF Users' Group at the following address:

EDIF Users' Group
P.O. Box 25542
Tempe, Arizona 85285-5542, USA

It is not expected that a new user of EDIF will use this document alone to gain an understanding of EDIF, nor to learn the correct application of EDIF. For this purpose an EDIF user guide and several EDIF style guides are planned which will further explain the overall structure of EDIF and the application of EDIF to specific areas of technology.

The reader is cautioned to exercise care in creating an EDIF file. Under no circumstances should syntax be guessed or invented to solve a problem or to be used as a shortcut.

In tests using previous versions of EDIF, some of the more common errors found were: (1) use of floating point numbers such as 100.000; (2) improper keyword abbreviations, i.e. use of keywords that were not given keyword definitions; (3) use of human-readable object names such as CMOS_Library to carry semantic weight in the EDIF file; and (4) missing EDIF Level and EDIF Version information. In each case the reader of the information is forced to guess at the meaning or interpretation or forced to write some form of special software just to read this particular file.

This manual is divided into the following sections:

- Introduction. The information within this section provides an overview of EDIF basics.

- Reference. This section describes in detail the constructs of all levels of EDIF. Once the reader is familiar with EDIF, this section may be used as a basic reference source.

- Grammar. This section describes the grammar of EDIF. It may be used by experienced EDIF programmers for initial coding of a scanner and parser, and for quick reference while developing translators.

For EDIF, upward compatibility is interpreted to mean that software which is designed to read a future EDIF version (e.g. a future EDIF Version 3 0 0) will also be able to read and correctly interpret a file which was written by software designed for an older EDIF version (such as EDIF Version 2 0 0). This capability requires compatibility at three levels of interpretation: the lexical level, the syntactic level, and the semantic level.

The most basic level of compatibility - semantic compatibility - already exists between EDIF Versions 1 0 0, 1 1 0 and the current version of EDIF, since the underlying data models of the earlier EDIF versions have been retained in the current version. Hence, anything which was expressible with the earlier EDIF versions is still expressible using EDIF Version 2 0 0. The EDIF technical contributors and reviewers considered carefully the requirements for upward compatibility at all three of these levels while preparing this version of EDIF. Everything which is included in EDIF Version 2 0 0 is expected to be completely upward compatible for the future, but this is not guaranteed at this time.

To guard against the possibility of uncovering some subtle problem in actual use which would violate upward compatibility, the EDIF reviewers have elected to wait until after some period of production use before attempting to identify the parts of EDIF which will be upward compatible. At that time certain keywords and groups of keywords will be identified as frozen or upwardly compatible. From this point on any changes to those keywords and their constructs will be made only in an upward compatible way. All future EDIF versions will maintain the syntax and semantics of those keywords, adding only optional or extended constructs within the keywords. The upward compatibility of the keywords which allow user-definable semantics (*userData* and *property*) cannot be controlled by the EDIF technical contributors but only by the originators of these constructs to which semantic interpretation is applied.

The capability to read a new EDIF file with obsolete software ("downward" compatibility) is not planned, since any significant changes to EDIF will involve the addition of new capabilities to EDIF with new and presumably significant information present in a file written using the new version. Obsolete software must be modified to handle the new information if only to know that the information may be safely ignored. An EDIF reader can be written in such a way that both the current EDIF version 2 0 0 and future versions could be read correctly without requiring modifications to the program, unless the new information is required.

December 13, 1989

TABLE OF CONTENTS

TABLE OF CONTENTS [continued]

LIST OF FIGURES

INTRODUCTION TO EDIF

This section provides an overview of basic EDIF concepts. These include the levels of EDIF, and the syntax and the meta–syntax used throughout the document. All concepts described in this section apply to all levels of EDIF.

An interchange format for electronic design data must meet the needs of a wide range of users – from those wishing to transfer mask artwork data in its final form, to those desiring to transfer a behavioral description of a microcomputer. A procedural format could be used to describe the mask artwork data, but the data can be expressed as effectively using simple geometric primitives.

A primary requirement of an interchange format is unambiguous description of the data it is transmitting. Consequently, it is important that all readers and writers of the format possess exactly the same understanding of how the file is to be interpreted.

To avoid complicating the simple tasks and still provide the power of procedural descriptions for those who need them, EDIF descriptions can be specified in three different levels of complexity. These are:

- Level 0 : The basic level – only literal constants are permitted.

- Level 1 : Level 0 with the addition of parameters and expressions.

- Level 2 : Level 1 with the addition of control–flow constructs.

Since Level 1 is a proper subset of Level 2, and Level 0 is a proper subset of Level 1, it is possible to move down a level by evaluating functions and expressions and by replacing parametric values with a constant value. Such a conversion would be necessary to move from a sophisticated design environment to a more straightforward system and would involve the loss of parametric information.

Reference page titles are followed by EDIF level in chevrons, unless the construct is the same for all levels: <0>, <1>, or <2>. In a similar way, constructs involved in keyword abbreviations are separated into keyword levels, indicated by <k0>, <k1>, <k2>, or <k3>. These keyword levels allow no abbreviations, simple keyword abbreviations, noniterative keyword definitions and iterative keyword definitions respectively.

EDIF Meta–Syntax

The meta–syntax used in the following sections to describe EDIF constructs obeys the following rules:

i. Syntactic categories (nonterminals) are printed in *italics*; literal words and characters (terminal strings) are **emboldened**. Symbolic constants are printed in roman and are in **UPPERCASE**; single characters are represented as '**+**' and parentheses represent themselves.

ii. If a construct is enclosed in [square brackets], it is optional.

iii. If a construct is enclosed in {curly braces}, it may be repeated zero or more times in any order.

iv. A choice is indicated with a vertical bar |. Only one of the options may be chosen. A list of items enclosed within {curly braces} and separated by vertical bars indicates that any number of each item may be present and that the items may occur in any order. Inside such a list, if an item is permitted to occur at most once, it is enclosed within <chevrons>.

v. Notes on the right–hand side are comments and are not part of the syntax.

vi. An ellipsis ... is used to indicate that further items have been omitted within an example.

vii. All EDIF names must be defined before they are referenced.

EDIF Syntax

EDIF uses a Lisp–like syntax. The syntax was chosen for ease of parsing and provision of a uniform method of extension of the format. A construct begins with an opening parenthesis and a keyword; this is followed by a list of items ending with a closing parenthesis. Those items may be other constructs which build a nested structure, or they may be tokens consisting of data items, such as integer tokens or string tokens, or EDIF identifiers. Delimiters may occur on either side of parentheses in EDIF constructs but are not required. EDIF delimiters are the ASCII characters space, tab, carriage–return, and linefeed.

The list of legal identifiers that play the role of EDIF keywords is defined by this document. Users of the format can define their own keywords in terms of existing EDIF keywords with the *keywordAlias* and *keywordDefine* constructs. Case is not significant in keywords, symbolic constants, or identifiers.

The specification of a particular construct is summarized between horizontal lines and in the paragraphs following the entry.

Names

Denoting Names or Identifiers

Identifiers are used in an EDIF description to uniquely identify objects. EDIF attaches no special meaning to the choice of identifier spelling; the basic semantics of an EDIF file is not changed if one or more of the identifiers is uniformly changed for a new (and valid) identifier both in the original definition which names an object and in all uses of the identifier to refer to that object. All structural semantics should be identical; the only change would be in the appearance of the name itself. No meaning should be assumed or expected with respect to the actual choice of names. This sharply contrasts with native EDIF keywords (and symbolic constants), whose semantic meaning is fully defined by this manual.

The Role of Names in EDIF

There are two mechanisms in EDIF to express relationships between objects: containment and name reference.

Containment is a purely lexical mechanism and relates to the textual enclosure of object descriptions within the matching parentheses of another description (construct).

Many relationships are expressed using simple containment. A *cell* definition being part of a *library*, and a *view* being within a particular *cell* are examples of this type. However, containment alone is only adequate to describe simple, one-dimensional structures. There are many relationships between objects in a typical CAD database which require more flexibility, such as the instantiation of one cell within another and netlist connectivity.

The details of naming structures within EDIF descriptions are derived partially from the need to represent such relationships and partly from common identification schemes used in typical systems. As far as possible, minimum real restrictions are placed on originating naming schemes. In particular, there are no reserved identifiers in EDIF.

To make the format as explicit as possible, there are no assumed relationships between the names of distinct classes of objects such as cells, ports, and nets. For example, a port may be declared with the same name as a cell without any implied significance or semantic implication: it is simply a coincidence of spelling.

Another important aspect of the naming mechanism is that each name *must* be defined before it may be referenced.

Very few design systems employ flat naming schemes: names are typically valid within a well-defined scope. For example, the name chosen for a port in one cell cannot be confused with a port of another cell that happens to have the same name spelling. Such local names require some form of qualification before the local object can be referenced from another context. For example, to reference an instance port requires both the instance name and the name given to the corresponding port within the definition of the cell.

Name Class

The concept of *name class* is an essential aspect of object referencing in EDIF. The type of object being named determines the class of its name, such as cell name or logic–value name. Any identifier used as a reference is associated with an object class by its immediate context.

The various name classes are all subject to the same scoping rules and are parallel, independent naming schemes. There is no connection or interference between names of different class, even when such names happen to involve the same identifier spelling and have overlapping ranges. In addition, none of these classes have any conflict with identifiers used as keywords or symbolic constants: a cell could be named **and** or even **cell** without implying any connection with the corresponding keywords.

Some name classes are used for more than one keyword. For example, *external* and *library* both define library names.

Name Scope

The *scope* of a name is always defined by lexical containment within a certain construct, such as *library*, *cell*, or *view*. The range of direct accessibility of a named object extends from just after its description to just before the end of the smallest enclosing name scope.

It is illegal for two objects of the same class to be given the same name if they also have the same scope. For example, no two cells in the same library may be given the same name.

The major name scopes created within EDIF are illustrated by the following example:

```
(edif example
    (edifVersion 2 0 0)
    (edifLevel 0)
    (keywordMap (keywordLevel 0))
    (library lib1
        (edifLevel 0)
        (technology
            (numberDefinition ...)
            (simulationInfo (logicValue low ...))
            (figureGroup m2 ...))
        (cell c1 (cellType Generic)
            (view v1 (viewType Netlist)
                (interface (port data ...))
                (contents
                    (instance inv12 ...)
                    (net q ...))))))))
```

In this example the scopes of **low, m2,** and **c1** extends from just after their definitions to the end of the library. The scope of **v1** extends from just after its definition to the end of the cell. The scope of **data** extends from just after its definition to the end of the view. The scopes of **inv12** and **q** extend from just after their definitions to the end of the contents.

Renaming for External Use

When the sending system allows more freedom in spelling than EDIF, there is a mechanism for recording the original spelling of the name. This is necessary when the external identifier does not meet the naming restrictions of EDIF. For this situation, the *rename* construct is provided. The *rename* provides a legal EDIF name for the illegal identifier. That name is used throughout the scope of the identifier and can be mapped back to the original identifier on output, if desired. For example, rather than:

(cell dollar   ...)

the rename would be used as:

(cell (rename dollar "$")   ...)

This defines a cell named **dollar,** and records the fact that it used to be called $ in the originating system. The legal identifier **dollar** is then the only name used within the rest of the file. A receiving translator should attempt to preserve the original names if possible; this could improve human communication. This has to be an individual design choice: few systems accept unrestricted identifier spellings completely.

Values

A second important general category of object is the *value*. In the following sections, the primitive value types supported by EDIF are described.

Numbers

A number is either an integer or scaled–integer quantity, and either one may be used in any EDIF description that expects a number. The integer portion of a number is restricted to lie in the range $+2^{31}-1 \geq m \geq -2^{31}+1$. This restriction guarantees that a program processing the file can represent any integer, or mantissa, using a 32–bit one's or two's complement integer. All of the following are legal integer tokens:

100
0
−123454321
+64

A scale factor can be applied to an integer to represent fractional numbers or numbers greater than can be expressed using an integer alone. These scaled integers are represented in the form: **(e** *integerToken integerToken*). The first integer is the mantissa; the second integer is the exponent of the scale factor, and the resulting number has a value of mantissa x $10^{exponent}$. While a restriction is not applied to the values of the scale factor itself, the resulting scaled integer must lie within the range ± 1 x 10^{35}, so that it may be expressed as a floating–point real number on most conventional computer systems.

Real numbers are represented as *scaledIntegers*; therefore, real–number notation is not allowed in EDIF. Integers of 32 bits can be used to store any mantissa values for both *integerTokens* and *scaledIntegers*. A 64–bit (double) floating–point number can store any *scaledInteger* within the range specified above. In a system that does not have double–precision floating point, a 32–bit integer can be used to store the mantissa, and a separate byte can be used to store the exponent. The following examples show numbers expressed in real–number notation and the *scaledInteger* equivalent:

100.0 →	**(e 1000 −1)**
0.8 →	**(e 8 −1)**
−2321. →	**(e −2321 0)**
+6E12 →	**(e 6 12)**

Numbers are used to represent a variety of types of data. For example, numbers are used for the width of paths (a distance) and the delay of a logic gate (a time). Numbers may be translated upon output to dimensioned quantities via the *scale* construct. That is, while a path width may be expressed as **3**, it is converted to 3μm or 3 meters depending on the value of the distance scale factor for the current library.

Strings

String tokens are delimited by quotation marks (") and can contain legal EDIF characters. A string has no limit to its length and there is no implication that adjacent strings are concatenated. Within strings, arbitrary ASCII characters can be included by using the *asciiCharacter* mechanism.

Booleans

Boolean constants can take only one of two values: **(true)** or **(false)**. This is extended in Level 1 descriptions to include Boolean expressions.

Points

A point value is the data type used to describe all geometric figures, including both line drawings and filled areas. It is defined by the keyword *pt* followed by two integer values. The first integer is the x–location and the second integer is the y–location of the point. For example: **(pt 100 200)**.

Ranges of Numbers

Another possible value for some constructs is the *mnm* construct. It is used to specify minimum, nominal and maximum values. For example: **(mnm 95 100 105)**.

REFERENCE

edif	*$goal*

The grammatical goal of an EDIF description is the *edif* form, possibly surrounded by *whiteSpace* characters.

Such a file need not be logically complete, since external library declarations may be used. The design or designs may also be partially described or not fully developed.

A legal EDIF file may be created to communicate a design that contains design errors (such as violations of physical design rules), possibly for verification or correction at another location.

See also:

design, edif, edifLevel, external, form, identifier, integerToken, keywordLevel, library, nameDef, nameRef, stringToken, viewType, and *whiteSpace.*

(**abs** *numberValue*)

abs

abs

Abs is a number function that returns the absolute value of its argument; it may be used only in Level 1 and Level 2 descriptions. In the special case where *abs* is applied to an *integerValue* the expression may also be used as an *integerValue*.

Example:

(**pt** (**abs** −5) (**abs** 4))

In this example the integer value **5** is returned as the x–coordinate of the point; the integer value **4** is returned as the y–coordinate of the point.

Used in:

integerValue, and *numberValue.*

See also:

divide, edifLevel, max, min, mod, negate, subtract, and *sum.*

	acLoad
(acLoad *miNoMaxValue* | *miNoMaxDisplay*)	*acLoad*

AcLoad is an attribute of a port and is used to express the external load capacitance of the port. This quantity has the units of CAPACITANCE. The total capacitance seen at the output port of a gate is the sum of the *acLoad* values of all connected ports.

Values of *acLoad* scale between *libraries* using the factors defined for CAPACITANCE values.

Example:

(acLoad (e 25 −15))

This example specifies an *acLoad* value of **25 fF,** assuming a scale factor of **1.**

Used in:

port, portBackAnnotate, and *portInstance.*

See also:

keywordDisplay, loadDelay, scale, and *unit.*

(actual *formalNameRef*)

actual

actual

Actual generates the actual token or form that corresponds in position within the use of the keyword being defined, to the formal parameter definition within the *keywordDefine* form. If the *formal* parameter is bound to several forms, the *actual* expands to several forms – unless it is used within a *forEach* statement which references the same formal parameter.

This is only appropriate within descriptions expressed at keyword level 2 or higher.

Example:

```
(keywordDefine EG
    (keywordParameters
        (formal layer)
        . . . )
    (generate
        (build figure
            (actual layer)
            . . . ) ) )
```

This will, if given the usage **(EG POLY . . .)**, generate the form **(figure POLY . . .)** during the keyword expansion.

Used in:

build, forEach, generate, and *optional.*

See also:

formal, keywordDefine, keywordLevel, and *literal.*

```
(after  miNoMaxValue
    { logicAssign |
    follow |
    maintain |
    comment |
    userData }
)
```

After is used to specify a time delay prior to execution of a series of actions in logic modeling. The time delay may not be negative. *After* differs from *delay*. Its actions are evaluated after the specified time; *delay* simply delays propagation of the result of an action. This is useful for checking values a specified time after a *trigger* has occurred.

Example:

```
(when
    (trigger (change CLK (becomes T)))
    (logicAssign OUT (logicRef X) (delay 2))
    (after 5
        (logicAssign OUT (portRef IN))))
```

In the above example the *logicAssign* statement takes the logic value **X** at the time of the *trigger* and will apply the value to **OUT,** **2** time units later. The *after* statement causes a delay of **5** time units after the *trigger* before taking the value of **IN** and applying it to **OUT** immediately. By that time, the value of port **IN** may have changed.

Used in:

when.

See also:

delay, follow, logicAssign, and *maintain.*

---

alpha

'A' | 'B' | 'C' | 'D' | 'E' | 'F' | 'G' | 'H' | 'I' | 'J' | 'K' | 'L' | 'M' |
'N' | 'O' | 'P' | 'Q' | 'R' | 'S' | 'T' | 'U' | 'V' | 'W' | 'X' | 'Y' | 'Z' |

'a' | 'b' | 'c' | 'd' | 'e' | 'f' | 'g' | 'h' | 'i' | 'j' | 'k' | 'l' | 'm' |
'n' | 'o' | 'p' | 'q' | 'r' | 's' | 't' | 'u' | 'v' | 'w' | 'x' | 'y' | 'z'

alpha

Alpha is a character of the set A..Z or a..z which is used within string tokens and identifiers. Case is significant within string tokens but not in identifiers (for the purpose of comparison).

Example:

netA
neta
"a string"
"A string"

In this example, the two identifiers are equivalent, but the two string tokens are distinct.

Used in:

identifier, and *stringToken.*

See also:

digit, and *specialCharacter.*

(and *{ booleanValue }* **)**

and

and

   And is a Boolean function that returns the logical conjunction of its arguments. It is *false* if any of its arguments are *false;* otherwise it returns *true.* If used with no arguments, it returns *true.*

Example:

   (constant x (integer 2))
   (constant y (integer 2))
   (constant z (integer 3))
   ...
   (and (equal x y) (equal y z))

In the above example, **x = y = 2,** and **z = 3;** therefore, **(equal x y)** is *true,* and **(equal y z)** is *false.* The *and* thus returns the Boolean value *false.*

Used in:

booleanValue.

See also:

equal, not, or, and *xor.*

(annotate *stringValue | stringDisplay*)

Annotate is used in *commentGraphics* for associating comment text with an object. The string value has an association with the object which the *commentGraphics* is contained within. The string has no interpretation and is equivalent to a comment in a programming language.

Annotate may also be used within a *symbol* to associate textual display that should appear within contexts that use the symbol.

The string can be displayed using *stringDisplay*. The *stringDisplay* contains *display* forms which are used to define the location and system attributes necessary to display the string value.

Example:

> **(commentGraphics**
>> **(annotate**
>>> **(stringDisplay "This is an example of annotate"**
>>> **(display textDisplay (origin (pt 12 13))))))**

In this example the string **"This is an example of annotate"** will be displayed at **(12, 13),** according to the display attributes associated with the figure group named **textDisplay,** which must have been defined previously.

Used in:

commentGraphics, and *symbol.*

See also:

display, figureGroup, property, and *stringDisplay.*

(apply *cycle*
    { logicInput | inputs and their values
    logicOutput | outputs and expected results
    comment | user comments
    userData }   user−defined constructs
)

Apply is used within *simulate* to describe input stimuli and expected responses over a certain time interval. The *cycle* specifies the number of input and output cycles described and the interval between each application of a logical pattern. The remainder of the construct consists of logic input and output statements, which individually describe the respective behavior of their subject ports.

Example:

    (apply
        (cycle 7 (duration (e 5 −1)))
        (logicInput dataIn (logicWaveform T T F T F F T))
        (logicOutput dataOut (logicWaveform F T F F T F T)))

This example indicates that **7** test cycles are desired, each of which will take half a time unit.

During the first cycle, **T** is applied to **dataIn** and **F** is expected from **dataOut**.

During the Last cycle **T** is applied to **dataIn** and **T** is expected from **dataOut**.

Used in:

simulate.

See also:

logicInput, and *logicOutput.*

(**arc** *pointValue pointValue pointValue*)

Arc is used in describing shapes with curved edges. The first *pointValue* is
starting point of the arc, the second *pointValue* is any point on the *arc*, and
third *pointValue* is the end point of the arc.

The three points of the arc specification must be distinct.

Example:

```
(shape
    (curve
        (pt 20 100)
        (arc
            (pt 40  100)
            (pt 60  110)
            (pt 40  120))
        (pt 20 120)))
```

This example shows a *shape* describing a curved figure and the use of an *arc*
construct such a shape.

Used in:

curve.

See also:

figure, openShape, and *shape.*

---

array

(**array** *nameDef*   name of arrayed object
    integerValue { integerValue }   range for each index
)

array

    Array is used in place of *nameDef* in contexts in which array structures are appropriate for the class of object involved. The class of array name is the same as that of a simple name in the same context. The *array* specifies the size of each index dimension of the created array, in order. Such values must be positive integers. There is no limit to the number of dimensions.

    The use of *array* causes several objects of the given class to be created. Individual members may be accessed or referenced by using the *member* construct, which must contain the same number of indices as those in the *array;* each must be greater than or equal to zero and less than the corresponding dimension size. The first index varies the most slowly for the purpose of any expansion.

Example:

    (**array X 32**)

This example defines an array **X** of size **32,** running from (**member X 0**) through (**member X 31**).

    (**array Q 4 16**)

The second example defines a two–dimensional array **Q** of size **4** by **16,** running from (**member Q 0 0**) through (**member Q 0 15**) through (**member Q 3 15**).

Used in:

instanceNameDef, netNameDef, portNameDef, and *valueNameDef.*

See also:

member, and *nameDef.*

(arrayMacro *plug***)**

ArrayMacro identifies a *plug* which describes the customizing patterns used to create a predefined function when placed at a valid site location on a gate array. The construct also includes a *plug* definition which may be matched to a *socket* for placement of the macro cell.

Example:

    (arrayRelatedInfo
      (arrayMacro
        (plug ...)))

This indicates that the current cell is a macro and contains necessary *plug* information.

Used in:

arrayRelatedInfo.

See also:

plug, site, and *socket.*

(arrayRelatedInfo
   arrayMacro | arraySite | baseArray
   { comment |
   userData }
)

ArrayRelatedInfo is used to contain the EDIF constructs for describing physical placement rules which define the placement of customizing macrocells in a gate array. It may be used in the *interface* of views of type MASKLAYOUT, PCBLAYOUT, STRANGER, and SYMBOLIC.

Example:

```
(cell M299 (cellType generic)
  (view Site_definition (viewType Symbolic)
    (interface
      (arrayRelatedInfo
        (arrayMacro
          (plug
            (socketSet (symmetry)
              (site
                (viewRef Site (cellRef Site_cell))
                (Transform (orientation R90)))))))))))
```

This example specifies **cell M299,** which may be placed in site **Site_cell** after being rotated **270** degrees.

Used in:

interface.

See also:

cellType, plug, socket, and *viewType.*

(arraySite *socket*)   *arraySite*

                                                                      arraySite

---

     ArraySite is used to define a site location in a gate array which may be satisfied by a macrocell placement during implementation of a gate array. A cell of this type consists of geometry which defines the underlying base pattern for the generic portion of a gate array. Different sites may be defined for different classes of underlying circuitry or for different physical realizations of similar functions such as high–power and low–power sites.

Example:

```
(Cell Site_cell (cellType generic)
  (View Site_definition (viewType Symbolic)
    (Interface
      (ArrayRelatedInfo (ArraySite (Socket))))))
```

This example specifies cell **Site_cell,** which may be instantiated in a base array to provide the required sites for macro placement.

Used in:

arrayRelatedInfo.

See also:

arrayMacro, plug, and *socket.*

'%'   *asciiCharacter*

      { integerToken }

'%'

                                                         asciiCharacter

---

AsciiCharacter represents a sequence of characters within a *stringToken;* the value of each *integerToken* is interpreted as an ASCII code, and must lie between 0 and 127 inclusive. *WhiteSpace* may exist within this construct to separate consecutive integer tokens, but is optional before the first value and after the last value.

None of the special properties associated with various characters (such as quote and percent) should be attributed to these characters. This enables any ASCII character to be explicitly incorporated into a string token.

Example:

    "abc%9%def"

This string contains seven characters.

    "% 8 9 10 13 32 34 37 %"

The second example illustrates a *stringToken* which represents the characters: back–space, horizontal–tab, line–feed, carriage–return, space, quote, and percent.

Used in:

stringToken.

See also:

identifier, and *integerToken.*

---

	assign
(assign *valueNameRef*	variable to assign to
typedValue	
)	
	assign

After a variable has been defined by using the *variable* construct in Level 2, it is possible to assign a new value to it using the *assign* statement. The type of value must match the type of variable.

The *valueNameRef* may be an array, in which case the size and structure of the *boolean, integer, miNoMax, number, point,* or *string* construct must match the array dimensions as specified by the *array* in the *variable*.

The use of *assign* is not restricted by *viewType*.

Example:

> **(variable x (number 12))**
> **...**
> **(assign x**
> **(number**
> **(subtract (product b b) (product 4 a c))))**

This example reassigns the value of the variable **x** to $b^2 - 4ac$.

> **(assign xLoc**
> **(integer (xCoord Corner)))**

In the above example the variable **xLoc** is assigned the x coordinate of the identifier named **Corner** which must be of type *point*.

Used in:

contents, interface, page, and *statement.*

See also:

boolean, constant, integer, miNoMax, number, parameter, point, string, typedValue, and *variable.*

(atLeast *numberValue***)**

The *atLeast* construct is used to specify that the range of values in the enclosing *between* or *range* constructs is greater than or equal to *numberValue*. This is needed in the context of most physical design rules to describe acceptable values for various geometric measurements.

Example:

(figureWidth metal_width
    (figureGroupObject metal)
    (atLeast 2))

This example restricts the width of all **metal** figures to be at least **2** distance units.

Used in:

between, and *range.*

See also:

atMost, multipleValueSet, numberValue, and *physicalDesignRule.*

(atMost *numberValue*)

AtMost is used to specify that the range of values in the *between* or *range* constructs is less than or equal to *numberValue*. It is used in the context of most physical design rules.

Example:

> **(figureWidth metal_width**
>   **(figureGroupObject metal)**
>   **(atMost 2))**

This example restricts the width of all **metal** figures to be at most **2** distance units.

Used in:

between, and *range*.

See also:

atLeast, multipleValueSet, numberValue, and *physicalDesignRule*.

(**author** *stringToken*)

author

author

Author is used to identify the person or organization responsible for writing the file. This field is often used for identifying ownership of the design or for identifying a contact for more information about the design.

Example:

> (**written**
>   (**timeStamp 1987 3 4 12 34 54**)
>   (**author** ″**Kiki**″)
>   (**program** ″**EDIF_$Net**″ (**Version** ″**5.3**″)))

The above example specifies that the block of information was produced on **March 4, 1987** at **12:34:54 UTC** by the program named **EDIF_$Net** version **5.3,** and that the person named **Kiki** is responsible for the creation or modification of the data.

Used in:

written.

See also:

dataOrigin, program, status, timeStamp, version, and *written.*

      BaseArray is used to identify a view which describes the top level of the hierarchy defining the uncustomized portion of a gate array. A *baseArray* cell view will contain instances of *arraySite* cells which define the sites for customization as well as other information relating to the basic array.

Example:

```
(cell Cell1
    (cellType generic)
    (view View1 (viewType symbolic)
        (interface
            (arrayRelatedInfo
                (baseArray)))
        (contents ...)))
```

The above example identifies view **View1** of cell **Cell1** as a base–array cell.

Used in:

arrayRelatedInfo.

See also:

arrayMacro, and *arraySite.*

(**becomes** *logicNameRef* | *logicList* | *logicOneOf*)

Becomes is used to describe a logic state transition from any value to the given logic value.

LogicList is used in conjunction with lists or arrays of ports. When specified the size of the logic list must match the size of the port list.

LogicOneOf is used to provide a choice of logic values or logic lists. Any match in the *logicOneOf* is considered a match in the *becomes* statement.

Example:

    (**becomes L**)

The first example specifies any transition to the logic value **L**.

    (**becomes (logicOneOf H L)**)

The second example specifies any transition to either the logic value **H** or to the logic value **L**.

Used in:

change, event, netDelay, portDelay, and *steady.*

See also:

logicList, logicOneOf, pathDelay and *transition.*

---

between

(between
    atLeast | greaterThan
    atMost | lessThan
)

between

The *between* construct is used to specify a range of real number values with both an upper and lower limit for use in physical design rules as a *range*.

Example:

    (between (atLeast 5) (lessThan 10))

This example specifies the range of numbers that are greater than or equal to **5** and less than **10.**

Used in:

range.

See also:

atLeast, atMost, greaterThan, lessThan, multipleValueSet, and *physicalDesignRule.*

(block *{ statement }*)

block

block

The *block* construct allows a number of EDIF statements to be collected into a group. *Block* is not restricted by *viewType,* but the enclosed *statements* must be appropriate within the context of the *block.* It may only be used in Level 2 descriptions.

Names defined within a block are local to that block. *Escape* may be used to prematurely terminate a *block.* Other than that, the meaning of the *block* is the same as the individual statements, taken in the same sequential order.

Example:

```
(block
    (variable n (integer 1))
    (while (increasing n chainSize)
        (figure POLY (dot (pt n 0)))
        (assign n (integer (sum 1 n)))))
```

This example shows the use of *block* to collect Level 2 statements which could be part of a procedural layout.

Used in:

contents, interface, page, statement, and *technology.*

See also:

else, escape, if, iterate, nameDef, then, and *while.*

(**boolean** *{ booleanValue | booleanDisplay | boolean }*)

boolean

boolean

Boolean declares a *constant, parameter, property,* or *variable* value to be of type Boolean. An optional *booleanValue* can be specified, in which case the value serves as a default.

An array of boolean values can be defined by specifying multiple *booleanValues* within a *boolean*. Nesting of the *boolean* construct is required to specify array values of two or more dimensions. The number of items within the outermost *boolean* should match the size of the first dimension of the *array*. Each nested *boolean* must have structure corresponding to the dimension of the *array*.

Example:

  (**parameter refresh (boolean (false)))**

In this example the parameter **refresh** is declared to be of type Boolean. A default Boolean value of **(false)** is also specified.

  (**constant (array BA1 2) (boolean (true) (false)))**
  (**constant (array BA2 2 3)**
      (**boolean**
          (**boolean (true) (false) (true))**
          (**boolean (false) (true) (true))))**

In the above example the constant **BA1** is defined to be a one–dimensional Boolean array with the following value assignments:

  (**member BA1 0) = (true),**
  (**member BA1 1) = (false)**

and **BA2** is defined to be a two–dimensional Boolean array with the following value assignments:

  (**member BA2 0 0) = (true),**
  (**member BA2 0 1) = (false),**
  (**member BA2 0 2) = (true),**
  (**member BA2 1 0) = (false),**
  (**member BA2 1 1) = (true),**
  (**member BA2 1 2) = (true).**

Used in:

boolean, borderPattern, fillPattern, and *typedValue.*

See also:

array, booleanValue, false, integer, miNoMax, number, point, string, and *true.*

booleanDisplay

(booleanDisplay *booleanValue*
   { display }
)

booleanDisplay

BooleanDisplay is used for displaying Boolean design data. The actual form that a Boolean value has while being displayed is system–dependent and is not specified by EDIF. *BooleanDisplay* is allowed in constructs that normally contain design data and which exists in a coordinate space.

BooleanDisplay contains the data to be displayed, which must be a Boolean value and any number of *display* forms.

Example:

```
(net N1
    (joined (portRef A) (portRef B))
    (property WidthFrozen
        (boolean
            (booleanDisplay (true) (display text (origin (pt 4 6)))))...))
```

In the above example the *property* named **WidthFrozen** is in a coordinate space, and the value **(true)** can be displayed at point **(4,6).**

Used in:

boolean.

See also:

booleanValue, display, false, integerDisplay, miNoMaxDisplay, numberDisplay, pointDisplay, stringDisplay, and *true.*

(**booleanMap** *booleanValue*)

BooleanMap is an attribute of a logic value which declares whether the logic value is associated with Boolean values of *true* or *false*. Not all logic values will map into Boolean values.

Example:

```
(simulationInfo
    (logicValue T  (booleanMap (true)))
    (logicValue WT (booleanMap (true)))
    (logicValue F  (booleanMap (false)))
    (logicValue WF (booleanMap (false)))
    (logicValue X))
```

In the above example the logic values **T** and **WT** map to *true*. The logic value **F** and **WF** map to *false*. The logic value **X** does not correspond to any Boolean value.

Used in:

logicValue.

See also:

false, simulationInfo, and *true.*

---

	booleanValue
false	*true*	*booleanValue*

BooleanValue is used to describe the primitive Boolean set. The set for Level 0 includes the Boolean values *true* and *false*. This is extended in Level 1.

Example:

(parameterAssign triState (boolean (true)))

This statement could be used in a Level 0 instance of a higher–level view to assign the value *true* to the parameter named **triState.**

Used in:

boolean, booleanDisplay, booleanMap, and *visible.*

See also:

false, parameterAssign, property, and *true.*

---

booleanValue

> *false | true | valueNameRef |*
> *and | or | not | xor |*
> *equal | increasing | strictlyIncreasing*

booleanValue

In Level 1 EDIF descriptions, *booleanValue* is extended to incorporate any Boolean expression. This includes Boolean constants, a value reference, and functions that return Boolean values. The *valueNameRef* may refer to a *constant, parameter,* or *variable* definition of type *boolean.*

Example:

(constant b (boolean (true)))

. . .

(and b ...)

In the above example the **b** in the *and* function is a constant value reference. The *and* construct is a Boolean function.

Used in:

and, boolean, booleanDisplay, booleanMap, constraint, if, not, or, visible, while, and *xor.*

See also:

constant, integerValue, numberValue, parameter, pointValue, stringValue, and *variable.*

<table>
<tr><td>

(**borderPattern**
   integerValue
   integerValue
   boolean
)

</td><td>

borderPattern

number of pixels in X direction
number of pixels in Y direction
boolean array containing pixel pattern

borderPattern

</td></tr>
</table>

BorderPattern is used to specify the stipple or pixel pattern for a border or perimeter of a figure. The first integer value represents the number of pixels required for the pattern in the x direction, and the second integer value represents the number of pixels required for the pattern in the y direction. The two integer values also specify the dimensionality of the Boolean array in the same manner as the *array* construct.

The *boolean* construct is used to define an array of pattern values. It must define a Boolean value for each point of the matrix defined by the two integer values. The pixel size is not defined since it is dependent on the type of display used. The origin of the pattern is in the lower left corner, the x dimension increasing toward the right and the y dimension increasing toward the top.

The pattern values are defined such that (**member 0 0**) of the Boolean array is the pixel value at the pattern origin, (**member 1 0**) is the pixel value for the next adjacent pixel from the pattern origin in the positive x direction, (**member 0 1**) is the pixel value for the next adjacent pixel from the pattern origin in the positive y direction, and the array value for the member with maximum indices is the pixel value for the upper right corner of the pattern. A Boolean *true* indicates that the pixel is to be displayed in the specified color; a Boolean *false* indicates that the pixel is either unchanged or is displayed in the background color.

BorderPattern may be specified in the *figureGroup* form in the technology block of a library. In this case the pattern is the default border pattern to be used to outline all figures in the figure group. *BorderPattern* may also be specified in the *figureGroupOverride* form within the *figure* itself. In this case the border pattern specified is used to override the default border pattern.

The pattern only affects the display of figures, not their fabrication.

Example:

```
(borderPattern 4 6
    (boolean
        (boolean (true) (true) (false) (false) (false) (false))
        (boolean (true) (false) (false) (false) (true) (false))
        (boolean (true) (true) (true) (true) (true) (false))
        (boolean (false) (false) (false) (false) (true) (false))))
```

The above example specifies a border pattern which would fill the border with **J** character patterns.

Used in:

figureGroup, and *figureGroupOverride.*

See also:

array, boolean, booleanValue, borderWidth, color, fabricate, false, figure, fillPattern, integerValue, true, and *visible.*

(borderWidth *integerValue***)**	*borderWidth*
	borderWidth

The *borderWidth* construct is used to define the display or plot width of the border or edge of all figures in a figure group. The integer value is expressed in DISTANCE units. The value may be zero but may not be negative. A zero value implies that the border should not be displayed.

BorderWidth may be specified in the *figureGroup* construct in the technology block of a library. In this case the width is the default width to be used in all figures in the figure group. *BorderWidth* may also be specified in the *figureGroupOverride* construct in the *figure* itself. In this case the width value is used to temporarily override the default width value.

Example:

```
(numberDefinition
    (scale 1 (e 1 −3) (unit distance)))
(figureGroup Display
    (borderWidth 10)...))
```

The first example defines a default border width of **10 mm** in the *technology* section.

```
(figure
    (figureGroupOverride Display
        (borderWidth 15)...)
```

The second example overrides the default border width with a value of **15 mm** for this use.

Used in:

figureGroup, and *figureGroupOverride.*

See also:

borderPattern, figure, pathWidth, and *technology.*

(**boundingBox** *rectangle*)

BoundingBox is a simplified summary of the extent of a collection of figures, often used for display–clipping purposes. The bounding box is the minimum–sized rectangle which can contain all of the graphical information specified in the same context.

A *boundingBox* may be used in the *contents* of views of type **GRAPHIC, MASKLAYOUT, PCBLAYOUT, STRANGER** and **SYMBOLIC,** and in **SCHEMATIC** *pages.*

Example:

```
(symbol
    (boundingBox (rectangle (pt 38 65) (pt 110 250)))
    (figure Green
        (rectangle (pt 100 65) (pt 110 120)))
    (figure Orange
        (dot (pt 38 250))))
```

This example shows the use of a *boundingBox* within a symbol that used two figures.

Used in:

commentGraphics, contents, page, protectionFrame, and *symbol.*

See also:

figure, rectangle, and *viewType.*

<table>
<tr><td>

(build *keywordNameRef*
    { literal |
    actual |
    build |
    comment }
)

</td><td>

build
build for keyword Level 2

build constructs may nest

build

</td></tr>
</table>

Build is used within the context of a *keywordDefine* to generate nonprimitive output. It contains a *keywordNameRef* which is the name of an existing (or previously defined) keyword. *Build* expands into a *form* with *keywordNameRef* as its keyword and each component of the *build* replaced by the result of generating the enclosed constructs in the order specified. The enclosed *comments* generate nothing but provide documentation about the purpose or use of the *keywordDefine*.

Build may nest to create nested output *forms*.

Example:

```
(keywordDefine rev
    (keywordParameters
        (formal a) (formal b))
    (generate
        (build pt
            (actual b) (actual a))))
```

This example defines a keyword such that **(rev 1 2)** expands to **(pt 2 1).**

Used in:

build, generate, and *optional.*

See also:

keywordDefine, and *keywordLevel.*

(**build** *keywordNameRef*
　　{ *literal* |
　　actual |
　　build |
　　forEach |
　　comment }
)

build
build for keyword Level 3

build constructs may nest

build

　　Build is used within the context of a *keywordDefine* to generate nonprimitive output. It contains a *keywordNameRef,* which is the name of an existing (or previously defined) keyword. *Build* expands into a *form* with *keywordNameRef* as its keyword and each component of the *build* replaced by the result of generating the enclosed constructs in the order specified. The *comments* generate nothing but provide documentation about the purpose or use of the *keywordDefine.* At this level of keyword complexity, the *build* construct can use embedded *forEach* constructs to process lists of arbitrary length.

Example:

```
(keywordDefine inport
    (keywordParameters
        (formal name (collector))
        (formal load (collector)))
    (generate
        (forEach (formalList name load)
            (build port (actual name)
                (build direction (literal INPUT))
                (build acLoad (actual load))))))
```

This example defines a keyword which accepts any number of pairs consisting of a port name and a corresponding load value, such as (**inport p1 15 p2 20 p3 45**).

Used in:

build, forEach, generate, and *optional.*

See also:

keywordDefine, and *keywordLevel.*

(**ceiling** *numberValue*)   *ceiling*

ceiling

Ceiling is an integer function that takes in a number value and returns the smallest integer that is greater than or equal to the number argument.

Example:

    (ceiling 5)
    (ceiling −5)
    (ceiling (e 55 −1))
    (ceiling (e −55 −1))

The first function returns **5,** the second function returns **−5,** the third function returns **6,** and the last function returns **−5.**

Used in:

integerValue, and *numberValue.*

See also:

fix, and *floor.*

```
(cell  cellNameDef                                              cell
    cellType                           a named cell definition
    { < status > |                            type of cell
    view |                              status of the cell
    < viewMap > |                       different views of the cell
    property |           relates ports & instances of different views
    comment |                          properties of the cell
    userData }                              user comments
                                        user-defined constructs
)
                                                               cell
```

The *cell* construct is used to define a cell in terms of one or more views. A view of this cell may be instantiated later in another cell view to build a design hierarchy. It holds all the information that logically pertains to a specific cell.

Cell instances may occur in any order in the contents of views of other cells but only if the referenced *cells* were defined earlier in the file or if they belong to external libraries and have already been declared as such in an *external* construct.

View names must be unique within a cell, even if they are of different view types.

Example:

```
(library CMOS2M . . .
    (edifLevel 0)
    (technology ..)
    (cell MUX
        (cellType GENERIC)
        (view SCHEM1
            (viewType SCHEMATIC)
            (interface ...))
        (view MIL_MASK
            (viewType MASKLAYOUT)
            (interface ...)
            (contents ...))))
```

```
(external FOREIGN_LIBRARY
    (edifLevel 0)
    (technology ...)
    (cell MYSTERY
        (cellType GENERIC)
        (view GRAPH_MYSTERY
            (viewType GRAPHIC)
            (interface ...))))
```

The above examples illustrate the use of the *cell* construct in the context of a *library* and an *external* library.

Used in:

external, and *library.*

See also:

cellRef, cellType, instance, keywordDisplay, view, viewMap, viewRef, and *viewType.*

---

nameDef	*cellNameDef*
	cellNameDef

CellNameDef is used to create a name for a cell. It must be unique within each *library* or *external* declaration. The occurrence of cells with the same name in different libraries has no significance and does not imply any relationship between the cells.

CellNameDef must occur before any corresponding *cellNameRef*. It should not be assumed that the choice of names for *cells* has any effect on their interpretation.

Example:

(cell Nand_32 ...)

This example contains a cell name definition for **Nand_32.**

Used in:

cell.

See also:

cellNameRef, cellRef, external, and *library.*

nameRef	*cellNameRef*
	cellNameRef

CellNameRef is a simple reference to a previously defined cell, by name. The corresponding *cellNameDef* must have occurred earlier in the appropriate library.

Example:

(cellRef nand5 (libraryRef nmos))

This example contains a cell name reference **nand5,** with an explicit context of the library named **nmos.**

Used in:

cellRef.

See also:

cell, and *cellNameDef.*

---

	cellRef
(cellRef *cellNameRef [libraryRef]***)**	
	cellRef

CellRef is used to reference a previously defined *cell*. It contains a reference to the name of a cell defined by the *cell* construct and an optional *libraryRef*. The *cellRef* construct is used at any place where there is need to reference a cell that is not necessarily in the current library. If the cell being referenced belongs in a different library, then *cellRef* is required to have the *libraryRef* specified. The *cellRef* is part of the generic name referencing mechanism in EDIF that provides indirect referencing and extends the range of accessibility to an object from beyond its immediate range.

Example:

```
(design ALU_32
    (cellRef ALU_CMOS_32
        (libraryRef CMOS2M)))
```

In the first example the design named **ALU_32** references the cell named **ALU_CMOS_32** which is defined in the library named **CMOS2M.** *LibraryRef* is required in this context as *design* is not in the context of a *library*.

```
(viewRef MIL_SCHEMATIC
    (cellRef MUX))
```

In the second example the cell referenced, namely **MUX,** is assumed to be defined in the current library that provides context to the *viewRef*.

Used in:

design, and *viewRef.*

See also:

cellNameRef, instance, libraryRef, site, and *viewList.*

---

cellType

(cellType GENERIC | TIE | RIPPER)

cellType

CellType is an attribute of a *cell* which describes the use of the cell. This form is required and follows the name definition of the *cell*. The allowed cell types are **GENERIC**, **TIE**, and **RIPPER**.

The cell type **TIE** indicates that the cell is used in describing connectivity objects. **TIE** instances are allowed only in *net* and are used explicitly for joining subnets within a net. The **TIE** cell definition must contain only one port, port bundle or arrayed port definition in its interface. Multiple subnets may join to this single via port.

The cell type **RIPPER** indicates that the cell is used for describing connectivity objects. These instances are used to explicitly merge nets with different names, to describe permutations of nets, or to extract pieces of net arrays and net bundles. The **RIPPER** interface must contain at least two ports, arrayed ports or bundles of ports. Only one net may reference each port on a **RIPPER** instance. Instances of cells of type **RIPPER** may only occur in the *contents* or *page* constructs.

The cell type **GENERIC** indicates that the cell is a generic cell and covers all uses of *cell* other than **TIE** and **RIPPER**.

Example:

```
(cell C1 (cellType TIE)
   (view dot (viewType SCHEMATIC)
      (interface
         (port INO (direction INOUT)))))
...
(cell C2 ...
   (view ...
      (contents
        (net N1
           (joined (portRef A) (portRef B) (portRef C))
           (instance I1 (viewRef dot (cellRef C1)))
           (net Sub1 (joined (portRef A) (portRef INO (instanceRef I1))))
           (net Sub2 (joined (portRef B) (portRef INO (instanceRef I1))))
           (net Sub3 (joined (portRef C) (portRef INO (instanceRef I1))))))))))
```

The above example shows the definition and use of a cell with a cell type of **TIE**. The instance **I1** of the cell is found in the net **N1**.

Used in:

cell.

See also:

instance, net, netBundle, and *viewType.*

---

change

(change
    portNameRef | portRef | portList
    [transition | becomes]
)

change

Change is used in the *trigger* or *entry* constructs to specify when the value of a port or list of ports has changed. *Transition* or *becomes* may be used to restrict which transitions satisfy the *change*. When a list of ports is specified, the *change* is satisfied when all the ports have changed; the event occurs at the time of the last such change.

Example:

    (when (trigger (change IN1)) ...)

In the first example, the *trigger* is satisfied when port **IN1** takes on any new logic value.

    (when (trigger (change IN1 (becomes H))) ...)

In the second example, the *trigger* is satisfied when the logic value of port **IN1** becomes **H.**

    (when (trigger (change IN1 (transition L H))) ...)

In the third example, the *trigger* is satisfied when port **IN1** changes from the logic value **L** to the logic value **H.**

    (when (trigger (change (portList IN1 IN2 IN3 IN4))) ...)

In the fourth example, the *trigger* is satisfied when all of the ports **IN1** through **IN4** change.

    (when
       (trigger
         (change
            (portList IN1 IN2 IN3 IN4)
            (becomes (logicList H L H H)))) ...)

In the last example, the *trigger* is satisfied when the ports **IN1** through **IN4** have taken on the following logic values: **IN1 = H, IN2 = L, IN3 = H, IN4 = H.**

Used in:

entry, and *trigger.*

See also:

becomes, steady, and *transition.*

(**circle** *pointValue pointValue { property }*)

circle

circle

     Circle is used to describe a circle which has the specified points at either end of a diameter of the circle. It is a special case of *shape*.

Example:

    (**circle (pt 0 0) (pt 10 0)**)

This example produces a circle of radius **5** distance units whose center is at **(5,0)**.

Used in:

figure.

See also:

figureGroupOverride, rectangle, and *shape.*

(collector)	*collector*
	collector

   Collector allows a *formal* parameter to be bound to a list of values as opposed to a single value. It may only be used in a file which has been declared to have a keyword level of 3.

   If a *formal* parameter contains a nested *collector*, then it will be bound to all input arguments that are in excess of the number of *formal* parameters defined for the keyword. Any *formal* parameter following a *collector* parameter must also be a *collector* parameter. If there is more than one *collector* parameter, then the extra values will be evenly distributed among them in turn. The number of actual *forms* and tokens bound as a list to each *collector* parameter must be the same.

Example:

```
(keywordDefine EG
    (keywordParameters
        (formal a)
        (formal b)
        (formal c (collector))...))
```

This defines a new keyword **EG**. A later use, such as: **(EG 1 2 3 4 5 6)** would expand under the binding **a=1; b=2;** and **c=3,4,5,6.**

Used in:

formal.

See also:

build, forEach, keywordDefine, keywordLevel, keywordParameters, and *optional.*

---

	color
(color	
scaledInteger	red
scaledInteger	green
scaledInteger	blue
)	
	color

Color is used to express the color to be used for display purposes for fill patterns, border patterns, and text. The three scaled integer values represent the percentage of saturation of each of the spectrum primary colors in the order red, green, blue, respectively. The color specification of (**color 100 100 100**) represents white. The color specification of (**color 0 0 0**) represents black; if *color* is not specified black is the default color.

Color may be specified in the *figureGroup* form in the technology block of a library. In this case the color specified is the default color to be used in the figure group. *Color* may also be specified in the *figureGroupOverride* form within the *figure* itself. In this case the color specified is used to override the default color.

Example:

> **(figureGroup Metal**
> **(color 100 0 0)...)**

The first example defines a default color of red.

> **(figure**
> **(figureGroupOverride Metal**
> **(color 0 0 50)...))**

The second example overrides the default color for the figure group with a dark blue.

Used in:

figureGroup, and *figureGroupOverride*.

See also:

borderPattern, figure, fillPattern, and *visible.*

(comment
　　{ stringToken }
)

comment

user comment

comment

　　Comment contains information interpretable by humans only. If possible, the recipient should preserve this information within the target database in an equivalent structure; if not, the entire form can be ignored without loss of significant design data.

　　Comments are allowed in places explicitly indicated in the syntax of each keyword. *Comment* encloses an arbitrary number of strings. They are not restricted by *viewType*.

Example:

　　(comment "Type_three buffer cell")
　　...
　　(comment "<− I think this is the problem")
　　(comment "This polygon represents the VDD grid."
　　　　"There are two forms of this signal.%10 13%")

The first two comments each contain one string token; the last comment contains two, the second of which uses the percent mechanism to encode *asciiCharacters*.

Used in:

after, apply, arrayRelatedInfo, build, cell, commentGraphics, contents, design, edif, enclosureDistance, external, figure, figureArea, figureGroup, figureGroupOverride, figurePerimeter, figureWidth, forEach, generate, instance, instanceBackAnnotate, instanceMap, interface, interFigureGroupSpacing, intraFigureGroupSpacing, keywordMap, library, logicPort, logicValue, net, netBackAnnotate, netBundle, netMap notAllowed, notchSpacing, numberDefinition, offPageConnector, overhangDistance, overlapDistance, page, physicalDesignRule, port, portBackAnnotate, portBundle, portImplementation, portInstance, portMap, property, protectionFrame, rectangleSize, simulate, simulationInfo, statement, status, symbol, technology, timing, view, viewMap, when, and *written.*

See also:

annotate, and *stringToken.*

---

commentGraphics

(**commentGraphics**
    { annotate | textual annotations
    figure | figures
    instance | instances of **GRAPHIC** view
    < boundingBox > | bounding-box of comment graphics
    property |
    comment |
    userData }
)

commentGraphics

CommentGraphics is used to include comment figures and text within the cell implementation and has an association with certain design objects. It may contain figures, instances of view type **GRAPHIC**, annotative text, and user properties. When used in the contents of a cell, a symbol, protection frame, or within a schematic page, *commentGraphics* is not associated with an object. When used in a net or port implementation, *commentGraphics* is associated with the object. Graphics and displayable comment text, which are defined in the cell interface, are not present in instances of the cell.

The *viewTypes* which permit *commentGraphics* within *contents* are **GRAPHIC**, **MASKLAYOUT**, **PCBLAYOUT**, **STRANGER**, and **SYMBOLIC**. It is also allowed within the *pages* of views of type **SCHEMATIC**.

Example:

```
(contents
    (commentGraphics
        (figure graphics
            (rectangle (pt 0 0) (pt 7 3)))
        (annotate
            (stringDisplay "ABC"
                (display textGraphics
                    (origin (pt 0 0)))))...)
```

The above example describes a picture which contains the string **"ABC"** and a rectangle. The picture is defined in the cell implementation and is not associated with any object of the cell.

Used in:

contents, net, netBundle, page, portImplementation, protectionFrame, statement, and *symbol.*

See also:

annotate, and *figure.*

(compound *{ logicNameRef }* **)**

compound

compound

Compound is an attribute of a logic value which is used to specify a logic value that has a well-defined relationship to previously defined logic values. This allows the derivation of various degrees of unknown values (using other logic values that are defined using *compound*). This structure is intended to assist in the process of relating the logic name to those used in a particular target simulator. This does not imply any relationship for comparison of logic values in subsequent descriptions, such as may be specified in a *logicOneOf* construct.

Example:

(simulationInfo
 (logicValue WF ...)
 (logicValue WT ...)
 (logicValue SF ...)
 (logicValue ST ...)
 (logicValue F (compound WF SF))
 (logicValue T (compound WT ST))
 (logicValue W (compound WF WT))
 (logicValue S (compound SF ST))
 (logicValue U (compound WF WT SF ST)))

In the above example, the logic value **T** is a compound of the logic values **WT** and **ST**. **T** is treated as an individual value in later descriptions.

Used in:

logicValue.

See also:

logicOneOf, and *simulationInfo.*

(**concat** { *stringValue* })

concat

concat

  Concat is a string function that concatenates any number of strings together. The resulting string has as its leftmost character, i.e. subscript zero, the leftmost character of the first nonempty argument string (if any). The empty string is returned if no arguments are present.

Example:

  (**concat** "PORT" "2")

The first example returns the string value "PORT2".

  (**concat** "abc" "def" "ghi")

The second example returns the string value "**abcdefghi**".

Used in:

stringValue.

See also:

stringToken.

(connectLocation
   { figure }
)

connectLocation

indicates legal region for connection

connectLocation

ConnectLocation defines the portion of a cell view which may be used to make a connection to a specific port within the view.

ConnectLocation is not involved in determining connectivity in a normal schematic view, which must be explicitly declared using the *joined* statement within nets. It is, however, important for the subsequent maintenance and change of connectivity which may be performed with a graphical interface. It is also used to indicate connection targets.

Example:

(portImplementation VDD
   (connectLocation
      (figure Poly (dot (pt 100 50)))
      (figure Metal
         (rectangle (pt 50 50) (pt 100 55)))))

Two potential areas for connection to the port **VDD** are specified above.

Used in:

portImplementation.

See also:

figure, net, protectionFrame, and *symbol.*

(**constant** *valueNameDef typedValue*)

constant

constant

  Constant defines a value name which can be used in place of a *valueNameRef* wherever it is allowed. This is only appropriate for Level 1 and Level 2 descriptions. Constants may not be the subject (left hand side) of any assignment statement. Constant arrays are specified with the *array* construct and the *boolean, integer, miNoMax, number, point,* and *string* constructs. The value of a *constant* must not involve any reference to a *parameter* or *variable.*

  Constants defined in the *technology* section are available to all cells of the library. Constants defined in the *interface* of a view are available to the entire view; constants defined in the *contents* of a view are available only within the contents of the view. There are no *viewType* restrictions on the use of *constant.*

Example:

  (**constant capLoad (number (e 5 0)))**

In this example the constant **capLoad** is defined to have a number value of **5.0.**

  (**constant (array TruthTable 4 3)**
   (**boolean**
    (**boolean (false) (false) (false))**
    (**boolean (false) (true) (false))**
    (**boolean (true) (true) (false))**
    (**boolean (true) (true) (true))))**

In the above example a constant array **TruthTable** of type *boolean* is specified. Nested *boolean* constructs are used to define the value of the array.

Used in:

contents, interface, page, statement, and *technology.*

See also:

array, boolean, integer, miNoMax, number, point, string, typedValue, and *variable.*

---

constraint

(constraint *booleanValue*
 { property }
)

constraint

  Constraint is used to express assertions about the design. *Constraint* can be used in the *technology, interface,* or *contents* of a *view* to express constraints. This may not be used in Level 0 descriptions.

  There are no *viewType* restrictions on the use of *constraint.*

Example:

  (constraint
   (equal
    (xCoord Output)
    (xCoord Input)))

This example specifies a constraint for a symbolic layout system; the x−coordinate of the point **Output** must always equal the x−coordinate of the point **Input.**

Used in:

contents, interface, page, statement, and *technology.*

See also:

boolean, and *booleanValue.*

(contents
  { instance |
  offPageConnector |
  figure |
  section |
  net |
  netBundle |
  page |
  commentGraphics |
  portImplementation |
  timing |
  simulate |
  when |
  follow |
  logicPort |
  < boundingBox > |
  comment |
  userData }
)

Contents consists of a detailed implementation of a view of a cell. While all the above-mentioned constructs are legal in one or more types of views, some of them may not be permitted in certain types of views. In particular, *offPageConnector* and *page* are only legal in views of type **SCHEMATIC** or **STRANGER.**

Section is available for **DOCUMENT** views; *follow, when,* and *logicPort* are for **LOGICMODEL;** *figure* is for **GRAPHIC, MASKLAYOUT,** and **PCBLAYOUT** views. Where appropriate, the description of each construct includes any *viewType* restrictions. Objects defined within contents may only be externally referenced in the context of *timing* or *viewMap.*

Used in:

view.

See also:

cell, interface, page, and *viewType.*

---

contents

(contents
    { instance |
    offPageConnector |
    figure |
    section |
    net |
    netBundle |
    page |
    commentGraphics |
    portImplementation |
    timing |
    simulate |
    when |
    follow |
    logicPort |
    < boundingBox > |
    constant |
    constraint |
    variable |
    comment |
    userData }
)

contents

Contents for Level 1 cells is the same as *contents* for Level 0 with the addition of *constant, constraint,* and *variable.*

Used in:

view.

See also:

cell, interface, and *viewType.*

---

contents

(**contents**
    { instance |
    offPageConnector |
    figure |
    section |
    net |
    netBundle |
    page |
    commentGraphics |
    portImplementation |
    timing |
    simulate |
    when |
    follow |
    logicPort |
    < boundingBox > |
    constant |
    constraint |
    variable |
    assign |
    block |
    if |
    iterate |
    while |
    comment |
    userData }
)

contents

    Contents for Level 2 is the same as contents for Level 1 with the addition of *assign, block, if, iterate,* and *while* constructs. These are used for the procedural descriptions in Level 2.

Used in:

view.

See also:

cell, interface, technology, viewMap, and *viewType.*

(cornerType EXTEND | ROUND | TRUNCATE)

CornerType specifies the type of corners of paths in a figure group. It encloses one of three possible symbolic constants. The possible values are **EXTEND, TRUNCATE,** and **ROUND.** The corners are formed by two consecutive segments of the same path.

If *cornerType* is used in *figureGroup* in the *technology* section of a library, the specified corner type is the default corner type to be used for all path corners in the figure group. *CornerType* may also be specified in *figureGroupOverride* within the *figure* itself to override the default corner type. A description of its use in *oversize* can be seen in the description of that keyword.

In all cases, the inside of a corner is formed by a single point when the expansion of the two edges meet. For *cornerType* **ROUND,** an arc with radius of half the value of the associated *pathWidth* forms the outer corner. Such specifications are not universally acceptable for **MASKLAYOUT** descriptions.

EndType and *cornerType* apply to cases in which one or two *arcs* are used, by using the tangents to those *arcs* (at the point of intersection) in the role of the simple center-lines referred to in the above definitions.

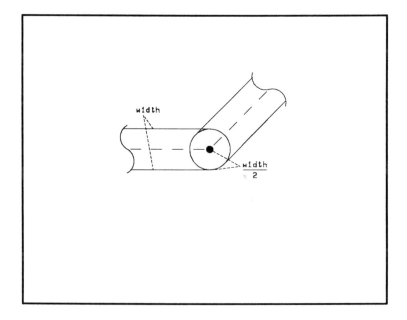

Figure 1   Corner-type round

If the corner forms an obtuse angle, both the remaining *cornerTypes* specify an outer corner with a single point.

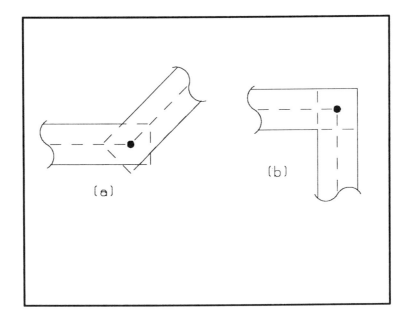

Figure 2 Corner-type extend for obtuse angles

For acute angles, **TRUNCATE** produces an additional edge which joins the two points that would have been produced by *endType* **TRUNCATE** applied to each edge separately. For example, this generates the "stop sign" or octagonal corner for a right angle.

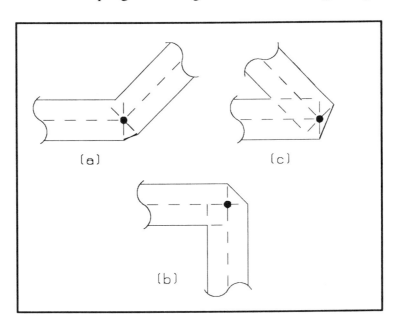

Figure 3 Corner-type truncate

The final case is the outer expansion of an acute angled corner with *cornerType* **EXTEND.** This specifies the addition of two extra symmetrical line segments at the corner. They should be perpendicular to the original centerline edges and be within the two edges that would have been produced by *endType* **EXTEND** applied to each edge separately. These are indicated as **tangent 1** and **tangent 2** in the following figure.

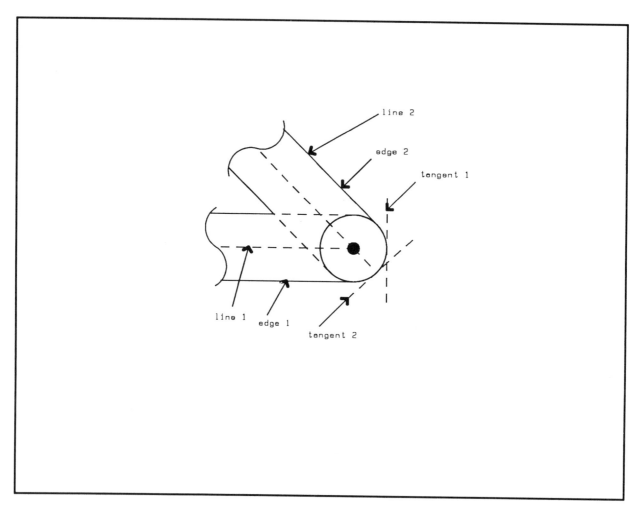

Figure 2-4 Corner-type extend for acute angles

Example:

```
(figureGroup Metal
    (cornerType EXTEND)
    (comment "specifies a default corner type of EXTEND")
    (pathWidth 10))
...
(figure
    (figureGroupOverride Metal
        (cornerType TRUNCATE)
        (comment "override default corner type")) ...)
```

This example shows the definition of **Metal** with a defined *cornerType* of EXTEND and the local change to TRUNCATE within a *figure* statement.

Used in:

figureGroup, figureGroupOverride, and *oversize.*

See also:

endType, and *pathWidth.*

(criticality *integerValue* | *integerDisplay***)**

The *criticality* attribute is used to describe the relative importance of a net compared to other nets, for routing purposes. The integer may be positive or negative. A net with a low value for its criticality is given a lower priority for routing purposes than a net with a higher value for its criticality. If the criticality for a net is not specified, the default is zero.

In a circuit net that is composed hierarchically of a number of instances and therefore possibly a number of nets or where nets are joined through **RIPPER** cells, the net criticality is a local value and does not interact with other nets.

Example:

> **(net CLOCK (joined ...)**
>   **(criticality 100))**

> **(net LSSD (joined ...)**
>   **(criticality −50))**

In this example, net **LSSD** is declared to be less critical than net **CLOCK** and also less critical than any nets that do not have a specified criticality value.

Used in:

net, and *netBackAnnotate.*

See also:

joined, and *viewType.*

(currentMap *miNoMaxValue*)

CurrentMap is an attribute of a logic value which is used to specify its electrical characteristics. *CurrentMap* gives a value or range of values to specify what the accepted current values are for the given logic value. The value is expressed in **CURRENT** units.

A logic value associated with a positive current indicates conventional current flow into a cell when observed on a port. When the same logic value is assigned to a port, this indicates conventional current flowing *out* of the cell. Reverse flows are appropriate if a negative value is used within *currentMap*.

Example:

```
(technology
   (numberDefinition
      (scale 1 (e 1 −3) (unit current))...)
   (simulationInfo
      (logicValue T
         (currentMap (e 2 −1)))))
```

In the above example, the accepted current for the logic value **T** is defined to be **0.2 mA.** As this is positive, it implies current flow from an input port or to an output port.

Used in:

logicValue.

See also:

simulationInfo, unit, and *voltageMap.*

(curve *{ arc | pointValue }*)

curve

curve

Curve contains an ordered list of points intermingled with arcs. A point preceding an arc forms a line segment with the first point specified within the arc. A point following an arc forms a line segment with the last point specified by the arc within figures. Two or more points in sequence represent one or more line segments.

A final line segment from the last point to the first point is obtained in the context of the *shape* figure.

Example:

```
(shape
    (curve
        (pt 20 100)
        (arc
            (pt 40 100)
            (pt 60 110)
            (pt 40 120))
        (pt 20 120)))
```

This example consists of one arc from **(40, 100)** through **(60, 110)** to **(40, 120)** and three straight line segments – from **(40, 120)** to **(20, 120)**, from **(20, 120)** back to **(20, 100)**, and from **(20, 100)** to **(40, 100)**.

Used in:

openShape, and *shape.*

See also:

figure.

(cycle *integerValue [duration]***)**

Cycle is used within *apply* to describe the number of cycles and duration of each cycle of the *apply*. The first integer value specifies the number of input and output cycles described, and must be strictly positive. The following *duration* specifies the interval between each application of a logical pattern. If the *duration* is omitted, this indicates that each pattern should only be applied after all activity is complete.

Example:

```
(apply (cycle 7 (duration (e 5 -1)))
   (logicInput dataIn (logicWaveform T T F T F F T))
   (logicOutput dataOut (logicWaveform F T F F T F T)))
```

This example indicates that **7** test cycles are desired, each of which will take half a time unit.

During the first cycle, **T** is applied to **dataIn** and **F** is expected from **dataOut.**

During the last cycle, **T** is applied to **dataIn** and **T** is expected from **dataOut.**

Used in:

apply.

See also:

duration, logicInput, and *logicOutput.*

(dataOrigin	*dataOrigin*
stringToken	location where the data was created
[version]	local version number of transmitted data
)	
	dataOrigin

DataOrigin identifies the actual location where a particular part of the EDIF file was created and its local version identification. This may be as specific or as general as required, identifying a particular office or an entire country. *DataOrigin* is intended for human interpretation and should serve as an aid in problem analysis. The *version* is nested within *dataOrigin* as the conventions for data versions are taken to be specific to each location.

Example:

(dataOrigin "EDIF Inc., Santa Clara Division"
     (version "12−A5"))

This identifies the **Santa Clara Division** of **EDIF Inc.** (a fictitious company) as the source of the data, which has a local version identification of **"12−A5"**.

Used in:

written.

See also:

author, program, status, timeStamp, and *version.*

(dcFaninLoad *numberValue | numberDisplay*)

DcFaninLoad is used to specify an EDIF attribute of ports. The value specified is used to compute the fan–in load contributed by an **OUTPUT** or **INOUT** port. No units are specified for this quantity. See *dcMaxFanin* for further description.

Example:

   (dcFaninLoad 25)

The above example specifies a port to have a *dcFaninLoad* value of **25.**

Used in:

port, portBackAnnotate, and *portInstance.*

See also:

dcFanoutLoad, dcMaxFanin, dcMaxFanout, direction, and *keywordDisplay.*

(dcFanoutLoad *numberValue | numberDisplay*)

DcFanoutLoad specifies an EDIF attribute of ports. The value specified is the fan-out load on an **INPUT** or **INOUT** port. No units are specified for this quantity. See *dcMaxFanout* for further description.

Example:

(dcFanoutLoad 30)

The above example specifies that the fan-out load of a port is **30.**

Used in:

port, portBackAnnotate, and *portInstance.*

See also:

dcFaninLoad, dcMaxFanin, dcMaxFanout, direction, and *keywordDisplay.*

(**dcMaxFanin** *numberValue | numberDisplay*)

DcMaxFanin is used to specify the maximum allowed fan−in load of an **INPUT** or an **INOUT** port. This is an upper limit for the accumulated fan−in loads contributed by all ports that drive the port under consideration. No units are specified for this quantity.

Example:

(**dcMaxFanin** **100**)

The above example specifies that the DC fan−in limit of a port is **100.** When used in a particular net the sum of the *dcFaninLoad* values of other ports must not exceed **100.**

Used in:

port, portBackAnnotate, and *portInstance.*

See also:

dcFaninLoad, dcFanoutLoad, dcMaxFanout, direction, and *keywordDisplay.*

(**dcMaxFanout** *numberValue | numberDisplay*)   *dcMaxFanout*

dcMaxFanout

DcMaxFanout is a *port* attribute which is used to specify the maximum fan-out capability of a port. This is an upper limit of an **OUTPUT** or **INOUT** port of all the accumulated fan-out load values in all **INPUT** or **INOUT** ports which it drives. No units are specified for this quantity.

Example:

   (**dcMaxFanout 100**)

The above example specifies that the maximum DC fan-out capability of a port is **100.** When the port is included in a particular net, the sum of the *dcFanoutLoad* values of other ports in the net should not exceed **100.**

Used in:

port, portBackAnnotate, and *portInstance.*

See also:

dcFaninLoad, dcFanoutLoad, dcMaxFanin, direction, and *keywordDisplay.*

---

	delay
(delay *miNoMaxValue* | *miNoMaxDisplay***)**	
	delay

Delay is used to specify the amount of delay in propagating a signal. The value may be a single time value or a range of time values, specified with a *miNoMaxValue*. Values are scaled using the scale for TIME specified in *technology*. Values may not be negative.

MiNoMaxDisplay may be used to display the value of the delay. This may be used in place of the number value or range when the delay exists in a coordinate space and is a displayable value.

Example:

    (delay (mnm (e 5 0) (undefined) (undefined)))
    ....
    (logicAssign OUT (logicRef T) (delay 6))

The first example specifies a delay minimum of **5.0** time units; nominal and maximum delays are undefined. The second example specifies a delay of **6** time units within a logic assignment.

Used in:

entry, follow, logicAssign, maintain, netDelay, pathDelay, portDelay, and *tableDefault.*

See also:

loadDelay, miNoMaxValue, miNoMaxDisplay, and *unit.*

(delta *{ pointValue }*)

Arrays of instances may be placed by using *delta* within the transform of geometric instances. It is expressed in terms of coordinates before any associated *orientation.*

Each *pointValue* in *delta* defines, for the corresponding index defined in the *array,* the delta–x and delta–y distance between the origins of neighboring array elements. The first *pointValue* in *delta* corresponds to the first index in *array,* the second *pointValue* corresponds to the second index, and so on.

More precisely, if an **n** dimensional instance array **Z** is defined:

(instance (array Z B1 B2 ... Bn)
   (viewRef V (cellRef C))
   (transform
      (delta PT1 PT2 ... PTn)
      (origin PT0)))

where

PT0 = (pt X0 Y0)
PT1 = (pt X1 Y1)
PT2 = (pt X2 Y2)
...
...
PTn = (pt Xn Yn)

then the location of **(member Z I1 I2 ... In)** is **(pt X Y)** where

$$X = X0 + I1 * X1 + I2 * X2 + ... + In * Xn$$

$$Y = Y0 + I1 * Y1 + I2 * Y2 + ... + In * Yn$$

Delta must contain the same number of *pointValues* as there are array index bounds in the corresponding *array.* If *delta* is not specified then the default is: **(delta (pt 0 0) ...).** The location of the origin of each element in an instance array is fully determined by the *origin, orientation,* and *delta* constructs.

Example:

```
(instance (array Foo 3 3)
    (transform ...
        (delta (pt 3 0) (pt 0 4)) (origin (pt 0 0))))
```

In the above example the location of: **(member Foo 1 0)** is at location **(3,0)**, **(member Foo 0 1)** is at location **(0,4)**, and **(member Foo 2 2)** is at location **(6,8)**.

```
(instance (array Fee 3 4) ...
    (transform ...
        (delta (pt 3 1) (pt 2 4)) (origin (pt 100 0))))
```

In the above example **(member Fee 1 0)** is at location **(103,1)**, **(member Fee 0 1)** is at location **(102,4)**, and **(member Fee 2 3)** is at location **(112,14)**.

Used in:

transform.

See also:

array, instance, orientation, origin, scaleX, and *scaleY.*

(**derivation** CALCULATED | MEASURED | REQUIRED)

derivation

derivation

Derivation is used to identify the classification of the timing information being provided. If specified as **CALCULATED,** the information has been derived from computations or simulation. If specified as **MEASURED,** the information has been derived from a measurement of the physical device. If specified as **REQUIRED,** the information has been derived from the design specification.

Example:

    (portDelay
        (derivation calculated)
        (delay ...))

In this example, the port delay timing information has been calculated.

Used in:

netDelay, portDelay, and *timing.*

See also:

forbiddenEvent.

---

design

(design *designNameDef*
    cellRef
    { < status > |
    property |
    comment |
    userData }
)

design

Design identifies the cell at the top level of the hierarchy of a particular design within a library. Since a single EDIF file may contain many designs, the reader–translator must always know the name of the design and view to be processed if only a single design is desired.

Within *design* the *cellRef* must always contain a *libraryRef,* as no *cells* are directly visible from that context.

Example:

    (design root
        (cellRef TopOfDesignCell
            (libraryRef CMOSLibrary)))

In the above example, the design **root** is specified to start at the cell named **TopOfDesignCell,** which can be found in the library called **CMOSLibrary.**

Used in:

edif.

See also:

cell, cellRef, library, libraryRef, and *status.*

(**designator** *stringValue* / *stringDisplay*)

Designator is used to specify the designated number or name of a port on a cell or an instance of a cell. In the PCB environment, the designators on ports are usually referred to as pin numbers, and the designators on cell instances are usually referred to as component reference designators.

Designator may not be used within the context of views of type **DOCUMENT** or **GRAPHIC**.

Example:

```
(cell Foo ...
   (view V1 ...
      (interface
         (designator "U000")
         (port A (designator "a")))))
(cell Fer ...
   (view V1 ...
      (contents
         (instance I1 (viewRef V1 (cellRef Foo))
            (designator "U123")
            (portInstance A (designator "1"))))))
(cell Fee ...
   (view V1 ...
      (contents
         (instance I2 (viewRef V1 (cellRef Foo)))))
      (viewMap
         (instanceBackAnnotate
            (instanceRef I2 (viewRef V1))
            (designator "U42"))
         (portBackAnnotate
            (portRef A (instanceRef I2 (viewRef V1)))
            (designator "2"))))
```

In the above example, a cell named **Foo** is defined with a default component reference designator of **"U000"** and port named **A** with a default pin name of **"a"**. A cell named **Fer** is defined in which the cell **Foo** is instantiated with an instance name of **I1** and assigned the component reference designator of **"U123"**; the port instance of port **A** is assigned the pin number designator of **"1"**. Finally, a cell named **Fee** is defined in which the cell **Foo** is instantiated with an instance name of **I2**. In cell **Fee,** the component reference designator for instance **I2** is back-annotated as **"U42"**. The pin number designator for the port instance of port **A** is back-annotated as **"2"**.

Used in:

instance,   instanceBackAnnotate,   interface,   port,   portBackAnnotate,   and *portInstance.*

See also:

keywordDisplay, stringDisplay, viewMap, and *viewType.*

---

nameDef   *designNameDef*

designNameDef

The *designNameDef* is provided for design identification external to the EDIF file. Such a reference should incorporate the EDIF file name to avoid ambiguity.

A name of this class does not conflict with any other names, such as those of libraries. However, it should be different from any other design name within the EDIF file.

Example:

(design micro99 ...)

This statement contains a design name definition for **micro99.**

Used in:

design.

See also:

edif.

(difference
   figureGroupRef | figureOp
   { figureGroupRef | figureOp }
)

    Difference defines the intersection of the first specified set of figure-group objects with the inverse of the union of all remaining sets of figure group objects. A location is contained within the *difference* if it is contained within the first figure group object but none of the following figure-group objects.

Example:

    (difference
       (figureGroupRef Poly)
       (intersection
          (figureGroupRef Poly)
          (figureGroupRef Diff)))

The above example specifies a new set of figure-group objects which are formed by subtracting the intersection of **Poly** and **Diff** from **Poly.** This is the same as **(difference (figureGroupRef Poly) (figureGroupRef Diff)).**

Used in:

figureOp.

See also:

includeFigureGroup, and *physicalDesignRule.*

$'0'$ | $'1'$ | $'2'$ | $'3'$ | $'4'$ | $'5'$ | $'6'$ | $'7'$ | $'8'$ | $'9'$	*digit*
	digit

In an *integerToken* or *asciiCharacter* this represents a normal decimal digit. In the other tokens, these are simply literal characters.

Example:

300   a10   "abc123"   "a%9%b"

The above tokens use digits in a variety of different contexts.

Used in:

identifier, integerToken, and *stringToken.*

See also:

alpha, specialCharacter, and *whiteSpace.*

(direction INOUT | INPUT | OUTPUT)

This attribute is used to specify the direction of signal information flow at a port. The permitted values are **INPUT**, **OUTPUT**, and **INOUT**; they indicate that the signal flows into the cell, out of the cell, or both ways, respectively, at the port.

Direction specifies information flow, not current flow.

Example:

(port A (direction INPUT))
(port B (direction OUTPUT))
(port (array DataBus 32) (direction INOUT))

In the above example, a port named **A** is defined to be an input port, a port named **B** is defined to be an output port, and an array of ports named **DataBus** is defined to be bidirectional.

Used in:

port.

See also:

acLoad, dcFaninLoad, dcFanoutLoad, dcMaxFanin, and *dcMaxFanout.*

(display
    figureGroupNameRef | *figureGroupOverride*

    [justify]   default: **LOWERLEFT**
    [orientation]   default: **R0**
    [origin]   default: **(pt 0 0)**
)

display

The *display* is used within the *name* and typed display constructs to indicate the desire to display information. It is only appropriate within the context of *page*, *symbol*, *protectionFrame*, or the *contents* of a view of type **GRAPHIC**, **MASKLAYOUT**, **PCBLAYOUT**, **STRANGER**, or **SYMBOLIC**. The contained elements give various attributes of the information to be displayed and should occur in the order shown above. The reference to a *figureGroupNameRef* provides normal graphical attributes, such as color, which may be overridden in the *figureGroupOverride* statement.

The *justify* and *orientation* attributes together control the relative placement and aspect of the displayed text. The origin is specified in the coordinate space of the object in which the text exists, as opposed to the coordinate space of the text. The height of the text display is determined by the *textHeight* attribute within *figureGroup* or *figureGroupOverride*. The default values for these attributes are **LOWERLEFT, R0,** and **(pt 0 0)** respectively. *Display* is not intended to be used on fabricated figure groups, as there is uncertainty in the derived font geometries.

Example:

    (integerDisplay 9999
        (display Green
            (justify LOWERCENTER) (orientation R90) (origin (pt 25 30))))

In the above example the integer **9999** is displayed in the **Green** figure group. The bottom center of the text is at the **x** and **y** coordinates of **25** and **30** units respectively, and the text is rotated counterclockwise by **90** degrees.

Used in:

booleanDisplay, integerDisplay, keywordDisplay, miNoMaxDisplay, name, numberDisplay, parameterDisplay, pointDisplay, propertyDisplay, and *stringDisplay.*

See also:

figureGroupOverride, justify, orientation, origin, protectionFrame, symbol, textHeight, viewType, and *visible.*

(divide *numberValue { numberValue })*	*divide*
	divide

     Divide is a Level 1 number function which successively divides the first argument by each of the remaining arguments, none of which may evaluate to zero. The result that is returned is a number value. At least one number is required. If a single argument is present, it is the trivial result of the function.

Example:

    (divide 24 4 2)

    (divide 24 (product 4 2))

The above examples both return the number value **3.**

Used in:

numberValue.

See also:

abs, subtract, product, max, min, negate, and *sum.*

(**dominates**   *{ logicNameRef }*)

dominates

Dominates is an attribute of a logic value used to specify the outcome of net contention when the logic value being defined is one of the values in contention when on a net. *Dominates* specifies that the logic value being defined will be the logic value seen when it is applied to a net at the same time as any of the other specified values.

The logic values referenced must have been previously defined. Unless overridden by an explicit *resolves* statement, each logic value should be taken to dominate itself.

Example:

> (**logicValue T**
>   (**dominates WT Z WF**))

In the above example if **T** and **WT, Z,** or **WF** are applied to a net at the same time, the net will take on the value of **T.**

Used in:

logicValue.

See also:

resolves, simulationInfo, strong, and *weak.*

(dot *pointValue { property }***)**

The *dot* is the geometric entity defined by a single point and is intended for use in schematic diagrams and other places where a marker is required. Neither the size of the dot nor its shape is specified and may be chosen by the implementor.

Dot is intended to be used for display purposes only and should not be used for fabrication. A common use of this figure would be as a connect dot associated with a TIE cell in schematic diagrams.

Example:

　　(dot (pt 100 200))

In the above example a *dot* is specified at the point **(100, 200)**.

Used in:

figure.

See also:

connectLocation, portImplementation, protectionFrame, and *symbol.*

(**duration** *numberValue*)

Duration is used to specify the duration of a time interval. The value specified is scaled by the TIME scaling defined in the technology block, and must be positive.

Example:

  (**duration** (**e 10 1**))

This example specifies a duration of **100** time units.

Used in:

cycle, steady, and *timeInterval.*

See also:

forbiddenEvent, numberDefinition, and *timing.*

---

e

(e

    integerToken   mantissa

    integerToken   exponent

)

e

A scale factor can be applied to an integer to represent fractional numbers or numbers too large to be expressed using an integer alone. The e construct consists of two integer tokens, representing the mantissa and exponent respectively. Its value is the mantissa times ten raised to the power of the exponent. The absolute value of this expression must be equal to zero or lie within the range 10^{-35} to 10^{+35}.

Only integer tokens are permitted in this context, even within Level 1 expressions.

Example:

    (e 100 1)
    (e 42 0)
    (e 9 −1)
    (e −12325 −3)
    (e −644 4)

The above examples represent the values **1000, 42, 0.9, −12.325,** and **−6440000** respectively.

Used in:

scaledInteger.

See also:

integerValue, and *number.*

---

edif

(edif	
edifFileNameDef	name of EDIF file (for external use)
edifVersion	version of EDIF used
edifLevel	level of EDIF file
keywordMap	user-defined keyword macros and aliases
{ < status > /	status block for file
external /	used for specifying external libraries
library /	libraries containing cell definitions
design /	the starting points for this file
comment /	user comments
userData }	user-defined constructs
)	

edif

The *edif* keyword marks the highest-level structure within the EDIF hierarchy, containing, directly or indirectly, all information transmitted within the file. The corresponding set of matching parentheses delimit that logical file. The initial substructures, *edifFileNameDef, edifVersion, edifLevel,* and *keywordMap,* contain the information required to read the file. Subsequent structures embody the actual design data and may occur in any order, subject only to the restriction that all references to any name defined within the file occur after the named construct.

An EDIF file may contain several designs and several libraries of cell definitions. The libraries serve to group relevant design information according to common characteristics. The designs indicate the particular cells within the libraries that convey the top-level, or root, descriptions of the design hierarchies.

Reference to this file cannot be made by name from within the file. The name defined by the *edifFileNameDef* has meaning only outside of the EDIF file, where it might be used by external file-handling mechanisms. This occurrence does not serve to define this name within any contained name space. Thus, the name is free for further use within the EDIF file.

Example:

```
(edif Prototype
    (edifVersion 2 0 0)
    (edifLevel 2)
    (keywordMap (keywordLevel 0))
    (status ...)
    (external Standard_Cells ...)
    (library VHSIC_CMOS
       (edifLevel 0)
```

```
        (technology ...)
        (cell B_Shift ...) ...)
    (design Barrel_Shifter (cellRef B_Shift (libraryRef VHSIC_CMOS))))
```

In the example, the file named **Prototype** contains (at least) a design named **Barrel_Shifter** drawn from the **VHSIC_CMOS** library. The reference to **Barrel_Shifter** occurs after the defining occurrence within its library. The file is written in Level 2 EDIF, Version 2 0 0 and has no mapped keywords.

Used in:

$goal.

See also:

edifLevel, edifVersion, keywordLevel, and *status.*

nameDef	*edifFileNameDef*
	edifFileNameDef

An *edifFileNameDef* is used to identify the entire EDIF file. Further information is desirable to document the source of any such file, but this name may be of value in distinguishing EDIF files from the same source.

Used in:

edif.

See also:

designNameDef, and *libraryNameDef.*

(edifLevel	*edifLevel*
integerToken	EDIF Level number (0, 1, or 2)
)	
	edifLevel

EdifLevel tells the reader the greatest EDIF level that will be found when processing the file or library. The integer token may take the value zero, one, or two only. A Level 0 structure will contain only the most primitive of the EDIF constructs. At Level 1, a superset of Level 0, *constants, parameters, variables,* and expressions may be employed to describe the design information. At Level 2, a superset of both Levels 0 and 1 and the highest level currently defined, procedural constructs may be used, enabling concise expression of data.

A Level 0 cell may always be processed as Level 1 or Level 2, since each level is a superset of all lower levels. Also, a view described at one level may instantiate a view of another cell described at a higher or lower level from a different library. *Parameters* may only be declared within the context of an *external* construct in Level 0.

Example:

```
(library nMOS_X
    (edifLevel 1)
    (technology ...)
    (cell ...)
    ...)
```

The example indicates that the library has been created using Level 1 EDIF constructs. A Level 0 reader may not be able to process the material.

Used in:

edif, external, and *library.*

See also:

edifVersion, and *keywordLevel.*

---

	edifVersion
(edifVersion *integerToken integerToken integerToken***)**	*edifVersion*

  EdifVersion indicates the version of EDIF used to create the file. The three integers are constrained to be those representing valid EDIF versions as defined by the EDIF Steering Committee. At present, this comprises the following versions: 1 0 0, 1 1 0, or 2 0 0.

Example:

  (edifVersion 2 0 0)

The example indicates a file written in the current version of EDIF.

Used in:

edif.

See also:

edifLevel.

(else *{ statement }*)   *else*

                                                                     else

---

    Else is a flow–of–control form used in conjunction with the *if* and *then* forms to achieve conditional invocation of *statements.* The *if* form takes a Boolean test expression. If the Boolean value evaluates to *true,* then the statements within the *then* form are executed. If the Boolean value evaluates to *false* and there is an *else* statement, the statements within the *else* are executed; otherwise, no statements are executed.

    Else is not restricted by *viewType* although the nested *statements* must be appropriate to the context.

Example:

```
(if (strictlyIncreasing n 5)
    (then (assign m (integer 1)))
    (else (assign m (integer (sum n 1)))))
```

In this example if **n** is less than **5** then **m** will be assigned the value **1.** If **n** is **5** or higher, **m** will be assigned the value **n+1.**

Used in:

if.

See also:

statement, and *then.*

(enclosureDistance *ruleNameDef*
   figureGroupObject
   figureGroupObject
   range / *singleValueSet*
   { comment /
   userData }
)

EnclosureDistance is used to specify the required distance by which the first figure-group object must be enclosed within the second figure-group object. Two different *figureGroups* are to be considered; pairs of edges (one from each figure group) are selected as follows: an edge from the first *figureGroupObject* which is totally inside a figure of the second *figureGroupObject,* and an edge from the enclosing figure of the second *figureGroupObject* with the same orientation as the first edge. The distance between the selected edges must satisfy the value range.

   (enclosureDistance ...
      (figureGroupObject A)
      (figureGroupObject B) ...)

In the above example, edges from **A** which are inside figures from **B** are selected. The distance between a selected edge from **A** and an edge from **B** with the same orientation must satisfy the value range. The order of *figureGroupObjects* is significant in this context.

Example:

   (enclosureDistance MET_ENCL_CONT
      (figureGroupObject CONTACT)
      (figureGroupObject METAL)
      (atLeast 2))

The above example rule requires that **CONTACT** be enclosed within **METAL** by a value greater than or equal to **2** distance units.

Used in:

physicalDesignRule.

See also:

figureGroupObject, overhangDistance, range, ruleNameDef, and *singleValueSet.*

(endType EXTEND | ROUND | TRUNCATE)

EndType is used to describe the ends of paths in figure groups. It may be specified in *figureGroup* in the technology block of a library. In this case, the end type is the default end type to be used for all path ends in the figure group. *EndType* may also be specified in *figureGroupOverride* within the *figure* itself. In this case, the end type specified is used to override the default end type.

With **EXTEND,** the end is extended by half the value of the associated *pathWidth*. **ROUND** ends are terminated with a semicircle centered at the end point with its radius half the value of the *pathWidth*. The figure ends exactly at the specified end point in the case where *endType* is **TRUNCATE**.

Caution should be used when using **ROUND** in the context of **MASKLAYOUT** *views;* such expansions are not universally acceptable.

EndType and *cornerType* apply to cases in which one or two *arcs* are used, by using the tangents to those *arcs* (at the point of intersection) in the role of the simple center-lines referred to in the above definitions.

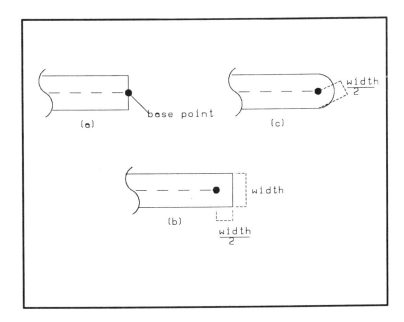

Figure 5 End types: (a) truncate (b) extend (c) round

Example:

```
(figureGroup Metal
    (endType EXTEND)
    (comment "specifies a default end type of EXTEND"))
. . .
(figure (figureGroupOverride Metal
    (endType TRUNCATE)
    (comment "override end type with TRUNCATE end type")
    (path ...))
```

This example illustrates the use of *endType* to establish a default expansion attribute and to override that attribute within a *figure* statement.

Used in:

figureGroup, and *figureGroupOverride.*

See also:

cornerType, and *pathWidth.*

(entry
    match | change | steady
    logicRef | portRef | noChange | table
    [delay | loadDelay]
)

Entry is used within the *table* construct in **LOGICMODEL** views. Any number of entries may be present in a table. The first *entry* satisfied will return the value for the table. Each table should have an action for all possible conditions. To help with this *tableDefault* is provided. *NoChange* inhibits the effect of the enclosing *follow* or *logicAssign*.

The *logicRef* should reference a logic value defined within the same library.

Example:

    (table
        (entry (match IN T) (logicRef F))
        (entry (match IN F) (logicRef T))
        (entry (change ENABLE) (logicRef Z))
        (tableDefault (logicRef X)))

In this example if the value of port **IN** is **T,** then the value **F** is returned. If the value of port **IN** is **F,** then value **T** is returned. If the value of port **IN** is neither **T** nor **F,** and the value of port **ENABLE** has just changed, then the value **Z** is returned. If none of the above conditions are satisfied, then the value **X** is returned.

Used in:

table.

See also:

change, maintain, match, noChange, steady, and *tableDefault.*

(**equal**   *numberValue { numberValue })*

equal

equal

     Equal is a function that returns *true* if all its arguments are numerically the same; it returns *false* otherwise. It is used within Level 1 and Level 2 descriptions.

Example:

    (**equal (yCoord TOPLEFT) (yCoord TOPRIGHT))**

The above example returns *true* if points **TOPLEFT** and **TOPRIGHT** have the same y–coordinate value.

Used in:

booleanValue.

See also:

increasing, and *strictlyIncreasing.*

(escape)

Escape is a flow–of–control form which provides for the exit from blocks and iterative looping structures. The invocation of *escape* results in control being passed to the end of the smallest containing *block, iterate,* or *while.* Conditional execution of the *escape* form can be achieved by including it within a *then* or *else.*

Example:

```
(block
    (variable n (integer 0))
    (iterate
        (if (increasing 100 n))
        (then (escape))
        (else
            (figure POLY (dot (pt n n)))
            (assign n (integer (sum 1 n)))))))
```

This describes a series of **100** *dot* figures in a procedural (Level 2) schematic.

Used in:

statement.

See also:

block, if, iterate, and *while.*

(event
    portRef | portList | portGroup | netRef | netGroup
    { transition | becomes }
)

Event is used to describe an event on a port or on a net using logic state transitions. Events can also be described for unordered groups of ports or nets using *portGroup* or *netGroup*. An ordered list of ports may also be used using a *portList*. If an ordered list of ports is specified and transitions are also specified, the size of the logic list and the port list must be equal. If no transitions are specified, then the default meaning is any logic state change.

Example:

    (event (portRef A) (transition H L))

In the first example the event described is port **A** changing from logic state **H** to logic state **L.**

    (event (portGroup A B))

In the second example the event described is any logic state change which occurs on port **A** or port **B.**

    (event (portList A B C)
      (transition (logicList L H X) (logicList X L H)))

In the third example the event described is a logic state change from **L** to **X** on port **A** *and* a logic state change from **H** to **L** on port **B** *and* a logic state change from **X** to **H** on port **C.** The event is satisfied when the all ports have made the transitions; the event occurs at the time of the last such change. None of the ports should have changed value more than once during the time since the first port transition.

Used in:

forbiddenEvent, offsetEvent, pathDelay, and *timeInterval.*

See also:

becomes, and *transition.*

(exactly *numberValue*)

The *exactly* construct is used to specify that a value is exactly equal to *numberValue*. It may also be used in conjunction with other ranges to include an isolated value. This is used within the context of physical design rules.

Example:

(exactly 3)

This example specifies that a design–rule measurement is required to be exactly equal to **3** units.

Used in:

range.

See also:

atLeast, atMost, multipleValueSet, numberValue, and *physicalDesignRule.*

---

	external
(external *libraryNameDef*	
edifLevel	a required EDIF level
technology	a required technology block
{ < status > |	status of the external library
cell |	cells may not contain contents
comment |	
userData }	
)	
	external

The *external* construct declares a library to which reference is made, but which is not actually present within the current EDIF file. This may include any library which has been exchanged by means outside the current EDIF file.

The structure and semantics of *external* are parallel to those of *library* except that *external* is known to be incomplete; *external* libraries that are declared should only contain minimal information. Any information present, such as *status,* must agree with the information available in the reader's *library* of the same name. *External* represents one way in which reference can be made to external information from within an EDIF file.

External should occur within a file only with prior consent of the intended receiving party, since it must be assumed that the missing library has already been transmitted. This statement provides an explicit means of declaring libraries, providing a simple check for data completeness. It also provides a mechanism for renaming an external library, since the *rename* construct may be used here. Cells in *external* may not have *contents* sections. Any object referenced later should be defined here, including all names and *interface* declarations.

In Level 0, *parameter* declarations are only permitted within the context of *cells* within *external* constructs.

Example:

```
(external ECL_H
    (edifLevel 1)
    (technology ...)
    (cell ...)
    (comment "Access to this library is restricted"))
```

This example shows the declaration of an external Level 1 library.

Used in:

edif.

See also:

cell, interface, library, libraryNameDef, parameter, status, and *technology.*

(**fabricate** *layerNameDef*
      figureGroupNameRef
)

This construct is used to declare that certain figure groups are intended to be used for physical fabrication. It also introduces a corresponding layer name.

Example:

    (**technology**
        (**figureGroup Poly** ...)
        . . .
        (**fabricate Mask_step_15 Poly**))

This example creates a layer name **Mask_step_15** and relates it to the figure group **Poly.**

Used in:

technology.

See also:

figureGroup, and *figureOp.*

(false)

false

false

       False is a Boolean value. It is expressed as a keyword to avoid clashes with *constant* and *variable* names in Levels 1 and 2.

Example:

    (property highlight
       (boolean
          (false)))

The above example defines a property named **highlight** whose value is *false*.

Used in:

booleanValue.

See also:

true.

figure

(figure *figureGroupNameRef | figureGroupOverride*
    { circle |
    dot |
    openShape |
    path |
    polygon |
    rectangle |
    shape |
    comment |
    userData }
)

figure

A *figure* is a classification of geometric entities which can be used to describe mask layers, colors for plots, or pictures. The *figure* plays a central role in the geometric layout views. The *figure* refers to a set of default characteristics defined in a *figureGroup* construct. More than one *figure* statement may use the same *figureGroupNameRef* in the same context.

The *figure* statement accumulates geometrical figures into the referenced figure group, which must have been previously defined with a *figureGroup* statement within the context of the same *library* or *external* construct. This is only allowed directly in the contents of views of type **GRAPHIC, MASKLAYOUT, PCBLAYOUT,** and **STRANGER.** It may be used indirectly in a **SCHEMATIC** *page,* **SYMBOLIC** *contents* (within *net, commentGraphics,* and *portImplementation),* and in various *interface* constructs.

Example:

    (figure
        (figureGroupOverride POLY (pathWidth 5))
            (path (pointList (pt 0 0) (pt 0 10))) (path (pointList (pt 9 0) (pt 9 10))))

This example describes two paths with a width of **5** distance units.

Used in:

commentGraphics, connectLocation, contents, net, netBundle, portImplementation, protectionFrame, statement, and *symbol.*

See also:

display, figureGroup, figureGroupOverride, and *viewType.*

(figureArea *ruleNameDef*
    figureGroupObject
    range | singleValueSet
    { comment |
    userData }
)

The *figureArea* construct is used to specify the required area of figure–group objects. A single figure group is to be considered; each figure–group object is to be selected. Any figure–group object whose area does not satisfy the specified value range is in violation of the rule.

Example:

    (figureArea CONT_AREA
        (figureGroupObject CONTACT)
        (singleValueSet
            (between (atLeast 10) (atMost 15))
            (exactly 25)))

The above example rule requires that **CONTACT** area be greater than or equal to **10** and less than or equal to **15,** or exactly equal to **25.**

Used in:

physicalDesignRule.

See also:

figureGroupObject, figurePerimeter, ruleNameDef, range, and *singleValueSet.*

---

figureGroup

(figureGroup *figureGroupNameDef*
    { < cornerType > |
    < endType > |
    < pathWidth > |
    < borderWidth > |
    < color > |
    < fillPattern > |
    < borderPattern > |
    < textHeight > |
    < visible > |
    includeFigureGroup |
    property | property of an entire figure group
    comment |
    userData }
)

figureGroup

Default figure–group attributes are defined in the *technology* block in the *figureGroup* form. Such a definition must exist for every collection of geometries referred to within any *display* or *figure* statement in the library. Each of the included attributes defines the default parameters to be used by the figure group, and each can be overridden with a *figureGroupOverride* within a *display* or *figure* statement.

Any properties used here are related to the entire figure group. Geometry is accumulated into figure groups by later *figure* statements in the context of *cells* within a design, or indirectly through an *includeFigureGroup* construct.

Example:

    (figureGroup Metal
        (pathWidth 3))

In this example, the default width for **Metal** paths is **3** distance units.

    (figure
        (figureGroupOverride Metal
            (pathWidth 5)) ...)

The second example overrides the default width with a value of **5** distance units.

    (figure Metal (path ...))

The final *figure* statement describes a path of width **3**, using the defined default value again.

Used in:

physicalDesignRule, and *technology.*

See also:

display, fabricate, figure, figureGroupOverride, and *library.*

---

nameDef

figureGroupNameDef

figureGroupNameDef

FigureGroupNameDefs must be declared for all figure groups that may be used within a library.

Figure-group names defined within a *physicalDesignRule* are local to that context. Otherwise they have a scope from the end of the *figureGroup* to the end of the local *library* or *external* context.

Used in:

figureGroup.

See also:

figureGroupNameRef.

---

nameRef

figureGroupNameRef

figureGroupNameRef

FigureGroupNameRef is an identifier used to refer to an object defined with the corresponding *figureGroupNameDef*.

Used in:

display, *fabricate,* *figure,* *figureGroupObject,* *figureGroupOverride,* and *figureGroupRef.*

See also:

figureGroupNameDef.

---

figureGroupObject

(figureGroupObject
    figureGroupNameRef | figureGroupRef | figureOp
)

figureGroupObject

The *figureGroupObject* construct contains one of several alternative methods for specifying a set of figure–group objects: by using a *figureGroupNameRef,* a *figureGroupNameRef* qualified by a library name, and by operations on figure–group objects.

Example:

    (figureGroupObject Metal1)

In the first example a set of figure–group objects is specified by the figure–group name **Metal1.**

    (figureGroupObject (figureGroupRef Poly (libraryRef Std_Lib)))

In the second example a set of figure–group objects is specified by the figure–group name **Poly,** which is defined in the *library* named **Std_Lib.**

    (FigureGroupObject
        (intersection (figureGroupRef Poly) (figureGroupRef Diff)))

In the third example a set of figure–group objects is specified as the intersection of the figure groups named **Poly** and **Diff.**

Used in:

enclosureDistance, figureArea, figurePerimeter, figureWidth, interFigureGroupSpacing, intraFigureGroupSpacing, notAllowed, notchSpacing, overhangDistance, overlapDistance, and *rectangleSize.*

See also:

figureGroupNameRef, figureGroupRef, figureOp, and *physicalDesignRule.*

(figureGroupOverride *figureGroupNameRef*
    { < cornerType > |
    < endType > |
    < pathWidth > |
    < borderWidth > |
    < color > |
    < fillPattern > |
    < borderPattern > |
    < textHeight > |
    < visible > |
    property |
    comment |
    userData }
)

figureGroupOverride

FigureGroupOverride is used in *figure* statements to override default attributes defined in the *figureGroup*. The *figureGroupNameRef* refers to a *figureGroup* defined in the technology block of the local library. After the enclosing *display* or *figure* construct, the default figure attributes originally defined in the *figureGroup* are once again effective.

Example:

    (figureGroupOverride Name_text
      (color 0 100 0))

This example shows the method used to change the default color of **Name_text** to green for a particular use.

Used in:

display, and *figure.*

See also:

figureGroup.

(figureGroupRef *figureGroupNameRef* [*libraryRef*])

FigureGroupRef is used to specify a reference to a figure group. The referenced figure group can be defined in another library, in which case the *libraryRef* construct is used. If the referenced library is defined outside of the current EDIF file, then it must also be specified in an *external* construct.

Example:

> **(figureGroupRef Poly (libraryRef Std_Lib))**

In the above example a figure group named **Poly** is referenced which is defined in the library named **Std_Lib.**

Used in:

difference, figureGroupObject, includeFigureGroup, intersection, inverse, oversize, and *union.*

See also:

figureGroup, figureGroupNameRef, figureGroupOverride, figureOp, and *libraryRef.*

difference | intersection | inverse | oversize | union   *figureOp*

                                                                          figureOp

FigureOp is not itself a keyword but is used for ease of reference. It provides a grouping of geometric operations for specifying new sets of figure–group objects. Their input and output is EDIF figures (polygons, shapes, etc.).

Example:

> (intersection
>   (union (figureGroupRef Poly) (figureGroupRef Buried))
>   (inverse (figureGroupRef Diff)))

In the above example the *figureOp* constructs *intersection, union,* and *inverse* are used to define a new set of figure–group objects.

Used in:

difference, figureGroupObject, includeFigureGroup, intersection, inverse, oversize, and *union.*

See also:

dot, circle, figure, figureGroup, figureGroupOverride, openShape, path, polygon, rectangle, and *shape.*

(figurePerimeter *ruleNameDef*
    figureGroupObject
    range | *singleValueSet*
    { comment |
    userData }
)

The *figurePerimeter* construct is used to specify the required perimeter size of figure–group objects. A single figure group is to be considered; each figure–group figure is to be selected. Perimeter is defined as the sum of the lengths of the external edges of any figure–group object. The perimeter of each figure–group object must satisfy the specified value range.

Example:

> **(figurePerimeter CONT_PERIM**
>   **(figureGroupObject CONTACTS)**
>   **(atLeast 16))**

The above example rule requires that **CONTACTS** perimeter be greater than or equal to **16** distance units.

Used in:

physicalDesignRule.

See also:

figureArea, figureGroupObject, ruleNameDef, range, and *singleValueSet.*

(figureWidth *ruleNameDef*
    figureGroupObject
    range | singleValueSet
    { comment |
    userData }
)

The *figureWidth* construct is used for specifying the required interior width of figure–group objects. A single input figure group is to be considered; pairs of edges within the same figure–group object which have their inside orientations facing are to be selected. The distance between these edges must satisfy the specified value range for these edges to satisfy the rule.

Example:

    (figureWidth POLY_WIDTH
        (figureGroupObject POLY)
        (atLeast 5))

The above example rule requires that **POLY** width be greater than or equal to **5** distance units.

Used in:

physicalDesignRule.

See also:

figureGroupObject, ruleNameDef, range, and *singleValueSet.*

---

	fillPattern
(fillPattern	
integerValue	number of pixels in X direction
integerValue	number of pixels in Y direction
boolean	boolean array containing pixel pattern
)	
	fillPattern

The *fillPattern* construct specifies the stipple or pixel pattern which is used to fill the interior of a figure. The first integer value represents the number of pixels required for the pattern in the x direction, and the second integer value represents the number of pixels required for the pattern in the y direction. The two integer values also specify the dimensionality of the boolean array in the same manner as the *array* construct. *Boolean* is used to define an array of pattern values. It must define a Boolean value for each point of the matrix defined by the two integer values. The pixel size is not defined since it is dependent of the type of display used.

The origin of the pattern is in the lower left corner, the x dimension increasing toward the right and the y dimension increasing toward the top. The pattern values are defined such that **(member 0 0)** of the Boolean array is the pixel value at the pattern origin, **(member 1 0)** is the pixel value for the next adjacent pixel from the pattern origin in the positive x direction, **(member 0 1)** is the pixel value for the next adjacent pixel from the pattern origin in the positive y direction, and the array value for the member with maximum indices is the pixel value for the upper right corner of the pattern. A Boolean *true* indicates that the pixel is to be displayed in the specified color of the figure. A Boolean *false* indicates that the pixel is unchanged: the present color of this pixel, which may be the background color or which may have been set previously by another overlapping *figure,* should not be altered.

FillPattern may be specified in the *figureGroup* form in the technology block of a library. In this case, the pattern is the default pattern fill to be used to fill all figures in the figure group. *FillPattern* may also be specified in the *figureGroupOverride* form within the *figure* itself. In this case, the fill pattern specified is used to override the default fill pattern.

This pattern only affects the display of a figure, not its fabrication.

Example:

```
(fillPattern 4 6
    (boolean
        (boolean (true) (true) (true) (true) (true) (false))
        (boolean (false) (false) (true) (false) (true) (false))
        (boolean (false) (false) (true) (false) (true) (false))
        (boolean (false) (false) (false) (false) (false) (false))))
```

The above example defines a fill pattern which would fill figures with **F** character patterns.

Used in:

figureGroup, and *figureGroupOverride.*

See also:

array, boolean, booleanValue, borderPattern, color, false, figure, integerValue, true, and *visible.*

(fix *numberValue***)**

fix

fix

Fix is an integer function which truncates its argument towards zero and returns the result. The result is the integer of the same sign as the argument and which has the greatest absolute value less than or equal to the argument.

Example:

> **(fix (e 52 −1))**
> **(fix (e −52 −1))**

The first example returns the integer value **5.** The second example returns the integer value **−5.**

Used in:

integerValue, and *numberValue.*

See also:

ceiling, and *floor.*

(floor *numberValue*)

floor

floor

      Floor is an integer function that returns the greatest integer less than or equal to its argument. It truncates its argument towards negative infinity.

Example:

    (floor (e −52 −1))

This example returns the integer value **−6.**

Used in:

integerValue, and *numberValue.*

See also:

ceiling, and *fix.*

follow

(follow
  portNameRef | portRef
  portRef | table
  [delay | loadDelay]
)

follow

Follow is used within the contents of the **LOGICMODEL** or **STRANGER** views, or within the *when* or *after* constructs to specify that a port will follow the value from a *table* construct or the value of some other *port*. A *follow* will continue to be in effect on a port until another action accesses that port such as a *logicAssign, maintain,* or another *follow.*

The first argument identifies which *port* will be affected by this statement. A *portRef* used as a second argument is used to determine which logic values should be transferred to the first *port*. The *delay* specifies the time taken for a change in the second value (or the activation of this statement) to affect the given port.

Example:

  (contents (follow OUT (portRef IN) (delay 5)))

The first example describes a simple buffer. Any change in the value of port **IN** will cause the same change to take place in the value of port **OUT, 5** TIME units later.

  (follow OUT
    (table
      (entry (match IN T) (logicRef F))
      (entry (match IN F) (logicRef T)))
    (delay 5))

The second example describes a simple inverter.

Used in:

after, contents, statement, and *when.*

See also:

logicAssign, maintain, and *table.*

(**forbiddenEvent** *timeInterval*
   { event }
)

    ForbiddenEvent lists *events* which are forbidden during a period of time which is specified by *timeInterval*. *ForbiddenEvent* may be used to describe minimum required setup and hold times, minimum pulse widths, and other timing constraints.

Example:

    (**forbiddenEvent**
       (**timeInterval**
          (**event** (**portRef CLK**) (**becomes H**)
          (**event** (**portRef CLK**) (**becomes L**))
       (**event** (**portRef D**)))

In this example no transitions can occur on port **D** during the time that port **CLK** becomes **H** to the time that port **CLK** becomes **L**.

    (**forbiddenEvent**
       (**timeInterval**
          (**event** (**portRef CK**) (**transition L H**))
          (**duration** (**E 78 −1**)))
       (**event** (**portRef CK**) (**becomes L**)))

In the second example, for **7.8** time units after a **L** to **H** transition on port **CK** there must not be a transition back to **L** on the same port. This is equivalent to port **CK** having a minimum **H** pulse width of **7.8** time units.

Used in:

timing.

See also:

event, and *timeInterval.*

(forEach *formalNameRef | formalList*
    { build |
    actual |
    literal |
    forEach |
    comment }
)

ForEach is a looping construct that is used to build *forms* iteratively. It may only be used in files declared to have a keyword level of 3. It is used in conjunction with the keyword builder constructs *build* and *generate*. The builders specified within the *forEach* will be expanded as long as the list of values bound to the *formal* parameter (or parameters) specified in the *forEach* is not exhausted.

In other words, the builders contained within *forEach* will be expanded for each value that is bound to the *formal* parameters that are specified. *ForEach* is used to generate *forms* that use *formal* parameters which are defined as *collector* parameters.

Any *actual* statements within *forEach* which reference the same formal parameter should expand to a single value on each iteration.

Example:

```
(keywordDefine inport
    (keywordParameters
        (formal name (collector))
        (formal load (collector)))
    (generate
        (forEach
            (formalList name load)
            (build port (actual name)
                (build direction (literal INPUT))
                (build acLoad (actual load)))))))
```

This example defines a keyword that will create several input *port* declarations and specify an *acLoad* value for each. This could later be used in a statement such as:

(inport portA 12 portB 15 portC 6)

The name **Inport** is not a native EDIF keyword and would not be legal without the appropriate definition.

This would generate:

(port portA (direction input) (acLoad 12))
(port portB (direction input) (acLoad 15))
(port portC (direction input) (acLoad 6))

Used in:

build, forEach, and *generate.*

See also:

actual, collector, formalList, keywordDefine, and *keywordLevel.*

---

form

'(' *keywordNameRef*
    { *integerToken* | *stringToken* | *identifier* | *form* }
')'

form

The *form* construct includes the generic class of all EDIF constructs. It is only directly used in certain low−level statements, in which only the parenthetical nesting is significant. It is also used to evoke a keyword−abbreviation defined within *keywordMap* at keyword level 1 or higher.

The *keywordNameRef* is an *identifier* which must be either a native EDIF keyword (defined within this document) or correspond to a *keywordNameDef* in a *keywordAlias* or *keywordDefine*.

WhiteSpace may be added or removed next to the parentheses of a *form* without affecting its interpretation.

Example:

(userData userName
        (sum x y . . .))

In this example the user−defined data of type **userName** uses a *form* with keyword name **sum.**

Used in:

form, literal, and *userData.*

See also:

keywordAlias, keywordDefine, keywordMap, keywordNameRef, and *whiteSpace.*

---

formal

(formal *formalNameDef*
    [optional]
)

formal

This construct is used to specify a formal parameter for use with the *keywordParameters* section of a *keywordDefine* form. These *formal* parameters will be substituted for positionally, by actual parameter values, in subsequent invocation of the defined keyword. The *optional* form allows the use of formal parameters which need not be included in every use of the new keyword. Any *formal* parameter following an *optional* parameter must also be *optional*.

This is only legal within keyword definitions at a keyword level 2 or higher.

Example:

```
(keywordDefine wait
    (keywordParameters
        (formal time)
        (formal load
            (optional (literal 5))))
    (generate
        (build loadDelay
            (actual time)
            (actual load))))
```

This keyword definition creates a *loadDelay* construct. However, load value is optional with a default value of **5**. A later use such as **(wait 10)** or **(wait 15 20)** would be legal in any context in which *loadDelay* is legal.

Used in:

keywordParameters.

See also:

form, keywordDefine, and *optional.*

(formal *formalNameDef*   *formal*
   [optional | collector]
)

                                                      formal

This construct is used to specify a formal parameter for use with the *keywordParameters* section of a *keywordDefine* form. These formal parameters will be substituted for positionally, by actual parameter values, in subsequent use of the defined keyword. The *optional* form allows the use of formal parameters which need not be included in every use of the new keyword.

At this level of keyword complexity (keyword level 3), the *formal* construct provides for the existence of an embedded *collector* construct, which enables it to be bound to a list of values as opposed to a single value.

Optional and *collector* parameters may only be followed by formal parameters of the same type within *keywordParameters*.

Example:

```
(keywordDefine EG
    (keywordParameters
        (formal a)
        (formal b)
        (formal c (collector))) ...)
```

This example defines a new keyword **EG.** A later use, such as:

(EG 1 2 3 4 5 6)

would expand under the binding **a=1, b=2,** and **c** is a list of **3,4,5,6.**

Used in:

keywordParameters.

See also:

collector, keywordDefine, keywordLevel, keywordMap, and *optional.*

(formalList *{ formalNameRef }* **)**

FormalList contains a set of formal parameter references which are used to control the iterations of the *forEach* form. Such iteration should step through the collected values of each referenced formal parameter in parallel, each of which should be bound to the same number of actual values.

Example:

```
(keywordDefine inport
    (keywordParameters
        (formal name (collector))
        (formal load (collector)))
    (generate
        (forEach (formalList name load)
            (build port (actual name)
                (build direction (literal INPUT))
                (build acLoad (actual load)))))))
```

This example illustrates the collection and use of a series of *port* name and *acLoad* value pairs.

Used in:

forEach.

See also:

build, generate, and *keywordDefine.*

identifier	*formalNameDef*
	formalNameDef

FormalNameDef is a simple identifier used to name a formal parameter of a *keywordDefine*. It is local to that construct.

Used in:

formal.

See also:

keywordDefine, and *formalNameRef.*

identifier	*formalNameRef*
	formalNameRef

FormalNameRef is used within keyword level 2 and higher levels to reference formal parameters defined in the context of the same *keywordDefine*.

Used in:

actual, forEach, and *formalList.*

See also:

formalNameDef.

---

generate
generate for keyword Level 2

(generate
    { literal |
    actual |
    build |
    comment }
)

generate

Generate is used to specify the expansion of a *form* which references a defined keyword, at keyword level 2 or higher. Since this construct contains an arbitrary number of builders, the use of a *keywordDefine* can generate more than one *form*. In such cases it should not be used as a positional item within the enclosing construct.

Example:

    (keywordDefine polyFigure
        (keywordParameters (formal figure))
        (generate
            (build figure
                (literal POLY)
                (actual figure))))

This creates a keyword tailored for the specification of **POLY** figures. A later use such as **(polyFigure (rectangle ...))** should generate **(figure POLY (rectangle ...))**.

Used in:

keywordDefine.

See also:

actual, build, form, and *literal.*

---

generate
generate for keyword Level 3

(generate
    { literal |
    actual |
    build |
    forEach |
    comment }
)

generate

Generate is used to specify the expansion of a *form* which references a defined keyword, at keyword level 2 or higher. Since this construct contains an arbitrary number of builders, the use of a *keywordDefine* can generate more than one *form*. In such cases it should not be used as a positional item within the enclosing construct.

At keyword level 3 only, *generate* can use embedded *forEach* constructs to process lists of arbitrary length.

Example:

```
(keywordDefine inport
   (keywordParameters
      (formal name (collector))
      (formal load (collector)))
   (generate
      (forEach (formalList name load)
         (build port (actual name)
            (build direction (literal INPUT))
            (build acLoad (actual load))))))
```

This example shows the use of *forEach* within a *generate* keyword definition at keyword level 3. A typical use could be: **(inport IN1 10 IN2 20),** which would generate:

(port IN1 (direction INPUT) (acLoad 10))
(port IN2 (direction INPUT) (acLoad 20))

Used in:

keywordDefine.

See also:

actual, build, forEach, keywordLevel, and *literal.*

(globalPortRef *portNameRef*)

GlobalPortRef is used to specify implicitly a port reference for each master and instance port with the same *portNameRef* identifier. The *portNameRef* may not reference a member of an array.

GlobalPortRefs containing the same *portNameRef* may not appear in separate *nets*. It is intended that *globalPortRef* should provide a shorthand notation for referencing all instance ports with the same name within the current *view* and any master port with that name, should one exist. Therefore, all *instances* that reference *views* which define *ports* of the same name are required to precede the *globalPortRef* that contains that *portNameRef*. *GlobalPortRef* may not be used in the context of the interface.

Example:

```
(library lib1 ...
   (cell Foo ...
      (view V2 ...
         (interface ... (port VCC ...))))
   (cell Fer ...
      (view V1 ...
         (interface (port VCC ...)
         (contents
            (instance I1 (viewRef V2 (cellRef Foo)) ...)
            (instance I2 (viewRef V2 (cellRef Foo)) ...)
            (net VCC_net (joined (globalPortRef VCC)))))))
```

In the example above, the *globalPortRef* is used as an abbreviation for specifying port references to a master port and two instance ports of instance **I1** and **I2,** all with the same port name of **VCC,** thus implying:

(joined (portRef VCC) (portRef VCC (instanceRef I1)) (portRef VCC (instanceRef I2)))

Used in:

joined.

See also:

net, and *portRef.*

(greaterThan *numberValue***)**

GreaterThan is used to specify the range of values greater than *numberValue*. It forms part of the specification of physical design rules.

Example:

(greaterThan 8)

This example specifies that the corresponding design-rule value should be greater than **8** units.

Used in:

between, and *range.*

See also:

lessThan, multipleValueSet, numberValue, and *physicalDesignRules.*

---

gridMap

(gridMap
    numberValue   X direction
    numberValue   Y direction
)

gridMap

GridMap specifies the relationship between a symbolic layout description and normal coordinates, in which different factors are required for x-coordinates and y-coordinates. This mapping is performed on coordinate data within each cell of the appropriate library, prior to any transformations resulting from instantiation or scaling. *GridMap* thus augments the distance scale for the interpretation of points within a library.

A typical need for such nonuniform description arises in gate-array macrocell definitions, in which different x and y pitches often result from different spacings for the interconnect layers for those directions.

Example:

```
(library NMOS
    (edifLevel 0)
    (technology
        (numberDefinition
            (scale 1 (e 1 6) (unit distance))
        (gridMap 5 7)) ...) ...)
```

This example shows the technology block of a library in which cells are described on a grid of **5** microns in the x direction and **7** microns in the y direction, thus a point specified as **(pt 2 3)** on the grid is at **10** microns in the x direction and **21** microns in the y direction.

Used in:

numberDefinition.

See also:

scale, scaleX, and *scaleY.*

---

alpha | '**&**' { *alpha* | *digit* | '_' }   *identifier*

                                                            identifier

---

Identifier is a basic token type; it is used for name definition, name reference, keywords, and symbolic constants. It contains alphanumeric or underscore characters and must be preceded with an ampersand if the first character is not a letter. This will normally be recognized by a lexical scanner.

Case is not significant in *identifiers*. There are no reserved identifiers, except within *keywordNameDef*. The length of an *identifier* must be between 1 and 255 characters, excluding the optional ampersand character. *Identifiers* are terminated by *whiteSpace* or by a left or right parenthesis.

Rename can be used to express external names which do not conform to the *identifier* syntax.

Example:

    a12
    &a12
    A12
    abc
    &12s
    &12o

The first three identifiers in this example are identical. The last two must include the ampersand.

Used in:

form, formalNameDef, formalNameRef, keywordNameDef, keywordNameRef, literal, name, nameDef, nameRef, rename, and *userData*.

See also:

integerToken, stringToken, and *whiteSpace*.

if

```
(if   booleanValue
      then
      [ else ]
)
```

if

If is a flow–of–control form which is used in conjunction with the *else* and *then* forms to achieve conditional invocation of EDIF statements. The *if* statement takes a Boolean test expression. If the Boolean value evaluates to *true* then the statements within the *then* form are executed; if the Boolean value evaluates to *false* and there is an *else* statement, the statements within the *else* are executed; otherwise, no statements are executed.

This is only legal in Level 2 EDIF, and has no *viewType* restrictions.

Example:

```
(if (strictlyIncreasing n 5)
    (then (assign m (integer 1)))
    (else (assign m (integer (sum n 1)))))
```

In this example if **n < 5** then **m** will be assigned the value **1.** Otherwise, **m** will be assigned the value **n+1.**

Used in:

contents, interface, page, statement, and *technology.*

See also:

else, then, and *while.*

(ignore)   *ignore*

                                                                            ignore

---

Ignore is used in place of a logic value to specify that an input (or inout) should not be driven or that an output (or inout) should not be compared. This may be used in a *logicWaveForm* to inhibit the **INPUT** or **OUTPUT** characteristics of an **INOUT** port in the context of a *simulate* construct.

Example:

```
(match (portList IN0 IN1 IN2)
    (logicOneOf
        (logicList  T (ignore) T)
        (logicList  T T (ignore))))
```

In the above example, *match* is satisfied when **IN0** is **T** and either **IN1** or **IN2** is **T**.

Used in:

logicList, and *logicWaveForm.*

See also:

logicOneOf, simulate, and *waveValue.*

(includeFigureGroup *figureGroupRef | figureOp*)

IncludeFigureGroup is used to specify that the figures of the designated figure group are to be included in the definition of another figure group. The figures carry with them the default attributes of the original figure group, unless they were overridden in their specification (using a *figureGroupOverride* construct), in which case those values prevail. The main effect of this statement is to associate further geometries with a figure group. The referenced figure group may be part of another library, where cells may be instantiated within the local library.

Example:

    (figureGroup MyPoly
       (includeFigureGroup
          (figureGroupRef Poly (libraryRef TheirLib))))

In the first example a new figure named **MyPoly** is defined which includes all figures and their attributes of the figure name **Poly** which is defined in **TheirLib.**

    (figureGroup Transistors
       (includeFigureGroup
        (difference
          (intersection
            (figureGroupRef Poly) (figureGroupRef Diff))
          (figureGroupRef Buried))))

In the second example a new figure group named **Transistors** is defined to include all figures resulting from geometric operations on the figure groups named **Poly, Diff,** and **Buried.**

Used in:

figureGroup.

See also:

difference, figureGroupRef, figureOp, intersection, inverse, oversize, and *union.*

(**increasing** *numberValue { numberValue }*)

Increasing is a Boolean function which returns *true* if the sequence of its arguments is monotonically nondecreasing (i.e. arg1 $\leq$ arg2 $\leq$ ... $\leq$ argn). It returns *false* otherwise.

Example:

(**increasing channelWidth 5**)

This expression is *true* if **channelWidth** $\leq$ **5.**

Used in:

booleanValue.

See also:

equal, and *strictlyIncreasing.*

(initial)
initial

Initial is used in a *trigger* statement to specify the actions to be taken when first initializing a model. The *when* statement which contains a *trigger* which is specified as *initial* will be used only when the model is first being initialized for simulation, i.e. at time zero. The other *when* statements which implement the model will control the model's behavior for the duration of the simulation.

Example:

    (when
        (trigger (initial))
        (logicAssign CLKOUT (logicRef X)))

The above example shows that, upon initialization, port **CLKOUT** is to be assigned the logic value **X.**

Used in:

trigger.

See also:

when.

```
(instance  instanceNameDef
    viewRef | viewList
    { < transform > |
    parameterAssign |
    portInstance |
    < designator > |
    timing |
    property |
    comment |
    userData }
)
```

Instance allows a view to be referenced within another view to create the instance hierarchy of a design. It indicates the structured inclusion of a copy of the referenced view, possibly modified by the various attributes. An array of *instances* is created by use of an *array* for the *instanceNameDef*.

Instance may not be used in the *contents* of views of type BEHAVIOR or SCHEMATIC, but it may be used within SCHEMATIC *pages*.

Example:

```
(contents
    (instance nand12 (viewRef netlist2 (cellRef nand))) ...)
```

The above example describes an instance named **nand12** of the view named **netlist2** of the cell named **nand.**

Used in:

commentGraphics, contents, net, page, portImplementation, protectionFrame, section, statement, and *symbol.*

See also:

array, delta, keywordDisplay, transform, view, and *viewType.*

---

	instanceBackAnnotate
(instanceBackAnnotate *instanceRef*	
{ < designator > |	instance (reference) designator
timing	
property |	properties to be back annotated
comment }	
)	
	instanceBackAnnotate

InstanceBackAnnotate is used to back–annotate EDIF attributes and user properties which are associated with instances. The EDIF attribute for instances is *designator*. User properties are specified with the *property* construct. *InstanceBackAnnotate* is used within *viewMap;* in this context, the *designator* serves to back–annotate an instance (reference) designator.

Example:

    (cell Foo ...
       (view V2 ...
          (interface ...
             (property packageType (string) (owner ″EDIFCo″)))
          (contents ... (instance I1 ...))))
    (cell Fer...
       (view V1 ...
          (contents ... (instance I2 (viewRef V2 (cellRef Foo)) ...)))
       (viewMap
          (instanceBackAnnotate
             (instanceRef I1 (instanceRef I2 (viewRef V1)))
             (designator ″U123″)
             (property packageType (string ″SIP″) (owner ″EDIFCo″)))))

In the above example, the component–designator attribute and the user–property **packageType** owned by **″EDIFCo″** on instance **I1** of view **V2** of cell **Foo** are back–annotated through the instance hierarchy via instance **I2** of view **V1** of cell **Fer.**

Used in:

viewMap.

See also:

designator, instanceMap, instanceRef, netBackAnnotate, portBackAnnotate, and *property.*

(instanceGroup *{ instanceRef }***)**

InstanceGroup is used to indicate a group of instance references. The group is not an ordered list but a set. By grouping instances, a relationship between a group and a single instance or another group can be established, e.g. the relationship that four primitive gates in one view taken together correspond to one component in another view. All the instances referenced within *instanceGroup* must belong to the same view.

Example:

```
(instanceMap
  (instanceGroup
    (instanceRef inst1 (viewRef V1))
    (instanceRef inst2 (viewRef V1))
    (instanceRef inst3 (viewRef V1))
    (instanceRef inst4 (viewRef V1)))
  (instanceRef I1 (viewRef V2)))
```

The example above indicates that **inst1, inst2, inst3,** and **inst4** in view **V1** are the same as **I1** in **V2**. There is no relationship implied between **inst1, inst2, inst3,** and **inst4**.

Used in:

instanceMap.

See also:

instanceRef, viewMap, and *viewRef.*

(instanceMap
    { instanceRef |
    instanceGroup |
    comment |
    userData }
)

InstanceMap is used in the *viewMap* construct to explicitly associate instances in different views which are the same object. An *instanceMap* may be used to map several instance objects of one view with one or more instance objects of other views. Groups of instances are specified with the *instanceGroup* construct. A common use of *instanceMap* would be to map an instance of a single primitive gate of a **SCHEMATIC** or **NETLIST** view to an instance within a **MASKLAYOUT** or **PCBLAYOUT** view. *InstanceMap* does not affect attribute or property values.

Example:

(viewMap ...
    (instanceMap
      (instanceGroup
        (instanceRef instance1 (viewRef ic))
        (instanceRef instance2 (viewRef ic)))
      (instanceRef instance1 (viewRef nets))))

The example above specifies explicitly that instances named **instance1** and **instance2** in the view named **ic** represent the same object as the instance named **instance1** in the view named **nets.**

Used in:

viewMap.

See also:

instanceGroup, instanceRef, netMap, portMap, and *viewRef.*

---

nameDef | *array*	*instanceNameDef*
	instanceNameDef

InstanceNameDef is used to create a name for an *instance* or *page*. Such names are scoped to the end of the smallest enclosing *view*, *net*, or *page*.

The *array* is used to create an array of *instances*, but may not be used for *pages*.

Used in:

instance, and *page*.

See also:

array, delta, instanceNameRef, instanceRef, net, and *view*.

---

nameRef	*member*	*instanceNameRef*
	instanceNameRef

An *instanceNameRef* is a name used to reference a previously defined instance or page with a matching *instanceNameDef*.

The *member* may only be used if the corresponding *instanceNameDef* was an *array*.

Used in:

instanceRef.

See also:

instanceNameDef, and *member.*

(**instanceRef** *instanceNameRef*
    [instanceRef | viewRef]
)

The *instanceRef* construct is used to reference an *instance* or *page* by name or by optional reference through the instance hierarchy. Nested *instanceRef* constructs, e.g. (**instanceRef ... (instanceRef ...**)) are used to reference an instance through the instance hierarchy. The first or outermost *instanceNameRef* in the syntax is the target, where the nested constructs which follow define a reference path in a bottom–up manner. The *viewRef* is only legal if the *instanceRef* originated from the context of a *viewMap*. *InstanceRef* may only be nested in the context of *viewMap* and *timing* statements.

Example:

(**instanceRef I1 (instanceRef (member I2 5) (viewRef V1)))**

Here, an instance named **I1** is referenced through the instance hierarchy via an instance array named **I2** which is specified in the contents of a view named **V1**.

(**portRef P1 (instanceRef I1))**

In the second example a port instance named **P1** belonging to the instance named **I1** is referenced.

(**portRef P1 (instanceRef I1 (instanceRef I2))**

In the third example a port instance named **P1** belonging to the instance named **I1** is referenced through the instance hierarchy via an instance named **I2**.

Used in:

instanceBackAnnotate, instanceGroup, instanceMap, instanceRef, netRef, and *portRef.*

See also:

event, instance, instanceNameDef, instanceNameRef, joined, member, netBackAnnotate, netGroup, netMap, page, pathDelay, portBackAnnotate, portGroup, portList, portMap, viewMap, and *viewRef.*

---

integer

(**integer** { *integerValue* | *integerDisplay* | *integer* })

integer

Integer declares a *constant, parameter, property,* or *variable* value to be of type *integer.* An optional *integerValue* can be specified, in which case the value serves as the default.

An array of integer values can be defined by specifying multiple *integerValues* within an *integer.* Nesting of the *integer* construct is required to specify array values of two or more dimensions. The number of items directly within *integer* corresponds to the first dimension of an array.

Example:

(**parameter wordWidth (integer 16**))

In this example the parameter **wordWidth** is declared to be of type *integer* and has a default integer value of **16.**

(**constant (array IA1 2) (integer 5 25**))
(**constant (array IA2 2 3)**
    (**integer**
        (**integer 2 7 45**)
        (**integer 1 0 22**)))

In the above example the constant **IA1** is defined to be a one–dimensional integer array with the value assignments (**member IA1 0**) **= 5,** (**member IA1 1**) **= 25.** **IA2** is defined to be a two–dimensional integer array with the following values:

(**member IA2 0 0**) **= 2,** (**member IA2 0 1**) **= 7,** (**member IA2 0 2**) **= 45,**
(**member IA2 1 0**) **= 1,** (**member IA2 1 1**) **= 0,** (**member IA2 1 2**) **= 22.**

Used in:

integer, and *typedValue.*

See also:

array, boolean, integerValue, miNoMax, number, point, and *string.*

(integerDisplay   *integerValue*
    { display }
)

IntegerDisplay is used to display integer design data. It is allowed in constructs that normally contain design data and which may exist in a coordinate space. Many constructs may exist in places where there is a coordinate space as well as in places where there is no coordinate space. *IntegerDisplay* contains the data to be displayed, which must be an integer value and any number of *display* forms.

The *integerValue* also serves its normal role as a value in the appropriate context.

Example:

```
(net N1
    (joined (portRef A) (portRef B))
    (criticality
        (integerDisplay 50 (display text (origin (pt 4 6))))))...)
```

In the above example the *criticality* attribute is in a coordinate space, and the value **50** can be displayed at **(4,6)**.

Used in:

criticality, and *integer.*

See also:

display, numberDisplay, miNoMaxDisplay, and *stringDisplay.*

---

integerToken

$[$ '$-$' $|$ '$+$' $]$ *digit* $\{$ *digit* $\}$

integerToken

This is a basic EDIF token, expressed in normal decimal notation. Its absolute value must be less than 2^{31}. *IntegerTokens* are terminated by *whiteSpace* or before a left or right parenthesis or percent character within *asciiCharacter*. *WhiteSpace* must not occur within the token or after the optional sign.

This will normally be recognized by a lexical scanner.

Example:

0
123
−456
+789

This examples illustrates four integer tokens.

Used in:

asciiCharacter, e, edifLevel, edifVersion, form, integerValue, keywordLevel, literal, scaledInteger, timeStamp, and *userData.*

See also:

identifier, stringToken, and *whiteSpace.*

integerToken	*integerValue*
	integerValue

IntegerValue describes the primitive integer tokens at EDIF Level 0.

This construct is extended in higher-level EDIF to allow the use of integer expressions.

Example:

> **10**
> **5**
> **−5**

These tokens represent ten, five, and minus five respectively.

Used in:

array, borderPattern, borderWidth, criticality, cycle, fillPattern, integer, integerDisplay, member, oversize, pathWidth, pt, scaleX, scaleY, and *textHeight.*

See also:

edifLevel, numberValue, and *stringValue.*

---

integerValue

integerToken | valueNameRef | floor | ceiling |
fix | mod | xCoord | yCoord |
abs | max | min | negate | product | subtract | sum

integerValue

IntegerValue describes an expression that evaluates to an integer. This includes EDIF integer tokens, a value reference, and functions that return EDIF integer values. The *valueNameRef* must refer to a *constant, parameter,* or *variable* definition of type *integer.*

In the context of *integerValue* the arguments to *abs, max, min, negate, product, subtract,* and *sum* are restricted to be of type *integerValue.*

Example:

(constant x (integer 5))
...
(xCoord (pt x y))

In the above example the **x** in *pt* is a constant value reference. The *xCoord* construct is an integer function which will return **5** as its value.

Used in:

array, borderPattern, borderWidth, criticality, cycle, fillPattern, integer, integerDisplay, member, mod, oversize, pathWidth, pt, scaleX, scaleY, and *textHeight.*

See also:

booleanValue, constant, edifLevel, numberValue, parameter, pointValue, stringValue, and *variable.*

(interface
    { port |
    portBundle |
    < symbol > |
    < protectionFrame > |
    < arrayRelatedInfo > |
    parameter |
    joined |
    mustJoin |
    weakJoined |
    permutable |
    timing |
    simulate |
    < designator > |
    property |
    comment |
    userData }
)

The *interface* defines objects which can be seen and relationships which are guaranteed to be true for all instances of the *view*. Objects include the *ports*, the abstraction of the cell *(symbol* and *protectionFrame),* and properties and attributes defined in the *interface* and in the *ports*. Relationships include what *ports* of the *cell* are shorted together *(joined)* and what ports can be interchanged *(permutable)*.

Some constructs are restricted for different *viewTypes*. An *interface* of type **DOCUMENT** or **GRAPHIC** may not contain *arrayRelatedInfo, designator, joined, mustJoin, permutable, port, portBundle, protectionFrame, simulate, symbol, timing* or *weakJoined*.

Interfaces of type **BEHAVIOR, LOGICMODEL,** and **NETLIST** may not use *arrayRelatedInfo, protectionFrame,* or *symbol;* those of type **SCHEMATIC** may use *symbol* but not *arrayRelatedInfo* or *protectionFrame*.

There are no *viewType* restrictions on the *interface* of **MASKLAYOUT, PCBLAYOUT, STRANGER,** or **SYMBOLIC** views.

In Level 0 descriptions, *parameter* is only allowed in *interface* within the context of the *external* construct. This is permitted so that parameter names from an external library can be declared before use.

Example:

```
(cell CZ (cellType generic)
    (view CZNet (viewType netlist)
        (interface
            (port A (direction INPUT))
            (port B (direction INPUT))
            (port O (direction OUTPUT))
            (property basic (string "XXX"))
            (designator "000")
            (joined (portRef A) (portRef B)))...))
```

The above example specifies the interface of the view named **CZNet** of cell **CZ.** The objects defined include the ports **A,** **B,** and **O;** the property **basic;** and the *designator* attribute. The relationship that port **A** is joined to port **B** is also specified.

Used in:

view.

See also:

contents, and *viewType.*

---

interface

(interface
    { port |
    portBundle |
    < symbol > |
    < protectionFrame >|
    < arrayRelatedInfo > |
    parameter |
    joined |
    mustJoin |
    weakJoined |
    permutable |
    timing |
    simulate |
    < designator > |
    constant |
    constraint |
    variable |
    property |
    comment |
    userData }
)

interface

Interface for Level 1 cells is the same as *interface* for Level 0 with the addition of *constant, constraint,* and *variable.* Also, *parameters* may be declared in the context of normal *libraries.*

Example:

    (interface
        (parameter n (integer 32))
        (port (array IN n) (direction input))
        (port Out (direction output)))

This illustrates the declaration of an integer parameter named **n** with default value **32,** an array of ports named **IN** with **n** members, and an output port named **Out.**

Used in:

view.

See also:

constant, constraint, contents, variable, and *viewType.*

interface

(**interface**
    { port |
    portBundle |
    < symbol > |
    < protectionFrame >|
    < arrayRelatedInfo > |
    parameter |
    joined |
    mustJoin |
    weakJoined |
    permutable |
    timing |
    simulate |
    < designator > |
    constant |
    constraint |
    variable |
    assign |
    block |
    if |
    iterate |
    while |
    property |
    comment |
    userData }
)

interface

Interface for Level 2 is the same as *interface* for Level 1 with the addition of the *assign, block, if, iterate* and *while*. In this context *statement* is restricted to *assign, block, comment, constant, constraint, escape, if, iterate, property, simulate, timing, userData, variable,* and *while*.

Example:

```
(interface ...
    (parameter P1 (point (pt 0 0)))
    (variable P1X (integer 0))
    (variable P1Y (integer 0))
    (assign P1X (integer (xCoord P1)))
    (assign P1Y (integer (yCoord P1))))
```

The above example defines a point parameter **P1** and integer variables **P1X** and **P1Y** which are assigned the **x** and **y** coordinate values of **P1** respectively.

Used in:

view.

See also:

contents, technology, and *viewType.*

(**interFigureGroupSpacing** *ruleNameDef*
    figureGroupObject
    figureGroupObject
    range | singleValueSet
    { comment |
    userData }
)

InterFigureGroupSpacing is used to specify the required spacing between two figure–group objects. Normally, both figure groups are distinct; if they are the same figure group then the effect is that of the *intraFigureGroupSpacing* construct. Both figure groups are to be considered; pairs of edges (one from each figure group) which have their outside orientations facing are to be selected. The distance between these edges must satisfy the specified value range; otherwise the edges are in violation of the rule.

Example:

    (**physicalDesignRule**
        (**interFigureGroupSpacing DIFF_POLY_SP**
            (**figureGroupObject DIFF**)
            (**figureGroupObject POLY**)
            (**atLeast 7**)) ...)

The above example rule requires that the spacing between figure groups **DIFF** and **POLY** be greater than or equal to **7.**

Used in:

physicalDesignRule.

See also:

figureGroupObject,   *intraFigureGroupSpacing,*   *range,*   *ruleNameDef,*   and *singleValueSet.*

intersection

(intersection
    figureGroupRef | figureOp
    { figureGroupRef | figureOp }
)

intersection

Intersection describes the intersection of one or more sets of figure–group objects. A location is contained within the intersection if it is contained within each of the specified figure–group objects.

Example:

    (intersection
        (figureGroupRef Poly)
        (figureGroupRef Diff))

This example specifies a new set of figure–group objects which are formed by the intersection of figure groups **Poly** and **Diff.**

Used in:

figureOp.

See also:

difference, figureGroupRef, physicalDesignRule, and *union.*

intraFigureGroupSpacing

(intraFigureGroupSpacing *ruleNameDef*
   figureGroupObject
   range | singleValueSet
   { comment |
   userData }
)

intraFigureGroupSpacing

IntraFigureGroupSpacing is used to specify the required external spacing between separate figures from the same figure group, but possibly different *figure* statements. A single group of figures is to be considered; pairs of edges (each from a different figure) which have their outside orientation facing are to be selected. The distance between these edges must satisfy the specified value range; otherwise these edges are in violation of the rule.

Example:

```
(physicalDesignRule...
   (intraFigureGroupSpacing  MET_SP
      (figureGroupObject METAL)
      (atLeast 5)))
```

The above example rule requires that the spacing between **METAL** figures be greater than or equal to **5.**

Used in:

physicalDesignRule.

See also:

figureGroupObject, range, ruleNameDef, and *singleValueSet.*

(inverse *figureGroupRef | figureOp***)**

Inverse is used to describe the inverse of a figure–group object. Normally this operator is used within a *union, intersection,* or *difference* operator. If the *inverse* operator is used alone, e.g.

(figureGroupObject (inverse ...))

then an intersection with the universal set (the maximum geometric extent of the figure group for the design) is implied.

A location is contained within the inverse if it is not contained within the specified object.

Example:

(intersection
    (figureGroupRef Poly)
    (inverse (figureGroupRef BuriedContact)))

This example specifies a new set of figure–group objects which are inside **Poly** but outside **BuriedContact.**

Used in:

figureOp.

See also:

difference, and *figureGroupRef.*

(isolated)

isolated

isolated

Isolated is an attribute of a logic value and is used to indicate the logic value which is used for isolated or undriven nets, i.e. those without any source. There may be only one *logicValue* which contains *isolated* in a *simulationInfo* construct.

Example:

```
(simulationInfo
    (logicValue T)
    (logicValue F)
    (logicValue Z
        (isolated)))
```

This defines a logic value **Z** and declares that it is the isolated value.

Used in:

logicValue.

See also:

simulationInfo.

(iterate *{ statement }* **)**

The *iterate* construct provides a simple looping mechanism in Level 2 descriptions. It allows a number of *statements* to be collected into a group. *Iterate* acts as a wrapping similar to the *block* construct, except that the end of the list is considered to continue with the first element. Apart from statements which explicitly refer to the enclosing form, the meaning of the *iterate* is the same as the individual statements, taken in the same sequential order. *Iterate* is not restricted by *viewType,* but the enclosed *statements* must be appropriate within the context of the *iterate.*

An *escape* statement should be used to terminate this loop, usually within the context of an *if* statement.

Example:

```
(assign n 1)
(iterate
    (if (increasing 100 n) (then (escape)))
    (figure POLY (dot (pt n n)))
    (assign n (integer (sum 1 n))))
```

This creates **100** *dot* figures. This will loop until **n** exceeds **100.**

Used in:

contents, interface, page, statement, and *technology.*

See also:

block, else, if, then, and *while.*

(joined
    { portRef |
    portList |
    globalPortRef }
)

Joined is used to specify that certain ports are shorted together. In all cases, the sizes of the expanded references must be equal.

When used in the interface, the *joined* may refer only to master ports (ports defined in the interface). The *portRefs* in the joined may not contain an *instanceRef* or *viewRef*. The *joined* may be nested with *mustJoin* and *weakJoined* to specify complex relationships between master ports. This relationship forms a tree structure. Within the interface a port may be referenced at most once in *joined, mustJoined* and *weakJoined. GlobalPortRef* may not be used in a *joined* in the context of the interface.

When used in the *net* statement, the *joined* may refer to master ports, local ports *(offPageConnector)* and instance ports. When used in this context, the *portRef* may contain at most one *instanceRef*. Only ports of locally defined instances may be referenced.

When arrays of ports, bundles of ports, or port lists are specified in the *joined,* the individual members are joined in a parallel manner. The first members of each reference are joined, the second members of each reference are joined, etc. A *port* may only be referenced in more than one *joined* statement if it is a port instance of an *instance* within an enclosing *net*.

Joined may not be used in the context of **GRAPHIC** or **DOCUMENT** view types.

Example:

    (joined (portRef A) (portRef B))

The first example states that the master ports **A** and **B** are connected.

    (portBundle BP
      (listOfPorts
        (port &1)
        (port &2)))
    (port (array A 2))
    (port B)
    (port C)...
    (joined

```
        (portRef BP)
        (portRef A)
        (portList (portRef B) (portRef C)))
```

The second joined above states that port **1** of bundle port **BP**, member **0** of arrayed port **A**, and port **B** are all joined. It also states that port **2** of bundle port **BP**, member **1** of arrayed port **A**, and port **C** are all joined.

```
    (net a
        (joined
            (portRef in (instanceRef I1)
            (portRef out (instanceRef I2)
            (portRef QW)))
```

The last example defines a net **a** which joins port **in** on instance **I1**, port **out** on instance **I2**, and port **QW** (master or local).

Used in:

interface, mustJoin, net, and *weakJoined.*

See also:

globalPortRef, portList, portRef, and *viewType.*

(justify
>   UPPERLEFT | UPPERCENTER | UPPERRIGHT |
>   CENTERLEFT | CENTERCENTER | CENTERRIGHT |
>   LOWERLEFT | LOWERCENTER | LOWERRIGHT
)

Justify indicates where the origin point of text occurs relative to the text before orientation.

The following list indicates the desired origin location for each *justfy* type:

- **UPPERLEFT** top left corner of text;

- **UPPERCENTER** above the middle of the text;

- **UPPERRIGHT** top right corner of the text;

- **CENTERLEFT** at the left of the text;

- **CENTERCENTER** middle point of the text;

- **CENTERRIGHT** at the right of the text;

- **LOWERLEFT** lower left corner of the text;

- **LOWERCENTER** below the middle of the text;

- **LOWERRIGHT** at the lower right of the text.

Example:

```
(stringDisplay "RXT"
    (display textFG
        (justify LOWERLEFT)
        (orientation R90)
        (origin (pt 2 3))))
```

In the above example the string "**RXT**" will be justified such that the origin will be located at the lower left corner, below and left of the **R**. The string is rotated **90** degrees with respect to its origin and translated to point (**2,3**).

Used in:

display.

See also:

annotate, orientation, origin, and *textHeight.*

---

keywordAlias

(keywordAlias *keywordNameDef*
   keywordNameRef
)

keywordAlias

KeywordAlias is provided to allow users to compress files by abbreviating keyword names. Existing keyword names may not be redefined by this construct. It may be evoked by using a *form* which references the new keyword name. This has the same effect as using the original keyword name, which may still be used directly.

KeywordAlias may not be applied to a symbolic constant.

Example:

```
(edif ...
   (keywordMap (keywordLevel 1)
      (keywordAlias p pt))
   (library ...
      (p 1 10)...))
```

The above example defines **p** to be an alias for the **pt** keyword. The new **p** keyword is then used to define a point at **(1,10)**.

Used in:

keywordMap.

See also:

form, and *keywordLevel.*

keywordDefine

(keywordDefine *keywordNameDef*
    keywordParameters
    generate
)

keywordDefine

The *keywordDefine* construct provides the capability in EDIF of defining new keywords in terms of existing ones. It is intended to act as a reasonably powerful method of abbreviating EDIF descriptions, using a general method which could be resolved in a preprocessing input step. Keywords have to be defined within *keywordMap* at the top level of the EDIF file, i.e. they cannot be defined inside a design or library or anywhere other than a *keywordMap*.

In the above syntax, *keywordNameDef* is an identifier which is being defined to be a keyword, *keywordParameters* is a construct that defines all arguments to be passed to the *keywordDefine,* and *generate* is a construct that specifies what the *keywordDefine* form will generate when processed. The defined keyword is not available for use until after the end of the *keywordDefine* statement. Existing keyword names may not be redefined with this construct.

Example:

```
(keywordDefine rev
    (keywordParameters
        (formal a) (formal b))
    (generate
        (build pt
            (actual b) (actual a))))
```

This example defines a new keyword **rev** in terms of the native keyword **pt.** A subsequent use such as **(rev 1 2)** should be interpreted in the same way as its expansion **(pt 2 1).**

Used in:

keywordMap.

See also:

form, keywordAlias, generate, keywordLevel, and *keywordParameters.*

(**keywordDisplay** *keywordNameRef*
   { display }
)

The *keywordDisplay* construct is used for specifying a default display location and attributes for the display of EDIF keyword–property values, and instance and cell names. It is used in the *interface* in the constructs which have a coordinate space associated with them, namely *portImplementation, protectionFrame,* and *symbol.*

The value for which the display location and attributes are specified is referenced with the *keywordNameRef* of the construct in which it is defined. Only the following *keywordNameRef* identifiers are allowed within the *keywordDisplay: acLoad, cell, dcFaninLoad, dcFanoutLoad, dcMaxFanin, dcMaxFanout, designator,* and *instance.* The *keywordNameRef* **cell** refers to the *cellNameDef* of the current cell and the *keywordNameRef* **instance** refers to the *instanceNameDef* of an instance which instantiates the current cell and view. The default display location and attributes are specified in the *display* construct.

The corresponding attribute need not be present in order for the *keywordDisplay* to be legal. It may be given a value by back annotation in an *instance* or *viewMap* context.

Example:

```
(cell Foo (cellType generic)
   (view S1 (viewType schematic)
      (interface
         (designator "Uxxx" )
         (symbol
            (keywordDisplay designator
               (display SymbolLayer
                  (origin (pt 20 5))))
            (keywordDisplay cell
               (display SymbolLayer
                  (origin (pt 20 10))))
            (keywordDisplay instance
               (display SymbolLayer
                  (origin (pt 20 0)))))))))
```

The above example specifies the default display locations for the component reference designator "**Uxxx**", cell name **Foo,** and the name of any instance which references cell **Foo,** view **S1.** The defaults can be overridden in an *instance* construct by *stringDisplay* within *designator* by augmenting the *cellNameRef* and *instanceNameDef* with the *name* construct.

```
(port PORTA (direction Input) (designator "1") (acLoad 5))
(symbol
    (portImplementation PORTA
        (keywordDisplay designator
            (display SymbolLayer (origin (pt 10 5))))
        (keywordDisplay acLoad
            (display SymbolLayer (origin (pt 10 10))))))
```

In the above example the default display location is specified for the *acLoad* and pin number values of a port named **PORTA** in the symbol.

Used in:

portImplementation, protectionFrame, and *symbol.*

See also:

acLoad, cell, dcFaninLoad, dcFanoutLoad, dcMaxFanin, dcMaxFanout, designator, display, instance, keywordNameRef, name, and *viewMap.*

(keywordLevel
 integerToken
)

keywordLevel

keyword level number (0, 1, 2, or 3)

keywordLevel

  This construct is used to specify the level of complexity that keyword mappings will have in the EDIF file. The integer token must have the value 0, 1, 2, or 3.

These are:

- Level 0: no keyword mappings;
- Level 1: abbreviations only;
- Level 2: keyword macros with no iterative parameter binding;
- Level 3: keyword macros with iterative parameter binding.

Example:

 (keywordLevel 2)

This example specifies that the file may contain *keywordAlias* and *keywordDefine*, with no iterative parameter binding.

Used in:

keywordMap.

See also:

edifLevel, keywordAlias, and *keywordDefine.*

keywordMap
keywordMap for keyword level 0

(keywordMap
    keywordLevel
    { comment }
)

keywordMap

KeywordMap isolates all keyword mapping in one area of the EDIF file. In keyword level 0 no abbreviations or definitions of new keywords are permitted.

Example:

    (keywordMap (keywordLevel 0))

The keyword level associated with this *keywordMap* specifies that no keyword definition or abbreviation will be used in this EDIF file. Only raw EDIF will be used.

Used in:

edif.

See also:

keywordLevel.

(keywordMap
    keywordLevel
    { keywordAlias |
    comment }
)
	keywordMap
	keywordMap for keyword level 1

	keywordMap

    KeywordMap isolates all keyword mapping in one area of the EDIF file. Within keyword level 1 descriptions, *keywordAlias* is provided to allow users to change keyword names to compress files or for other purposes.

Example:

    (keywordMap
        (keywordLevel 1)
        (keywordAlias pi portImplementation ...))

After such a definition, **(pi portA ...)** means the same as **(portImplementation portA ...)** throughout the rest of the EDIF file.

Used in:

edif.

See also:

form, keywordAlias, and *keywordLevel.*

---

	keywordMap
(keywordMap	keywordMap for keyword levels 2 & 3
keywordLevel	
{ keywordAlias |	
keywordDefine |	
comment }	
)	
	keywordMap

KeywordMap isolates all keyword mapping in one area of the EDIF file. Within keyword level 2, *keywordAlias* is provided to allow users to change keyword names to compress files or for other purposes. Additionally, *keywordDefine* is provided to allow users to define new keywords in terms of existing ones.

The syntax for *keywordMap* at keyword level 3 is the same as this level.

Example:

```
(keywordMap
    (keywordLevel 2)
    (keywordAlias pi portImplementation)
    (keywordDefine diagonal
        (keywordParameters (formal a))
        (generate
            (build pt
                (actual a) (actual a)))))
```

This creates a keyword named **diagonal** such that **(diagonal 25)** is interpreted in the same way as **(pt 25 25).**

Used in:

edif.

See also:

form, keywordAlias, keywordDefine, and *keywordLevel.*

identifier	*keywordNameDef*
	keywordNameDef

A *keywordNameDef* must be a simple *identifier* and must not have been previously defined as a keyword name. Also, it must not match any native EDIF keywords of the same *edifVersion*.

The scope of a defined keyword is from the end of the enclosing *keywordAlias* or *keywordDefine* to the end of the entire *edif* construct.

Used in:

keywordAlias, and *keywordDefine.*

See also:

edifVersion, keywordMap, and *keywordNameRef.*

identifier	*keywordNameRef*
	keywordNameRef

KeywordNameRef must be a simple *identifier* which has been previously defined as a keyword name within the context of a *keywordMap* or be a native EDIF keyword of the same *edifVersion*.

Example:

(port   P   ...)

In this example, **port** is a native *keywordNameRef,* and **P** is a user–defined *portNameDef.*

Used in:

build, form, keywordAlias, and *keywordDisplay.*

See also:

edifVersion, keywordMap, and *keywordNameDef.*

(keywordParameters *{ formal }*)	*keywordParameters*
	keywordParameters

    KeywordParameters contains a list of formal parameters which should correspond to individual *forms* or tokens at the time of expansion of a use of the new keyword. *KeywordParameters* is available at keyword level 2 and higher.

    If any of the enclosed *formal* parameters are *optional* or *collectors* (at keyword level 3) then any subsequent *formal* parameters must be of the same type.

Example:

```
(keywordDefine EG
    (keywordParameters
        (formal a)  (formal b))
    (generate
        (build pt (actual a)  (actual b))))
```

This keyword definition shown in this example will generate the EDIF construct *pt* with values supplied by **a** and **b**. This shows the explicit definition of a keyword **EG** which has the same effect as a *keywordAlias* for **pt**.

Used in:

keywordDefine.

See also:

actual, collector, formal, generate, and *optional.*

nameDef	*layerNameDef*
	layerNameDef

LayerNameDef is an identifier for a layer, which may be renamed. In this version, there are no references to such layer names; this is intended to relate to external fabrication layer names. It should be unique within each *library* or *external* construct.

Used in:

fabricate.

See also:

external, figureGroup, and *library.*

---

	lessThan
(lessThan *numberValue***)**	*lessThan*

The *lessThan* construct is used to specify a range of values less than *numberValue* in the context of a design rule.

Example:

(lessThan 5)

This example specifies that the value is less than **5** units in the context of a physical design rule, such as a spacing rule.

Used in:

between, and *range.*

See also:

moreThan, multipleValueSet, numberValue, and *physicalDesignRule.*

	library
(library *libraryNameDef*	a named library
edifLevel	a required EDIF Level
technology	a required technology
{ < status > |	status of library
cell |	library cells
comment |	user comments
userData }	user–defined data
)	
	library

Library is a grouping of EDIF design information grouped according to some set of common characteristics. This grouping is arbitrary except for the technology information which is shared by all *cells* within the *library*. For this reason libraries are often grouped by technology definition (such as CMOS), but the same technology could also be defined by more than one *library* by repeating the information in *technology*. A library that is external to the EDIF file is defined using the *external* form in the *edif* form.

Example:

```
(edif HYBRID_DESIGNS
    (edifVersion 2 0 0)
    (edifLevel 0)
    (keywordMap ..)
    (library CMOS2M
        (edifLevel 0)
        (technology ...)
        (cell MUX ...)
        (cell FFT ...)))
```

This example shows the definition of a *library* named CMOS2M which contains *technology* and the definitions of *cells* named **MUX** and **FFT**.

Used in:

edif.

See also:

external, cell, and *technology.*

---

nameDef

libraryNameDef

libraryNameDef

LibraryNameDef is used to name internal or external libraries. All such names must be unique within an EDIF file and must be defined before use. They are not otherwise restricted.

It should not be assumed that the choice of names for *libraries* has any effect on their interpretation.

Used in:

external, and *library.*

See also:

libraryNameRef, and *libraryRef.*

nameRef	*libraryNameRef*
	libraryNameRef

A *libraryNameRef* is used to reference a previously defined *library* or *external* library. This is generally needed to establish a remote name context.

Example:

(cellRef nand3 (libraryRef lib2))

Here, the library name **lib2** is referenced to provide the context for the cell name **nand3.**

Used in:

libraryRef.

See also:

cellRef, and *libraryNameDef.*

(libraryRef *libraryNameRef*)

LibraryRef contains a reference to the name of a library that is defined in the EDIF file using either *external* or *library*. This is used in *cellRef* to qualify a cell as belonging to a particular library. It is also used in *figureGroupRef* to reference figure–group objects in another library and in *logicRef* to reference defined logic values. *LibraryRef* is part of the generic name referencing mechanism in EDIF that provides indirect referencing and extends the range of accessibility to an object from outside its immediate range.

Example:

```
(design ALU_32
    (cellRef ALU_CMOS_32
        (libraryRef CMOS2M)))
```

This example refers to a cell named **ALU_CMOS_32** in the library named **CMOS2M**. This library should have been defined earlier in the EDIF file using either the *library* or *external* constructs. The *libraryRef* is required in this context since the *design* form is not in the context of a *library*.

Used in:

cellRef, figureGroupRef, and *logicRef.*

See also:

design, external, includeFigureGroup, instance, library, site, viewList, and *viewRef.*

(listOfNets { *net* })

  ListOfNets describes an ordered list of net definitions. The enclosed *nets* are local to the context of the enclosing *netBundle* definition.

Example:

```
(netBundle NB
    (listOfNets
        (net a (joined ...))
        (net b (joined ...)))
    (figure ...) ...)
```

Net bundle **NB** is defined to contain two nested nets and associated graphics. The names **a** and **b** are local to the bundle and thus do not conflict with any externally defined nets.

Subsequent reference to these inner nets is made by nesting *netRef* statements, as in **(netRef a (netRef NB)).**

Used in:

netBundle.

See also:

net, netBundle, and *listOfPorts.*

(listOfPorts   *listOfPorts*
    { port |
    portBundle }
)

                                                               listOfPorts

---

ListOfPorts describes   an ordered list of port definitions used to designate the ports in a *portBundle*. It may contain nested *portBundle* definitions, which are local to the enclosing *portBundle*.

Example:

```
(view a (viewType netlist)
    (interface
        (portBundle multi_port
            (listOfPorts
                (port input1)
                (port input5)
                (port output6)
                (port VCC)))))
```

This example defines a port bundle called **multi_port,** which contains the definitions for four ports. The port **input5** can be accessed with **(portRef input5 (portRef multi_port)).**

Used in:

portBundle.

See also:

listOfNets, port, and *portList.*

---

	literal
(**literal** *{ integerToken | stringToken | identifier | form }*)	*literal*

Literal generates the *forms* and tokens specified within it, in the order specified. It is used in keyword level 2 and 3 constructs. This avoids conflict between formal names of a *keywordDefine* and identifiers or symbolic constants desired in the keyword expansion. The nested *forms* may require keyword expansion.

Example:

```
(keywordDefine EG
    (keywordParameters ...)
    (generate
        (build figure
            (literal POLY) ...)))
```

In this example, **POLY** is to be taken literally and should not be interpreted as a *formalNameRef.*

Used in:

build, forEach, generate, and *optional.*

See also:

actual, keywordDefine, and *keywordMap.*

(**loadDelay**   *loadDelay*

    miNoMaxValue / *miNoMaxDisplay*   delay

    miNoMaxValue / *miNoMaxDisplay*   ac-load factor

)

                                                                                 loadDelay

---

LoadDelay is used to specify a delay in propagating a signal. The first value or range of values specifies the delay in **TIME** units. The second value specifies the amount of delay per unit load capacitance as specified by the *acLoad* on each of the ports connected to the driving port. Neither of these values may be negative. *MiNoMaxDisplay* is allowed for displaying the value of the delay. This may be used in place of the number value or range when the delay exists in a coordinate space and is a displayable value.

Example:

    (**loadDelay (e 18 -1) (e 2 -1)**)

The first example describes a delay of **1.8** time units with a load-dependent delay of **0.2** time units per unit load capacitance.

    (**view V (viewType logicModel)**
       (**interface**
          (**port A (acLoad 1)) (port B (acLoad 3)) (port C)**
          (**joined (portRef A) (portRef B) (portRef C))) ...**
       (**contents ...**
          (**logicAssign (portRef C) (logicRef T) (loadDelay 4 2))))**

In the second example the port **A** is defined with an *acLoad* of **1**. Port **B** is defined with an *acLoad* of **3**. They are joined to port **C**. The total delay of **12** time units would be produced before port **C** would change to the logic value **T**. That is, the delay is equal to **4 + (2 * (1 + 3))**. This delay estimate will increase as further loading is provided in larger contexts that instantiate this view.

Used in:

entry, follow, logicAssign, maintain, portDelay, and *tableDefault.*

See also:

acLoad, delay, and *unit.*

(logicAssign
  portNameRef | portRef
  portRef | logicRef | table
  [delay | loadDelay]
)

LogicAssign is used within the *when* construct for logic modeling. The *logicAssign* construct is used to set a port to a value and maintain it until another action accesses that port. The *logicRef* should reference a logic value defined within the same library. If a *portRef* is used as the second argument, its present logic value should be used.

Delay or *loadDelay* may be used within *logicAssign* to delay its assignment.

Example:

(when
  (trigger (steady IN 5 (becomes F)))
  (logicAssign OUT (logicRef T))))

The above example specifies that the logic value **T** is to be assigned to port **OUT** when the logic value **F** has been steady on port **IN** for exactly **5** time units.

Used in:

after, and *when.*

See also:

delay, follow, loadDelay, logicValue, maintain, and *table.*

(logicInput
    portNameRef | portRef | portList
    logicWaveform
)

    LogicInput is used within *apply* to specify the logical stimulus to be given to certain ports for the duration of the appropriate apply statement. The first item indicates one or more ports; the second contains a number of logic values or lists, the size of which corresponds to the number of ports, taking array sizes into account. Each such structured logic value is applied to the port list in turn, one for each cycle of the apply statement. In this context, *logicOneOf* may not be used directly or indirectly inside the *logicWaveform*.

    If more cycles are specified than values, the last value (singular or arrayed) is repeatedly applied. The ports involved must be either **INPUT** or **INOUT**; the application of the value defined by *ignore* to an **INOUT** port means that the port is temporarily not driven. This may be used to inhibit its input characteristics. The *ignore* may also be incorporated into the value defined by *waveValue*.

Example:

    (logicInput dataIn (logicWaveform T T F T F F T))

This supplies a pattern of seven logic values to apply sequentially to port **dataIn** in the specified order.

Used in:

apply.

See also:

cycle, direction, ignore, logicOutput, logicWaveform, simulate, and *waveValue*.

(logicList { *logicNameRef* | *logicOneOf* | *ignore* }**)**

    LogicList creates an array of logic values. It is used within *logicWaveform* in *logicInput* and *logicOutput* constructs in those cases where an array or list of ports is involved. The number of elements in the *logicList* should be same as the number of ports specified in the corresponding *logicInput* or *logicOutput* forms.

Example:

```
(logicInput
    (portList A B C D)
    (logicWaveform
        (logicList T T F X)))
```

The example shows that a logic value of **T** is applied to ports **A** and **B,** a logic value of **F** is applied to port **C,** and a logic value of **X** is applied to port **D** during a single cycle.

Used in:

becomes, logicOneOf, logicWaveform, match, and *transition.*

See also:

logicInput, and *logicOutput.*

(logicMapInput *{ logicRef }*)

LogicMapInput is used in *logicValue* in *simulationInfo* to map the present logic value to values being input to the models in the present *library* from models in previously defined libraries. This construct is appropriate when models from multiple libraries or technologies are used during the same simulation.

Example:

    (logicValue T
        (logicMapInput (logicRef HI (libraryRef Blib)))

The above example describes that when the value **HI** is received from a model in library **Blib,** it should be treated as the local logic value **T.**

Used in:

logicValue.

See also:

logicMapOutput, and *simulationInfo.*

(logicMapOutput *{ logicRef }*)	*logicMapOutput*
	logicMapOutput

LogicMapOutput is used in *logicValue* in *simulationInfo* to map the present logic value to a value or values being output to models in a previously defined library or libraries. There should be no more than one logic reference for each such library. This construct is appropriate when models from multiple libraries or technologies are used during the same simulation.

Example:

```
(logicValue ST
    (logicMapOutput (logicRef HI (libraryRef Blib))))
```

The above example describes that the local logic value **ST** maps to the logic value **HI** in the library **Blib.**

Used in:

logicValue.

See also:

logicMapInput, and *simulationInfo.*

---

nameDef	*logicNameDef*
	logicNameDef

A *logicNameDef* is a name which is later used as a logical value. It has a scope to the end of the smallest enclosing *library, external* or *simulate* form.

Example:

(logicValue T ...)
(logicValue F ...)
(logicValue X ...)

In the above example, **T, F** and **X** are *logicNameDefs*. No significance should be directly assumed from the particular choice of names.

Used in:

logicValue, and *waveValue.*

See also:

external, library, logicNameRef, and *simulate.*

---

nameRef   *logicNameRef*

logicNameRef

A *logicNameRef* is a name used to refer to logic values, which must have been previously defined by a corresponding *logicNameDef*.

Used in:

becomes, compound, dominates, logicList, logicOneOf, logicRef, logicWaveform, match, resolves, strong, transition, and *weak.*

See also:

logicNameDef.

(logicOneOf *{ logicNameRef | logicList }***)**

LogicOneOf supplies a list of alternative logic values or logic lists. Where *logicList* is used, the sizes of the *logicLists* must all be equal. When used, any match in *logicOneOf* is considered as a match for the containing construct. It thus acts as a specific "don't care" condition.

Example:

   (logicList A B C (logicOneOf D E F))

This expression indicates a list **A, B, C (D or E or F).**

   (logicOneOf
      (logicList A B C D)
      (logicList A B C E)
      (logicList A B C F))

The second expression indicates a list which is one of three lists: **(A, B, C, D), (A, B, C, E),** or **(A, B, C, F).** The expressions are therefore equivalent.

Used in:

becomes, logicList, logicWaveForm, match, and *transition.*

See also:

compound, and *ignore.*

---

logicOutput

(logicOutput
    portNameRef | portRef | portList
    logicWaveform
)

logicOutput

LogicOutput is used within *apply* to specify the logical response to be expected from certain ports during a cycle of the appropriate *apply* statement. The first item indicates one or more ports; the second contains a number of logic values or lists, the size of which corresponds to the number of ports, taking array sizes into account. Each such structured logic value is compared with that of the port list in turn, one for each cycle of the *apply* statement.

If more cycles are specified than values, the last value (singular or arrayed) is repeatedly compared. The ports involved must be either **OUTPUT** or **INOUT**. The application of the *ignore* value means that the *port* should not be compared against any value for the corresponding cycle. This may be used to inhibit the output characteristics of an **INOUT** port. The *ignore* may also be incorporated into a value defined by *waveValue*.

Example:

    (logicOutput dataOut (logicWaveform F T F F T F T))

This example shows seven values expected to match the output value of port **dataOut** in sequence.

Used in:

apply.

See also:

cycle, direction, ignore, logicInput, logicWaveform, simulate, and *waveValue.*

(logicPort *portNameDef*
    { property |
    comment |
    userData }
)

LogicPort is used within the **LOGICMODEL** view to specify local signal ports. The logic port definition is in the name space of ports for the containing *view*. An array of *logicPorts* may be created by using the *array* form of *portNameDef*.

LogicPort may only be used in the context of views of type **LOGICMODEL** or **STRANGER.**

Example:

    (view view_1 (viewType logicModel)
        (interface
            (port D (direction input) ...))
        (contents
            (LogicPort HOLD1)
            (when
                (trigger (change D))
                (logicAssign HOLD1 (portRef D) (delay 5))) ...))

In the above example the port **HOLD1** is defined as a local port in the view **view_1.**

Used in:

contents, and *statement.*

See also:

array, offPageConnector, port, and *viewType.*

(logicRef *logicNameRef [libraryRef]*)	*logicRef*
	logicRef

LogicRef is used to reference a logic value by name. The optional library reference is for use within the context of *logicMapInput* and *logicMapOutput* constructs to reference other libraries.

The library reference should not be made within *entry, logicAssign,* or *tableDefault.*

Example:

(logicRef T)
(logicRef HI (libraryRef MyLib))

This references the logic value **T** defined in the local library and value **HI** defined in a previous library named **MyLib.**

Used in:

entry, logicAssign, logicMapInput, logicMapOutput, and *tableDefault.*

See also:

libraryRef, and *logicValue.*

(logicValue *logicNameDef*
    { < voltageMap > |
    < currentMap > |
    < booleanMap > |
    < compound > |
    < weak > |
    < strong > |
    < dominates > |
    < logicMapOutput > |
    < logicMapInput > |
    < isolated > |
    resolves |
    property |
    comment |
    userData }
)

LogicValue is used within *simulationInfo* to define a logic value to use for modeling in the *logicModel* view. A value can be specified by name and also by specifying the characteristics of the value. The characteristics can be electrical, Boolean, relational between other logic values, and relational between logic values specified in previously defined libraries.

Example:

    (logicValue ST
        (voltageMap (mnm 25 48 50)) (currentMap (mnm 10 15 20))
        (booleanMap (true))
        (strong T) (dominates T Z WT WF)
        (logicMapOutput (logicRef HI (libraryRef MyLib))))

This example defines a logic value **ST,** giving explicit electrical and Boolean mappings and wiring contention information.

Used in:

simulationInfo.

See also:

isolated, and *logicRef.*

(logicWaveform
    { logicNameRef |
    logicList |
    logicOneOf |
    ignore }

    LogicWaveform is used within *waveValue, logicInput,* and *logicOutput* to express a temporal sequence (starting with the first logic value) of singular or arrayed logic values. The values must have been previously defined within the appropriate technology block or by the *waveValue* statement.

    A *logicOneOf* construct used directly inside *logicWaveform,* or indirectly by being contained in *logicList* inside *logicWaveform,* is only permitted when the *logicWaveform* is used in a *logicOutput* statement.

Example:

    (logicWaveform F T F F T F T)

This example shows a temporal sequence of seven logic values starting with **F** and assumes that **T** and **F** have been previously defined as local logic values.

Used in:

logicInput, logicOutput, and *waveValue.*

See also:

logicList, logicValue, and *simulate.*

maintain

(maintain
    portNameRef | portRef
    [delay | loadDelay]
)

maintain

Maintain is used within the *when* construct for logic modeling. The *maintain* construct is used to maintain a port at a fixed value until another action accesses that port. This explicitly releases any influence that has been created by a previous *follow* statement. Whatever value the port has after the given delay should remain constant, even if the port previously specified in a *follow* changes value.

Example:

    (when
        (trigger (change CLK (transition T F)))
        (maintain OUT))

The above example describes that the present logic value on port **OUT** is to be maintained (fixed) whenever port **CLK** changes in value from **T** to **F**.

Used in:

after, and *when.*

See also:

delay, follow, loadDelay, logicAssign, logicValue, and *table.*

---

match

(match
   portNameRef | portRef | portList
   logicNameRef | logicList | logicOneOf
)

match

    Match is used within *entry* in the *logicModel* view to denote a static condition in which a port or list of ports matches a given logic value or list of logic values. In the case of a *portList* or reference to a *port* array, each member should be compared with the corresponding element of the following *logicList;* in this case the number of ports and logic values must be equal.

Example:

    (entry (match IN T) ...)

In the first example the *entry* is satisfied when port **IN** has the value **T.**

    (entry (match (portList IN D CLK) (logicList T F T)) ...)

In the second example the *entry* is satisfied when the ports **IN, D,** and **CLK** have the values **T, F,** and **T** respectively.

    (table
       (entry (match IN (logicOneOf T ST X)) (logicRef T))
       (entry ...))

In the third example the table entry is satisfied and returns a **T** when the logic value of port **IN** is either **T, ST,** or **X.**

Used in:

entry.

See also:

table, and *trigger.*

---

max

(max *numberValue { numberValue })*

max

    Max is a number function which returns the argument that is greatest (closest to positive infinity). There must be at least one argument to this function. If all the arguments of *max* are *integerValues* the expression may also be used as an *integerValue*.

Example:

    (max −50 −4 1 12)

This example returns the integer value **12.**

Used in:

integerValue, and *numberValue.*

See also:

abs, divide, min, mod, negate, product, subtract, and *sum.*

member

(member *nameRef*
    integerValue { integerValue }
)

member

    The *member* construct is used to reference elements of an array. Arrays are defined with the *array* construct. The *nameRef* is used to reference the array; the *integerValue* is an index into the array. *Member* must contain the same number of integer values as a corresponding *array*. If the array is defined as a one–dimensional array, then there must be exactly one *integerValue* following the *nameRef*. A two–dimensional array requires two *integerValues,* and so on. The indices of an EDIF array always start at zero. Thus, the first element of an array is referenced with index zero.

Example:

    (port (array P 25))
    (joined (portRef (member P 13)) ...)

In the first example, a one dimensional port–array named **P** of size **25** is defined. In the *joined* construct, the 14th member of the port–array **P** is referenced.

    (portBundle PB
      (listOfPorts
        (port (array PB1 2 4))
        (port (array PB2 6 4 2))))
    (joined
      (portRef (member PB1 1 3) (portRef PB))
      (portRef (member PB2 4 2 0) (portRef PB)))

In the second example a port bundle named **PB** is defined with two port arrays, **PB1** and **PB2.** Later members of the port arrays within the port bundle are referenced.

Used in:

instanceNameRef, netNameRef, portNameRef, and *valueNameRef.*

See also:

array, integerValue, and *nameRef.*

(min *numberValue { numberValue })*   *min*

                                                                  min

---

   Min is a number function which returns the argument that is least (closest to negative infinity). There must be at least one argument. In the special case where all of the arguments to *min* are *integerValues* the result may also be used as an *integerValue.*

Example:

   (min (e 5 −1) (e 3 −1) 20)

This example returns the number value **0.3.**

Used in:

integerValue, and *numberValue.*

See also:

abs, divide, max, mod, negate, product, subtract, and *sum.*

(miNoMax { *miNoMaxValue* | *miNoMaxDisplay* | *miNoMax* })

MiNoMax declares a *constant, parameter, property,* or *variable* value to be of type *miNoMax.* An optional *miNoMaxValue* can be specified, in which case the value serves as a default.

An array of *miNoMax* values can be defined by specifying multiple *miNoMaxValues* within a *miNoMax.* Nesting of *miNoMax* is required to specify array values of two or more dimensions.

Example:

> (parameter node (miNoMax (mnm 0 (e 55 −1) 10)))

In this example the parameter **node** is declared to be of type *miNoMax.* A default value of **(mnm 0 (e 55 −1) 10)** is also specified.

> (constant (array MA1 2)
>   (miNoMax (mnm 0 5 55) (mnm 100 200 300))
> (constant (array MA2 2 3)
>   (miNoMax
>   (miNoMax (mnm 0 5 10) (mnm 10 20 30) (mnm 100 200 300))
>   (miNoMax (mnm 0 5 10) (mnm −30 −20 −10) (mnm −300 −200
> −10))))

In the above example the constant **MA1** is defined to be a one–dimensional *miNoMax* array with the following value assignments:

(member MA1 0) = (mnm 0 5 55), (member MA1 1) = (mnm 100 200 300).

MA2 is defined to be a two–dimensional *miNoMax* array with the value assignments:

(member MA2 0 0) = (mnm 0 5 10),
(member MA2 0 1) = (mnm 10 20 30),
(member MA2 0 2) = (mnm 100 200 300),

(member MA2 1 0) = (mnm 0 5 10),
(member MA2 1 1) = (mnm −30 −20 −10),
(member MA2 1 2) = (mnm −300 −200 −10).

Used in:

miNoMax, and *typedValue.*

See also:

array, boolean, integer, miNoMaxValue, mnm, number, point, and *string.*

(miNoMaxDisplay *miNoMaxValue*
    { display }
)

    MiNoMaxDisplay is used for displaying range–type number values. It is allowed in constructs that normally contain design data and which may exist in a coordinate space. Many constructs may exist in places where there is a coordinate space as well as in places where there is no coordinate space.

    MiNoMaxDisplay contains the data to be displayed, which must be a *numberValue* or *mnm* form, and any number of *display* forms. Systems display range data in different forms. The *miNoMaxDisplay* is provided for systems that display range data as a single piece of data.

Example:

```
(property opTemp
    (miNoMax
        (miNoMaxDisplay (mnm 225 275 400)
            (display text (origin (pt 20 30)))))
    (unit temperature))
```

In the above example the *property* form is in a coordinate space, and its value can be displayed at point **(20,30).** Units are indicated for the property. If the scaling in the technology block is **1,** then the range of values for **opTemp** will be **225.0, 275.0, 400.0** degrees kelvin. The receiving system may then display the range of values in whatever form is appropriate for the system. For example the data may be displayed as **225.0,275.0,400.0** (a string with commas for delimiters) in one system or **225:275:400** (a string with colons for delimiters) in another system.

Used in:

acLoad, delay, loadDelay, and *miNoMax.*

See also:

display, integerDisplay, numberDisplay, and *stringDisplay.*

---

numberValue | mnm   *miNoMaxValue*

                                                             miNoMaxValue

---

MiNoMaxValue describes the primitive set of constructs used to specify a minimum–nominal–maximum value. The set for Level 0 includes *mnm* and any Level 0 *numberValue*. A single *numberValue* is equivalent to **(mnm (undefined)** *numberValue* **(undefined))**.

Example:

(mnm 2 (e 55 −1) (e 755 −2))

In the above example a *miNoMaxValue* of **2** minimum, **5.5** nominal, and **7.55** maximum is specified.

Used in:

acLoad, after, currentMap, delay, loadDelay, miNoMax, miNoMaxDisplay, and *voltageMap.*

See also:

mnm.

---

numberValue | *mnm*	*miNoMaxValue*
	miNoMaxValue

MiNoMaxValue describes the set of constructs used to specify a minimum–nominal–maximum value. The set for Level 1 includes *mnm* and *numberValue*. The *valueNameRef* alternative of *numberValue* may refer to a *constant, parameter* or *variable* of type *miNoMax, number* or *integer.*

Example:

```
(constant std_delay
    (miNoMax (mnm 2 (e 55 −1) (e 755 −2))))
...
(delay std_delay)
```

In the above example a *miNoMaxValue* of **2** minimum, **5.5** nominal, and **7.55** maximum is specified as the value for the constant **std_delay.** In the *delay* construct a value reference **std_delay** is used to specify the minimum–nominal–maximum value.

Used in:

acLoad, after, currentMap, delay, loadDelay, miNoMax, miNoMaxDisplay, and *voltageMap.*

See also:

mnm.

---

mnm

(mnm
  numberValue | *undefined* | *unconstrained*   minimal
  numberValue | *undefined* | *unconstrained*   nominal
  numberValue | *undefined* | *unconstrained*   maximal
)

mnm

  Mnm is used to specify a minimum, nominal, and maximum range of values. The *unconstrained* construct states that there is no restriction specified; the *undefined* construct states that no information is provided and its value is not to be assumed.

Example:

  (mnm 25 30 (e 335 −1))

This example specifies a range of **25** minimum and **33.5** maximum, with a nominal value of **30.**

  (mnm (unconstrained) (undefined) 60)

The above example specifies a range of values with an upper limit of **60,** no lower limit, and an unspecified nominal value.

Used in:

miNoMaxValue.

See also:

miNoMax, numberDisplay, numberValue, unconstrained, and *undefined.*

	mod
(mod *integerValue integerValue*)	
	mod

Mod is an integer function that performs a modulus operation on its two arguments and returns the result. It is the smallest integer in absolute magnitude which differs from the first argument by an integer multiple of the second argument and has the same sign as the first argument. The second argument must be a positive integer value.

Thus **(mod n d)** is equivalent to:
(subtract n (product d (fix (divide n d)))).

Example:

(mod 10 4)

In the above example the integer value **2** is returned.

(mod −8 3)

The second expression represents the value **−2.**

Used in:

integerValue, and *numberValue.*

See also:

abs, divide, max, min, negate, product, subtract, and *sum.*

(**multipleValueSet** *{ rangeVector }*)

The *multipleValueSet* is used to specify a set of range vectors. To satisfy the rule, at least one range vector must be satisfied.

Example:

```
(rectangleSize  CONTACT_SIZE
    (figureGroupObject CONTACT)
    (multipleValueSet
        (rangeVector (exactly 3) (exactly 5))
        (rangeVector (exactly 7) (exactly 8))))
```

The above example rule requires that **CONTACT** size be **3** by **5,** or **7** by **8.**

Used in:

rectangleSize.

See also:

physicalDesignRules, rangeVector, and *singleValueSet.*

(mustJoin
   { portRef |
   portList |
   weakJoined |
   joined }
)

MustJoin is used in *interface* to specify ports of a cell view which must be connected or joined externally for correct operation. Only *ports* defined in the *interface* of the local *view* (master ports) may be referenced within a *mustJoin*. *Joined* and *weakJoined* constructs may be nested with a *mustJoin* to state more complex relationships between master ports. This relationship forms a tree structure. Within the interface, a port may be referenced at most once in *joined, mustJoin* and *weakJoined*.

PortRef is used to reference master ports, port-arrays, or port-bundles. The *portRef* should not contain an *instanceRef* or *viewRef* when used within the context of the *mustJoin*.

PortList is used to form an ordered list of port references which are then associated with port-arrays, port-bundles, or other port-lists. See the *joined* construct for more information on *portList*.

MustJoin may be used in the *interface* of any type of view except **DOCUMENT** or **GRAPHIC**.

Example:

   (mustJoin (portRef A) (portRef B))

The first example states that the master ports **A** and **B** (defined in the *interface*) must be connected externally for the cell to operate properly.

   (mustJoin
     (weakJoined (portRef W1) (portRef W2))
     (joined (portRef J1) (portRef J2)))

The second example states that **W1** and **W2** are weak-joined internally and that **J1** and **J2** are joined internally, and that the pair **W1, W2** must be connected externally to the pair **J1, J2.** Since **J1** and **J2** are joined internally, either one may be connected with to satisfy a connection to the other. This is not true for **W1** and **W2** since they are weak-joined. Therefore, to satisfy the *mustJoin* construct, **W1** must be connected externally to either **J1** or **J2,** and **W2** must be connected externally to **J1** or **J2.**

Used in:

interface.

See also:

joined, portList, portRef, weakJoined, and *viewType.*

---

name

(**name** *identifier*
   { display }
)

name

Name is used to specify an identifier and its associated display information.

Any enclosed *display* statement indicates the desire to graphically display the identifier within an appropriate context. If a *rename* was used in the construct that contained the corresponding *nameDef,* and the *rename* was accepted by the receiving system, that value should be displayed instead of the EDIF *identifier*.

Example:

   (**name Clock**
     (**display ROMAN_12**
      (**justify LowerLeft**)))

This example indicates that the name **Clock** is to be displayed according to the specifications in the *figureGroup* called **ROMAN_12,** justified to the lower left.

Used in:

nameDef, nameRef, and *rename*.

See also:

display, and *identifier*.

---

	nameDef
*identifier	name	rename*	
	nameDef

Every name must have a defining occurrence as a *nameDef*, except for native EDIF keywords and symbolic constants or when used within *userData*. Subsequent references may be made to the object so named, using the same identifier in the role of a *nameRef*. Named constructs (and *block* statements in Level 2) always terminate the scope of any nested name definitions.

All names in EDIF must be defined before use. A simple identifier will frequently be all that is required for a name. This should be unique for the scope of the defining construct and for its name class, which is always determined by the immediate context of the name. There are no reserved names in EDIF other than keyword names. There is no semantic significance to the choice of identifier within a *nameDef* except for the structure established through corresponding *nameRefs* and the display of such names.

Name augments the simple identifier with display information, where appropriate. *Rename* defines an alias for use in later references, and records the original spelling of such a name.

Example:

```
(cell (rename TWOS_COMPLEMENT "2s-complement")
   (cellType generic)
   ...)
```

This example illustrates a cell defined to be **TWOS_COMPLEMENT,** a legal EDIF identifier, serving as an alias for the original illegal name, **"2s-complement".**

Used in:

array, cellNameDef, designNameDef, edifFileNameDef, figureGroupNameDef, instanceNameDef, layerNameDef, libraryNameDef, logicNameDef, netNameDef, portNameDef, propertyNameDef, ruleNameDef, simulateNameDef, valueNameDef, and *viewNameDef.*

See also:

identifier, name, nameRef, and *rename.*

---

identifier | name   *nameRef*

nameRef

A *nameRef* always corresponds to a previously defined *nameDef* of the same class and within the same scope. The class of the name is indicated by the prefix to the category, such as *cellNameRef* or *portNameRef*. The scope of a name is from the end of the defining construct to the end of the innermost (smallest) named form that encloses the original *nameDef*. In some explicitly documented cases further restrictions are placed on the scope, such as *figureGroupNameRef* within *physicalDesignRule* or names within *block*.

Name may be used to augment the simple identifier with display information where appropriate. Certain reference mechanisms such as *cellRef* and *portRef* explicitly identify the required name class and may access an indirect scope by including a nested reference.

Example:

(permutable p1 p2 p3)

The names **p1, p2,** and **p3** are references to three previously defined *ports*.

Used in:

cellNameRef, figureGroupNameRef, instanceNameRef, libraryNameRef, logicNameRef, member, netNameRef, portNameRef, propertyNameRef, valueNameRef, and *viewNameRef*.

See also:

nameDef.

(negate *numberValue*)

Negate is a number function that returns the negative of its argument. In the special case when *negate* is applied to an *integerValue* the expression may also be used as an *integerValue*.

Example:

(negate 5)

In the first example the number value **−5** is returned.

(negate (e −3 −1))

In the second example the number value **0.3** is returned.

Used in:

integerValue, and *numberValue.*

See also:

abs, divide, max, min, mod, product, subtract, and *sum.*

net

```
(net netNameDef
   joined                                              a required joined
   { < criticality > |                       net criticality for routing
   netDelay |                                              net delays
   figure |                                 figures to implement net
   net |                                                       subnets
   instance |                                        of cellType TIE
   commentGraphics |                  for annotative text and figures
   property |
   comment |
   userData }
)
```

net

The *net* construct is provided within the *contents* of a view in order to describe its connectivity. In views of type **SCHEMATIC**, *nets* may only be used within *page*. *Nets* may also be used in the *contents* of views of type **MASKLAYOUT**, **NETLIST**, **PCBLAYOUT**, **STRANGER**, or **SYMBOLIC**. *Net* must contain a single *joined* statement which determines its effect on connectivity. *Criticality* may be declared to aid in routing priorities. The remaining constructs serve to graphically illustrate or implement that connectivity.

An array of nets is created by using the *array* variant of *netNameDef*. The array variant must be used whenever the port references or *portLists* are arrays. In these cases, the number of individual ports represented by the port references and *portLists* within *joined* must be the same size as the net array.

Nets may nest to form a tree structure of subnets. Only views from cells of type **TIE** may be instantiated within *nets*. *Nets* directly within *contents* or *page* must not reference the same port. *Nets* defined within *nets* (subnets) may share references to a port defined on a locally instantiated *view* of a cell of type **TIE**.

Example:

```
(page P
   (net N1
      (joined (portRef P1) (portRef P2) (portRef P3))
      (instance T (viewRef symbol (cellRef tieCell)))
      (figure...)
      (net top
         (joined (portRef P1) (portRef P (instanceRef T)) (portRef P2))
         (figure...))
      (net upright
         (joined (portRef P3) (portRef P (instanceRef T)))
         (figure ...))))
```

This shows the definition of net **N1** which connects ports **P1, P2,** and **P3.** It has an inner structure of local subnets named **top** and **upright** and uses a TIE cell named **tieCell** to complete the tee junction.

Used in:

contents, listOfNets, net, page, and *statement.*

See also:

array, cellType, joined, netBundle, and *viewType.*

(**netBackAnnotate** *netRef*
 { netDelay |
 < criticality > |
 property | properties to be back annotated
 comment }   user comments
)

The *netBackAnnotate* construct is used to back−annotate EDIF attributes, user properties and *netDelays* which are associated with nets. The EDIF attribute for *nets* is *criticality*. The user properties are specified with the *property* construct. The *netBackAnnotate* is used with *viewMap*. The attribute values or user property values override any values previously assigned within the view being mapped to or supply new attributes or properties.

Example:

```
(cell Foo ...
    (view V2 (viewType SCHEMATIC) ...
        (contents ...
            (page P1 ...
                (net N1 ...
                    (property capacitance
                        (number)
                        (unit CAPACITANCE)
                        (owner "EDIFCo")))))))
(cell Fer ...
    (view V1 ...
        (contents ...
            (instance I2
                (viewRef V2 (cellRef Foo)) ...)))
    (viewMap
        (netBackAnnotate
            (netRef N1
                (instanceRef P1
                    (instanceRef I2 (viewRef V1))))
            (property capacitance
                (number (e 10 −12))
                (unit CAPACITANCE)
                (owner "EDIFCo")))))
```

In the above example the user property **capacitance** owned by "EDIFCo" on net **N1** of page **P1** of view **V2** of cell **Foo** is back−annotated through the instance hierarchy via instance **I2** of view **V1** of cell **Fer.**

Used in:

viewMap.

See also:

instanceRef, netMap, netRef, property, and *viewRef.*

---

                                                                                                  netBundle

(netBundle *netNameDef*
    listOfNets   nets comprising the bundle (ordered)
    { figure | picture of the bundle
    commentGraphics |
    property |
    comment |
    userData }
)

                                                                                                 netBundle

---

The *netBundle* construct is used to indicate collections of nets to which reference can subsequently be made by name. This may only be used within a **SCHEMATIC** *page* or in the contents of views of type **MASKLAYOUT**, **NETLIST**, **PCBLAYOUT**, **STRANGER**, or **SYMBOLIC**. The mandatory *listOfNets* presents an ordered list of the individual nets of the bundle. The *figures* are used to graphically represent the entire bundle.

Net names are local within a *netBundle* and do not conflict with other nets within the same *contents* or *page*. These may be *net* arrays, but the *netNameDef* of the *netBundle* itself must not use *array*.

Example:

    (netBundle Clocks
        (listOfNets
            (net clock (joined ...))
            (net clock_bar (joined ...)))
        (figure ...) ...)

Net bundle **Clocks** is defined to contain two nested nets and associated graphics. The names **clock** and **clock_bar** are local to the bundle and thus do not conflict with any externally defined nets.

Subsequent reference to these inner nets is made by nesting *netRef* statements, as in **(netRef clock (netRef Clocks))**.

Used in:

contents, page, and *statement.*

See also:

net, netRef, and *portBundle.*

---

netDelay

(netDelay
    derivation
    delay
    { transition | becomes }
)

netDelay

NetDelay is an attribute of a net which is used to specify a delay and its derivation for the given set of transitions. If no *transition* or *becomes* is specified, then the default is any transition.

Such a delay is effective between any two ports connected to the net and acts in addition to any specified port delays.

Example:

    (net N1
        (netDelay
            (derivation CALCULATED)
            (delay (e 3 1))
            (transition HS LR)))

The above example specifies a calculated delay of **30** time units when a transition from **HS** to **LR** occurs on net **N1.**

Used in:

net, and *netBackAnnotate.*

See also:

becomes, delay, derivation, pathDelay, portDelay, and *transition.*

(netGroup *{ netNameRef | netRef }***)**

NetGroup is used to indicate a group of net references. The group is not an ordered list but is a set. By grouping nets a relationship between a group and a single net or another group can be established, for example, the relationship that four nets in one view taken together are the same as one net in another view. All the nets referenced within *netGroup* must belong to the same view.

Example:

```
(netMap
  (netGroup
     (netRef net1 (viewRef V1))
     (netRef net2 (viewRef V1))
     (netRef net3 (viewRef V1))
     (netRef net4 (viewRef V1)))
  (netRef N1 (viewRef V2)))
```

The example above indicates that **net1, net2, net3,** and **net4** in view **V1** are the same as **N1** in **V2.** There is no relationship implied between **net1, net2, net3,** and **net4.**

Used in:

event, and *netMap.*

See also:

netNameRef, netRef, viewMap, and *viewRef.*

(netMap
    { netRef |
    netGroup |
    comment |
    userData }
)

NetMap is used in the *viewMap* construct to explicitly associate nets in different views which are the same object. A *netMap* may be used to map several net objects of one view with one or more net objects of other views. Groups of nets are specified with the *netGroup* construct. A common use is for mapping a net of a **SCHEMATIC** or **NETLIST** view to a net within a **MASKLAYOUT** or **PCBLAYOUT** view. No attribute inheritance is implied by the *netMap*.

Example:

    (netMap
      (netGroup
        (netRef net1 (viewRef ic))
        (netRef net2 (viewRef ic)))
      (netRef net1 (viewRef nets)))

The example above specifies explicitly that nets named **net1** and **net2** in the view named **ic** represent the same object as the net named **net1** in the view named **nets.**

Used in:

viewMap.

See also:

instanceRef, netGroup, netRef, and *viewRef.*

---

nameDef | array   *netNameDef*

                                                                netNameDef

---

NetNameDef is used to name *nets* and *netBundles*. When defined within another *net* or *netBundle,* this name is local to that context. Otherwise, net names are scoped by their enclosing *page* or *view,* as appropriate.

Array is used within *net* to create an array of nets. In such an array, the corresponding *joined* statement must contain port references and *portLists* of the same array length. *Array* should not be used for the name of a *netBundle.*

Used in:

net, and *netBundle.*

See also:

array, netNameRef, page, and *view.*

nameRef	*member*	*netNameRef*
	netNameRef

NetNameRef is used to reference a previously defined net name. This is used in the context of *viewMap* and timing statements. A simple *identifier* can be used to reference a single net or an entire net array.

Member should not be used to access a *netBundle,* although it may be used to specify an element of an array of nets.

Used in:

netGroup, and *netRef.*

See also:

member, and *netNameDef.*

(**netRef** *netNameRef*
    [*netRef* | *instanceRef* | *viewRef*]
)

NetRef is used to reference a net or net bundle by name and optionally through the instance hierarchy or a nested net hierarchy. The *member* construct is used to reference one net in an array of nets. Nested *netRef* constructs, e.g. (**netRef** ... (**netRef** ...)) are used to reference a net defined within a *net* or *netBundle*. Nested *instanceRef* constructs, e.g. (**instanceRef** ... (**instanceRef** ...)) are used to reference a net via the instance hierarchy. The first or outermost *netNameRef* in the syntax is the target net or net bundle, where the nested constructs which follow define a reference path in a bottom-up manner. The *instanceRef* construct is used when the instance hierarchy is part of the reference path to the target net. The *viewRef* is only legal if the *netRef* originated from the context of a *viewMap*.

Nested *instanceRef* and *viewRef* constructs are only appropriate within the context of *viewMap*.

Example:

    (**netRef AN1**
        (**netRef AN2**
            (**viewRef AV1**)))

The first example illustrates a reference to a net named **AN1** which is a subnet of the net or net bundle named **AN2** which is defined in the contents of the view named **AV1** in the current context.

    (**netRef**
        (**member BN1 2**)
        (**instanceRef**
            (**member BI2 5**)
            (**viewRef BV1**)))

In the second example, member **2** of a net array named **BN1** is referenced through the instance hierarchy via an instance array named **BI2** which is specified in the contents of a view named **BV1**.

    (**netRef CN1**
        (**netRef CN2**
            (**instanceRef CI1**
                (**instanceRef CI2**
                    (**viewRef CV1**)))))

The third example references a net named **CN1** which is a subnet of the net or net bundle named **CN2** which is referenced through the instance hierarchy via an instance named **CI1** of a view which is referenced by an instance named **CI2** which is defined in the contents of the view named **CV1.**

Used in:

event, netBackAnnotate, netGroup, netMap, and *netRef.*

See also:

instance, instanceNameDef, instanceNameRef, member, nameRef, net, netBundle, page, viewMap, and *viewRef.*

(noChange)

noChange

noChange

     NoChange is used by *entry* and *tableDefault* within *table* for logic modeling to indicate that no change is to take place. In other words, no change of value or status should occur on any port. In particular, a *follow* in effect on a *port* is not canceled.

Example:

```
(table
    (entry ... )
    (entry
        (match IN T)
        (noChange))
    (entry ...))
```

The above example describes an entry which, when the port **IN** is **T,** does not change the value or status of any ports.

Used in:

entry, and *tableDefault.*

See also:

table.

(nonPermutable
    { portRef |
    permutable }
)

NonPermutable is used to describe ports or groups of ports which cannot be interchanged. Used in conjunction, the *nonPermutable* and *permutable* constructs define a permutability tree structure of ports within the local *interface*. A port may be referenced at most once within a *permutable* or *nonPermutable* in a view.

References to *portBundles* or arrays are treated as if they were expanded to individual members, with the first index varying most slowly in arrays. In the context of a *permutable* construct, corresponding ports may be exchanged as a whole or not at all; partial exchanges are not permitted.

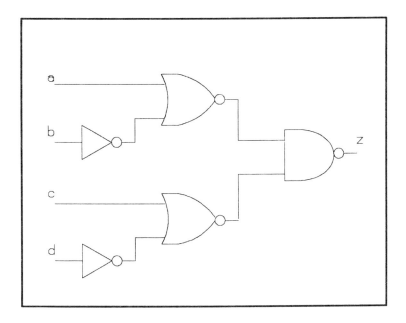

Figure 6 NonPermutable example

Example:

```
(permutable
    (nonPermutable (portRef A) (portRef B))
    (nonPermutable (portRef C) (portRef D)))
```

The example states that the ports **A** and **B** are not permutable and also that the ports **C** and **D** are not permutable. However, the ports **A** and **C** may be permuted as long as the ports **B** and **D** are permuted at the same time. This structure could be appropriate for the previously illustrated schematic.

Used in:

permutable.

See also:

interface, and *port.*

not

(not *booleanValue***)**

not

      Not is a Boolean function that returns the logical negation of its argument.

Example:

    (not x)

This example returns *true* if Boolean **x** has the value *false*. It returns *false* if Boolean **x** has the value *true*.

Used in:

booleanValue.

See also:

and, equal, or, and *xor.*

notAllowed

(**notAllowed** *ruleNameDef*
    figureGroupObject
    { comment |
    userData }
)

notAllowed

The *notAllowed* construct is used to specify the requirement that certain figure group objects (normally relationships between objects) are not allowed. A single figure group is to be considered. Any figure group object which exists is in violation of the rule.

Example:

```
(notAllowed CONTACT_TRANSISTOR
    (figureGroupObject
        (intersection
            (figureGroupRef CONTACT)
            (figureGroupRef TRANSISTOR))))
```

The above example rule requires that **CONTACT** figures and **TRANSISTOR** figures never intersect.

Used in:

physicalDesignRule.

See also:

figureGroupObject, and *ruleNameDef.*

(notchSpacing *ruleNameDef*
    figureGroupObject
    range | singleValueSet
    { comment |
    userData }
)

NotchSpacing is used to specify the required external spacing between nonadjacent edges of the same figure–group object. A single figure group is to be considered; pairs of edges from the same figure which have their outside orientations facing are to be selected. The distance between these edges must satisfy the specified value range for these edges to satisfy the rule.

Example:

    (notchSpacing MET_NOTCH
        (figureGroupObject METAL)
        (atLeast 3))

The above example rule requires that the exterior facing edges of a **METAL** figure must have a distance greater than or equal to **3.**

Used in:

physicalDesignRule.

See also:

figureGroupObject, range, ruleNameDef, and *singleValueSet.*

(**number** *{ numberValue | numberDisplay | number }*)

Number declares a *constant, parameter, property,* or *variable* value to be of type *number.* An optional *numberValue* can be specified, in which case the value serves as a default.

An array of number values can be defined by specifying multiple *numberValues* within a *number.* Nesting of the *number* construct is required to specify array values of two or more dimensions.

Example:

> (**parameter elementWidth** (**number** (**e 52 −1**)))

In this example parameter **elementWidth** is declared to be of type **number** and has a default number value of (**e 52 −1**), **5.2.**

> (**constant** (**array NA1 2**) (**number** (**e 54 −1**) **34**))
> (**constant** (**array NA2 2 3**)
>   (**number**
>   (**number** (**e 45 5**) **23 99**)
>   (**number** (**e 22 4**) **−22 −54**)))

In the above example the constant **NA1** is defined to be a one−dimensional number array with the assignments: (**member NA1 0**) = **5.4,** (**member NA1 1**) = **34.** **NA2** is defined to be a two−dimensional number array with the assignments:

> (**member NA2 0 0**) = **4500000,**
> (**member NA2 0 1**) = **23,**
> (**member NA2 0 2**) = **99,**
>
> (**member NA2 1 0**) = **220000,**
> (**member NA2 1 1**) = **−22,**
> (**member NA2 1 2**) = **−54.**

Used in:

number, and *typedValue.*

See also:

array, boolean, integer, miNoMax, numberValue, point, and *string.*

```
(numberDefinition
    { scale |
    <gridMap > |
    comment }
)
```

numberDefinition

NumberDefinition is used to collect all scaling information for a *library* at the top of its *technology* construct.

It may contain *scale* and *gridMap* to establish scales for each unit and for coordinates. These are used to relate values across *libraries* and to link them to physical units. At most one *scale* statement may be used within *numberDefinition* for each different *unit*. At most one *gridMap* may be used.

Example:

```
(technology
    (numberDefinition
        (scale 1 (e 1 −10) (unit distance))
        (scale ...) ...))
```

This illustrates a *numberDefinition* at the top of a *technology*. It establishes a local distance unit of one Angstrom.

Used in:

technology.

See also:

external, library, scale, and *unit.*

(numberDisplay *numberValue*
     { display }
)

NumberDisplay is used for displaying integer and real design data values. It is allowed in constructs that normally contain design data and which may exist in a coordinate space. Many constructs may exist in places where there is a coordinate space as well as in places where there is no coordinate space. *NumberDisplay* contains the data to be displayed, which must be an integer or number value, and any number of *display* forms.

The number value serves its normal role as a value in the appropriate context. Thus, if the *numberDisplay* were replaced by its *numberValue* the only change in the description would be the loss of display.

Example:

      (property opTemp
         (number
            (numberDisplay (e 3 2)
               (display text (origin (pt 20 30)))))
         (unit temperature))

In the above example the *property* form is in a coordinate space and its value **300.0** can be displayed at point **(20,30)** using the default attributes of figure group **text.** Units are indicated for the property. If the scaling in the technology block is **1,** then the value for **opTemp** will be **300.0** degrees kelvin. The receiving system may then display the value **300.0** in whatever form is appropriate for the system.

Used in:

dcFaninLoad, dcFanoutLoad, dcMaxFanin, dcMaxFanout, and *number.*

See also:

display, integerDisplay, miNoMaxDisplay, and *stringDisplay.*

---

scaledInteger	*numberValue*
	numberValue

In Level 0 an EDIF number can be either an integer token or an *e* construct. This is extended in Level 1.

Example:

5
(e 54323 −3)

These expressions represent the number values **5** and **54.323** respectively.

Used in:

atLeast, atMost, dcFaninLoad, dcFanoutLoad, dcMaxFanin, dcMaxFanout, duration, exactly, greaterThan, gridMap, lessThan, miNoMaxValue, mnm, number, numberDisplay, offsetEvent, scale, and *waveValue.*

See also:

e, integerValue, number, scaledInteger, and *stringValue.*

---

	numberValue
scaledInteger | *valueNameRef* | *floor* | *ceiling* | *fix* | *mod* | *xCoord* | *yCoord* | *divide* | *abs* | *max* | *min* | *negate* | *product* | *subtract* | *sum*	
	numberValue

NumberValue describes the number–value set. In Level 1 or 2 this includes numeric expressions. The *valueNameRef* may refer to a *constant, parameter,* or *variable* definition. Such a value must be of type *integer* or *number.* When used in the context of a *miNoMaxValue,* this may also reference a value of type *miNoMax.*

Example:

   (e 3 −1)

The above is an example of an EDIF number value.

   (constant x (number (e 3 4)))
   ...
   (negate x)

In the above example the **x** in the *negate* function is a constant value reference. The *negate* construct is a number function.

Used in:

abs, atLeast, atMost, ceiling, dcFaninLoad, dcFanoutLoad, dcMaxFanin, dcMaxFanout, divide, duration, equal, exactly, fix, floor, greaterThan, gridMap, increasing, lessThan, max, min, miNoMaxValue, mnm, negate, number, numberDisplay, offsetEvent, product, scale, strictlyIncreasing, subtract, sum, and *waveValue.*

See also:

booleanValue, integerValue, parameter, pointValue, scaledInteger, stringValue, and *valueNameRef.*

offPageConnector

(offPageConnector *portNameDef*
    { < unused > |
    property |
    comment |
    userData }
)

offPageConnector

OffPageConnector creates a local port for use within the *contents* of a schematic view. It is visible to each *page* and can thus be used within nets to establish connectivity between different pages. *Array* may be used to create an array of off-page connectors.

Each *page* may supply a different *portImplementation* for an *offPageConnector*, which may thus have different graphics in each page. This is only allowed in views of type **SCHEMATIC** and **STRANGER**. The *offPageConnector* port name is not directly visible outside the *view*.

Example:

```
(view V
   (viewType schematic)
   (interface
      (port IN  (direction input))
      (port OUT (direction output)))
   (contents
      (offPageConnector A)
      (page P1 ... )
      (page P2 ... )))
```

In this example, either page may reference the off-page connector **A** in the same way that they reference interface ports **IN** and **OUT.** However, in an instance of this view, there is no *portInstance* corresponding to **A;** it is private to the contents of the view.

Used in:

contents, and *statement.*

See also:

page, port, portImplementation, portNameDef, and *viewType.*

(offsetEvent
   event
   numberValue
)

offsetEvent

OffsetEvent is used to define a time relative to an event. A positive number value indicates a time after the specified event. A negative number value indicates a time before the specified event.

Example:

(offsetEvent
   (event
      (portRef CK)
      (transition H L))
   (e −48 −1))

This example defines a time **4.8** units before a transition from **H** to **L** on port **CK.**

Used in:

timeInterval.

See also:

event, and *forbiddenEvent.*

(**openShape** *curve*
  { property }
)

OpenShape is used for describing shapes which are open by definition. It uses the *curve* form and may thus describe an open figure containing *arcs*.

Example:

```
(openShape
    (curve
        (arc  (pt 0 4)  (pt 1 2)  (pt 0 0))))
    (shape
        (curve
            (arc  (pt 1 4)  (pt 4 3)  (pt 5 2))
            (arc  (pt 5 2)  (pt 4 1)  (pt 1 0))
            (arc  (pt 1 0)  (pt 2 2)  (pt 1 4))))
```

This example uses *openShape* as part of the graphics for a typical **xor** symbol.

Used in:

figure.

See also:

arc, path, and *shape.*

optional

(**optional**
    literal | *actual* | *build*
)

optional

Optional may appear within a *formal* keyword–parameter definition. It allows the use of formal parameters which need not be included in every use of a defined keyword. It contains the default value for its parameter. The default can be a literal value, the actual value of a parameter specified previously in the construct or the result of building a *form*. The default value should generate a single token or *form*.

An *optional* parameter may only be followed by further *optional* parameters in the same list of *keywordParameters*.

This is only appropriate for keyword level 2 or higher.

Example:

    (**keywordDefine wait**
       (**keywordParameters**
         (**formal time**)
         (**formal load**
            (**optional (literal 5)**)))
       (**generate**
         (**build loadDelay**
            (**actual time**)
            (**actual load**))))

This keyword definition creates a *loadDelay* construct. However, load value is optional with a default value of **5.** A later use such as (**wait 10**) or (**wait 15 20**) would be legal in any context in which *loadDelay* is legal.

Used in:

formal.

See also:

keywordDefine, keywordLevel, and *keywordParameters.*

(**or** *{ booleanValue }*)

or

or

      Or is a boolean function that returns the logical **or** of its arguments. It is *true* if any of its arguments are *true,* and *false* otherwise.

      If no arguments are present, it returns *false.*

Example:

    (**or**
        (equal X A)
        (equal X B))

This expression evaluates to *true* if **X** has a value equal to **A** or to **B.**

Used in:

booleanValue.

See also:

and, equal, not, and *xor.*

(orientation R0 | R90 | R180 | R270 | MX | MY | MYR90 | MXR90)

The *orientation* attribute provides the capability of specifying any one of eight possible orientations achieved by counter–clockwise rotation about the origin or by reflection in one of the two axes. Any rotation or reflection is applied before an object is translated to its final position, but after any scaling. The orientation of a placed view or text has no effect on the location of its origin.

Orientation fully determines the final direction of the axes of such objects relative to their enclosing context.

In the absence of other *transform* attributes, a typical point (**x**, **y**) will be mapped as follows:

- (**+x**, **−y**) for MX,

- (**+y**, **+x**) for MXR90,

- (**−x**, **+y**) for MY,

- (**−y**, **−x**) for MYR90,

- (**+x**, **+y**) for R0,

- (**−x**, **−y**) for R180,

- (**+y**, **−x**) for R270,

- (**−y**, **+x**) for R90.

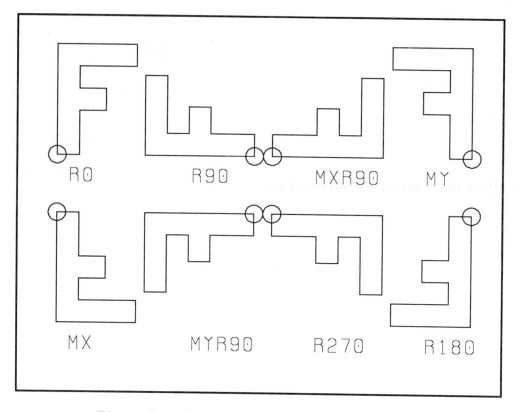

Figure 2-7 The eight orthogonal orientations

Example:

```
(instance NAND1
    (viewRef mask  (cellRef nand))
    (transform
        (orientation R90)
        (origin  (pt 100 0)))))
```

The first example specifies that the instance named **NAND1** of cell **nand** is to be placed so that its origin lies at point **(100,0)** and that the cell is rotated by **90** degrees counter-clockwise with respect to its origin.

```
(stringDisplay "U12"
    (display text
        (justify lowerLeft)
        (orientation r270)
        (origin (pt 4 6))))
```

The second example specifies that the string "U12" is to be displayed such that the origin is the lower left of the text (below and left of the "U"); then the text is rotated **270** degrees and finally placed such that the origin is at point **(4,6)**. The combined effect is a textual display which reads in a downward direction and lies below and to the right of the point **(4,6)**.

Used in:

display, and *transform.*

See also:

justify, and *origin.*

(origin *pointValue***)**

origin

origin

Origin is used to specify the translation point of an object when transforming. Translation of an object is always the last operation performed when transforming an instance or text.

The *pointValue* identifies the location (with respect to the enclosing context) which corresponds to the point with zero coordinates in an instanced *view,* or the point indicated by *justify* in a textual *display.*

Example:

```
(instance NAND1
    (viewRef mask (cellRef nand))
    (transform
        (origin (pt 100 0)))))
```

The first example specifies that the instance of cell nand named **NAND1** is to be placed so that its origin lies at point **(100,0).**

```
(stringDisplay "U12"
    (display text
        (justify lowerLeft)
        (orientation r270)
        (origin (pt 4 6))))
```

The second example specifies that the string **"U12"** is to be displayed such that the lower left of the text (below and left of the **"U"),** is at point **(4,6).**

Used in:

display, and *transform.*

See also:

instance, justify, and *orientation.*

(**overhangDistance** *ruleNameDef*
   figureGroupObject
   figureGroupObject
   range / *singleValueSet*
   { *comment* /
   userData }
)

OverhangDistance is used to specify the required distance by which the first *figureGroupObject* must overhang the second *figureGroupObject*. Two different *figureGroups* are to be considered; pairs of edges (one from each figure group) are selected as follows: an edge from the second *figureGroupObject* which is partially inside a figure of the first *figureGroupObject,* and an edge from the enclosing figure of the first *figureGroupObject* with the same orientation as the other edge. The distance between the selected edges must satisfy the value range.

   (**overhangDistance** ...
      (**figureGroupObject A**)
      (**figureGroupObject B**) ...)

This example selects edges from **A** and **B** such that the edges from **B** lie inside **A.** The distance between a selected edge from **B** and an edge from **A** which has the same orientation must satisfy the value range. The order of *figureGroupObjects* is significant in this construct.

Example:

   (**overhangDistance POLY_DIFF_OVERHANG**
      (**figureGroupObject POLY**)
      (**figureGroupObject DIFF**)
      (**atLeast 4**))

The above example rule requires that **POLY** must overhang **DIFF** by a value greater than or equal to **4.**

Used in:

physicalDesignRule.

See also:

enclosureDistance, figureGroupObject, range, ruleNameDef, and *singleValueSet.*

---

overlapDistance

(overlapDistance *ruleNameDef*
    figureGroupObject
    figureGroupObject
    range | singleValueSet
    { comment |
    userData }
)

overlapDistance

    OverlapDistance is used to specify the required overlap distance between two figure–group objects, with each in a different figure group. Two figure groups are to be considered; pairs of edges (one edge from each figure group) which have their inside orientations facing are to be selected. The value range specifies the allowable distances between a selected pair of edges.

Example:

    (overlapDistance POLY_DIFF_OVERLAP
        (figureGroupObject POLY)
        (figureGroupObject DIFF)
        (atLeast 7))

The above example rule requires that **POLY** and **DIFF** overlap be greater than or equal to **7.**

Used in:

physicalDesignRule.

See also:

figureGroupObject, range, ruleNameDef, and *singleValueSet.*

---

oversize

(oversize
    integerValue
    figureGroupRef | figureOp
    cornerType
)

oversize

The *oversize* construct is used to specify an operation which grows (oversizes) or shrinks (undersizes) figure–group objects. The result is an oversized or undersized set of figure–group objects. If the value of *integerValue* is positive then *oversize* is oversizing; if the value of *integerValue* is negative then *oversize* is undersizing. It gives the perpendicular distance between corresponding edges of the original figures and the oversized figures.

The geometric behavior of the *oversize* operation is specified by the *cornerType* construct. The **ROUND** *cornerType* requires that the oversize operation displaces the points along the edges of figures by the Euclidean distance, thus creating arcs at corners where necessary. The **TRUNCATE** *cornerType* requires that the oversize operation displaces the edges of figures by the distance specified and as defined by the **TRUNCATE** *cornerType*. The **EXTEND** *cornerType* requires that the oversize operation displaces the edges of figures by the distance specified and as defined by the **EXTEND** *cornerType*.

Example:

    (oversize −25
        (figureGroupRef Poly)
        (cornerType EXTEND))

This example specifies a new set of figure–group objects which are formed by undersizing **Poly** by **25** distance units using the **EXTEND** corner–type algorithm.

Used in:

figureOp.

See also:

cornerType,   *figureGroupRef,*   *includeFigureGroup,*   *numberValue,*   and *physicalDesignRule.*

(**owner** *stringToken*)

owner
name of "owner" of property
owner

The *owner* construct is provided to specify the owner or source of the enclosing *property*. This provides a source for the meaning or definition of the property. Some external understanding between the sender and receiver of the meaning of the owner string is necessary if this is to be treated as more than an annotation.

Example:

```
(property PRS
    (number (e 3 −2))
    (owner "SKIPPY"))
```

The above example specifies that the source of the property **PRS** is **SKIPPY**.

Used in:

property.

See also:

userData.

page

```
(page  instanceNameDef
    { instance |
    net |
    netBundle |
    commentGraphics |
    portImplementation |
    < pageSize > |
    < boundingBox > |
    comment |
    userData }
)
```

page

Page is used for implementing the pages of a schematic design. *Page* contains much of the same information found in the contents of other views of a cell. However, the *page* includes an *instanceNameDef*, which is in the name class of instances. That is, it is referenced with an *instanceNameRef* or *instanceRef*. *Array* may not be used in this context.

Page is only permitted within **SCHEMATIC** and **STRANGER** views. In the schematic view all schematics sheets are done as *page* whether the system supports a multiple page hierarchy or not. If a system does not support multiple page designs, only one page will exist per schematic view. Each *page* of a *view* must have a distinct name.

Each page has a local name space and a local coordinate space. Names defined within one *page* do not conflict with identical names in any other *page*. *Simulate* and *timing* are not allowed in *page,* but are permitted in the *contents* of a **SCHEMATIC** view. *Pages* communicate with each other through *ports* defined in the *interface* and *offPageConnectors* defined in the *contents*.

Example:

```
(cell BIG (cellType generic)
    (view V1 (viewType Schematic)
        (interface ...)
        (contents
            (offPageConnector C)
            (page &1
                (instance I1 ...)
                (instance I2 ...)
                (net N1 ...)
                (net N2 ...) ...)
```

```
(page &2
    (instance I1 ...)
    (instance I2 ...)
    (net N1 ...)
    (net N2 ...) ...))))
```

In the above example the view named **V1** of cell **BIG** is implemented with two schematic pages named **1** and **2**.

Used in:

contents.

See also:

offPageConnector, portImplementation, pageSize, and *viewType.*

page

```
(page   instanceNameDef
      { instance |
      net |
      netBundle |
      commentGraphics |
      portImplementation |
      < pageSize > |
      < boundingBox > |
      constant |
      constraint |
      variable |
      comment |
      userData }
)
```

page

In Level 1, a *page* may contain parametric constructs. This is used to describe SCHEMATIC diagrams in parametric designs.

Example:

```
(page p1
    (instance
        (array dynamicArray bitWidth)
        (viewRef symbol (cellRef inverter)) ...) ...)
```

In this example, the number of instances of the view named **symbol** from the cell named **inverter** is specified by the integer value named **bitWidth**.

Used in:

contents.

See also:

edifLevel.

page

(page *instanceNameDef*
    { instance |
    net |
    netBundle |
    commentGraphics |
    portImplementation |
    < pageSize > |
    < boundingBox > |
    constant |
    constraint |
    variable |
    assign |
    block |
    if |
    iterate |
    while |
    comment |
    userData }
)

page

In Level 2, a *page* may contain algorithmic constructs. This is used to describe **SCHEMATIC** diagrams in procedural designs.

Example:

    (page p2
       (if feedThrough
          (then
             (net optionalNet ...))) ...)

In this example, the net named **optionalNet** will only be included in page **p2** if the Boolean value named **feedThrough** is *true*.

Used in:

contents.

See also:

edifLevel.

(pageSize *rectangle***)**	*pageSize*
	pageSize

   PageSize is an attribute of the environment of *pages* and *symbols*. The *rectangle* indicates the extent of the page used for the schematic page or symbol.

   The page size does not indicate the absolute size of the page but the extent of the page in its environment. That is, the points in the page size are related to the points in the design data. *PageSize* is not the same as *boundingBox* which describes the minimum containing rectangle of the design information. The page size must cover the design information, but in many systems the page size will be larger than the extent of the design.

Example:

```
(symbol
    (pageSize
        (rectangle
            (pt −120 −100)
            (pt 120 100)))
    (figure ...))
```

In the above example the page size for the symbol is **(−120,−100)** to **(120,100)** distance units.

Used in:

page, and *symbol.*

See also:

boundingBox, and *rectangle.*

(parameter *valueNameDef*
    typedValue
    [unit]
)

Parameter is used within the *interface* of any view type to define a parameter, its type and optional default value, and an optional unit. In Level 0 descriptions, this may only be used in the context of *external* declarations.

Within the instance hierarchy a parameter may be assigned new values with the *parameterAssign* form within an *instance*. The type and default value of a parameter is specified with the *boolean, integer, miNoMax, number, point* or *string,* typed value. Parameter arrays are specified with the *array* construct and the nesting of typed values.

The scope of a parameter is the whole view whose interface it is defined in. A parameter may not be defined within the interface of a cell which is specified in a Level 0 *library*. A parameter may be defined within the *interface* of a cell which is specified in a Level 1 or 2 *library* or in a Level 0, 1, or 2 *external* statement.

Example:

    (interface
        (parameter capLoad
            (number (e 5 0))
            (unit capacitance)))

In the above example a parameter named **capLoad** is defined to be of type *number* with a default value of **5.0.** The values are specified to be in **CAPACITANCE** units.

    (parameter (array PA 2 3)
        (point
            (point (pt 0 0) (pt 0 1) (pt 0 2))
            (point (pt 1 0) (pt 1 1) (pt 1 2))))

In the above example a two-dimensional point parameter **PA** is defined with default value for **(member PA 0 0)** of **(pt 0 0),** **(member PA 0 1)** of **(pt 0 1),** and **(member PA 1 2)** of **(pt 1 2).**

Used in:

interface.

See also:

array, boolean, constant, external, integer, library, member, miNoMax, number, parameterAssign, point, scale, string, typedValue, unit, and *variable.*

(**parameterAssign** *valueNameRef typedValue*)

ParameterAssign is used within the *instance* statement to supply overriding values to parameters defined within the interface of the instantiated view. The *valueNameRef* must be a valid reference to an interface parameter of that view, which must have the same type and array structure as the given value. The type and structure of the given value is specified by a *boolean, integer, miNoMax, number, point,* or *string* construct. If the parameter value is of type *point,* then the value must have the inverse of the instance transformation applied to it before the value is passed into the instantiated cell.

Example:

>   (instance I1 (viewRef V1 (cellRef Foo))
>   (parameterAssign capLoad (number 5)))

In the above example, assuming the referenced cell and the current cell are in libraries at Level 1 or higher, the parameter named **capLoad** is assigned the number value of **5.0.** This parameter must have been defined as a *number* within the *interface* of the view named **V1** in the cell named **Foo.**

>   (instance I2 (viewRef V1 (cellRef Fer (libraryRef anotherLib)))
>   (parameterAssign PT1 (point (pt 25 30)))
>   (transform
>   (origin (pt 5 10))))

In the above example the inverse of the transform is applied to the point value of **(25,30)** yielding **(20,20),** which is supplied to the parameter variable **PT1** within the view named **V1** in cell **Fer** in library **anotherLib.** Note that *library* **anotherLib** must be at Level 1 or higher.

Used in:

instance.

See also:

boolean, integer, interface, miNoMax, number, parameter, point, string, and *typedValue.*

---

parameterDisplay

(**parameterDisplay** *valueNameRef*
  { display }
)

parameterDisplay

ParameterDisplay is used to specify display locations and display attributes for the display of parameter values. It is used in the *interface* in the constructs which have a coordinate space associated with them, namely *protectionFrame* and *symbol*. The parameter value to be displayed is referenced by the *valueNameRef* and must be defined in the *interface* of the current *view*. Its display location and attributes are specified in the *display* construct.

Example:

```
(interface
    (parameter IP (integer 2)) ...
    (symbol ...
        (parameterDisplay IP (display ...))))
```

In the above example the value of the parameter **IP** is displayed as part of the symbol. If the default value of the parameter has not been overridden, then the value **2** should be displayed.

Used in:

protectionFrame, and *symbol.*

See also:

display, name, parameter, and *valueNameRef.*

---

path

(**path** *pointList*
   { property }
)

path

A *path* is a collection of joining line segments with an associated width. The width is specified in the *figureGroup* attribute *pathWidth,* which applies when the path is used in a view.

Example:

    (symbol
        (figure black_line
            (path
                (pointList
                    (pt 3000 500)
                    (pt 3000 9500)
                    (pt 12000 5000)
                    (pt 3000 500)))
            (circle
                (pt 12000 5000)
                (pt 13000 5000))
            (path
                (pointList
                    (pt 0 5000)
                    (pt 3000 5000)))
            (path
                (pointList
                    (pt 13000 5000)
                    (pt 16000 5000)))))

This example describes a typical symbol for an inverter, using three paths and a circle.

Used in:

figure.

See also:

cornerType, endType, openShape, pathWidth, polygon, and *shape.*

(pathDelay *delay*
  { event }
)

PathDelay associates a delay with a specified chain of events. This does not specify the enabling conditions for the path but does state that whenever the given path is enabled it has the given delay range. The path is described by an ordered sequence of events on ports or on nets, or both; at least two events must be given. Not all of the transitions on nets or ports in the path need to be specified in detail.

The *delay* contains the time from first *event* in the path to the final *event* and must evaluate to a non−negative number. Each *event* is taken to be a contributing cause of the following *event*.

Example:

```
(pathDelay
    (delay (mnm (e 13 −1) (e 27 −1) (e 59 −1)))
    (event (portRef CK) (transition A B))
    (event (portRef Q) (transition B A)))
```

The above example describes the path from port **CK,** with a logic transition from **A** to **B,** to port **Q,** with a transition from **B** to **A.** The path has associated with it, a delay of **1.3** time units minimum, **2.7** time units nominal, and **5.9** time units maximum.

Used in:

timing.

See also:

delay, event, netDelay, and *portDelay.*

pathWidth

pathWidth

(pathWidth *integerValue*)

The *pathWidth* attribute is used to define the width of *paths* and *openShapes* in a figure group. The integer value is expressed in distance units. The value may be zero but may not be negative. It indicates the required perpendicular distance between pairs of edges in an expanded path, corresponding to each center line in the original path.

PathWidth may be specified within *figureGroup* in the technology block of a library. In this case the width is the default width to be used for all paths and curves in a figure group. *PathWidth* may also be specified within *figureGroupOverride* in the *figure* itself. In this case the width value is used to temporarily override the default path–width value.

PathWidth has no effect on the interpretation of *polygon, shape, rectangle, circle,* or *dot* figures. A *pathWidth* of **0** implies that no area is contributed to the *figure*, although this may cause a display.

Example:

```
(numberDefinition
    (scale 1 (e 1 −3) (unit distance)))
(figureGroup Display (pathWidth 10) ...)
```

The first example defines a default path width of **10** mm.

```
(figure
    (figureGroupOverride Display (pathWidth 15)) ...)
```

The second example overrides the default path width with a value of **15** mm. The default value of **10** mm is still in effect for subsequent *figures* which reference the **Display** figure group.

Used in:

figureGroup, and *figureGroupOverride.*

See also:

borderWidth, cornerType, endType, openShape, and *path.*

permutable

(permutable
    { portRef |
    permutable |
    nonPermutable }
)

permutable

Permutable is used to describe a relationship in which ports are interchangeable. The ports referenced within *permutable* may be individual, arrayed, or bundled. *Permutable* may also contain nested *permutable* and *nonPermutable* constructs. *Permutable* may be nested with *nonPermutable* to specify complex relationships between *ports* defined in the local *interface* (master ports). This explicitly provides a degree of freedom for the external routing of this view. A port may be referenced at most once within a *permutable* or *nonPermutable* in a view. *Permutable* may be used in the *interface* of any view type except **GRAPHIC** or **DOCUMENT.**

When arrays and bundles are specified in *permutable,* the permutability applies to the individual members of the array or bundle as if the bundle or port had been expanded to the individual members. Nested *nonPermutable* structures may be exchanged as a whole but not partially.

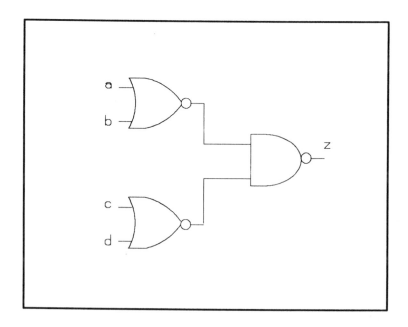

Figure 7 Nested permutable example

Example:

> **(port IN1)**
> **(port IN2)**
> **(permutable (portRef IN1) (portRef IN2)**

This states that connections to ports **IN1** and **IN2** may be interchanged during routing of this view without affecting the logical operation of the view.

> **(portBundle BP**
>   **(listOfPorts**
>   **(port A)**
>   **(port B)))...**
> **(permutable (portRef BP))**

This is equivalent to:

> **(permutable**
>   **(portRef A (portRef BP))**
>   **(portRef B (portRef BP)))**

The above example specifies that the ports **A** and **B** of port bundle **BP** are interchangeable in use.

> **(port (array a 2))**
> **(port (array b 2))**
> **(permutable (portRef a) (portRef b))**

This is equivalent to:

> **(permutable**
>   **(portRef (member a 0))**
>   **(portRef (member a 1))**
>   **(portRef (member b 0))**
>   **(portRef (member b 1)))**

The above example specifies that all members of arrays **a** and **b** are interchangeable.

> **(port (array a 2))**
> **(port (array b 2))**
> **(permutable**
>   **(nonPermutable (portRef a))**
>   **(nonPermutable (portRef b)))**

This is equivalent to:

```
(permutable
    (nonPermutable
        (portRef (member a 0))
        (portRef (member a 1)))
    (nonPermutable
        (portRef (member b 0))
        (portRef (member b 1))))
```

The above example specifies that arrays **a** and **b** are interchangeable as a whole; individual members of the arrays are not interchangeable.

Used in:

interface, nonPermutable, and *permutable.*

See also:

portRef, and *viewType.*

(physicalDesignRule
    { figureWidth |
    figureArea |
    rectangleSize |
    figurePerimeter |
    overlapDistance |
    overhangDistance |
    enclosureDistance |
    interFigureGroupSpacing |
    intraFigureGroupSpacing |
    notchSpacing |
    notAllowed |
    figureGroup |
    comment |
    userData }
)

The *physicalDesignRule* construct is provided to specify process or manufacturing physical design rules. This includes the definition of new figure groups which are temporarily created with the *figureGroup* construct and are only defined within the scope of the *physicalDesignRule*. Such a figure group name is not available for later use in *figure* statements.

Example:

```
(physicalDesignRule
    (figureGroup Transistors
        (includeFigureGroup
            (difference
                (intersection
                    (figureGroupRef Poly)
                    (figureGroupRef Diff))
                (figureGroupRef Buried))))
    (figureWidth Poly_Width (figureGroupObject Poly) (atLeast 5))
    (rectangleSize Transistor_Size
        (figureGroupObject Transistors)
        (multipleValueSet
            (rangeVector (exactly 7) (exactly 10))
            (rangeVector (exactly 5) (exactly 8))))
    (overHangDistance Poly_Overhang
        (figureGroupObject Poly) (figureGroupObject Transistors)
        (atLeast 5)))
```

In the above example three physical design rules, namely **Poly_Width, Transistor_Size,** and **Poly_Overhang,** are specified in the *physicalDesignRule* construct. Also, a temporary figure group named **Transistors** is defined and used within the physical design rule specification.

Used in:

technology.

See also:

enclosureDistance,   figureArea,   figureGroup,   figurePerimeter,   figureWidth, interFigureGroupSpacing,   intraFigureGroupSpacing,   notAllowed,   notchSpacing, overhangDistance, overlapDistance, and *rectangleSize.*

(plug *{ socketSet }*)

Plug is used to define the placement rules for a macrocell within a gate array. The *plug* defines a series of socket sets any of which can be used to correctly place this macrocell. If no *socketSet* is given, then no placement is possible.

Example:

```
(Cell M299
    (CellType Generic)
    (View Site_definition
        (ViewType Symbolic)
        (Interface
            (ArrayRelatedInfo
                (ArrayMacro
                    (Plug
                        (SocketSet
                            (Symmetry
                                (Transform
                                    (Orientation R90)))
                            (Site
                                (ViewRef Site
                                    (CellRef Site_cell)))))))))))
```

This example specifies cell **M299** which may be placed in site **Site_cell,** possibly after being rotated **270** degrees.

Used in:

arrayMacro.

See also:

arrayRelatedInfo, and *socket.*

(point *{ pointValue | pointDisplay | point }***)**

Point declares a *constant, parameter, property,* or *variable* to be of type point. An optional *pointValue* can be specified, in which case the value serves as a default. An array of point values can be defined by specifying multiple *pointValues* within a *point*. Nesting of the *point* construct is required to specify array values of two or more dimensions.

Example:

> **(parameter node (point (pt 0 10)))**

In this example the parameter **node** is declared to be of type *point*. A default point value of **(pt 0 10)** is also specified.

> **(constant (array PA1 2) (point (pt 0 0) (pt 100 100)))**
> **(constant (array PA2 2 3)**
>   **(point**
>   **(point (pt 0 0) (pt 10 10) (pt 100 100))**
>   **(point (pt 0 0) (pt −10 −10) (pt −100 −100))))**

In the above example the constant **PA1** is defined to be a one−dimensional point array with the following value assignments: **(member PA1 0)** = **(pt 0 0)**, **(member PA1 1)** = **(pt 100 100)**.

PA2 is defined to be a two−dimensional point array with the following value assignments: **(member PA2 0 0)** = **(pt 0 0)**, **(member PA2 0 1)** = **(pt 10 10)**, **(member PA2 0 2)** = **(pt 100 100)**, **(member PA2 1 0)** = **(pt 0 0)**, **(member PA2 1 1)** = **(pt −10 −10)**, **(member PA2 1 2)** = **(pt −100 −100)**.

Used in:

point, and *typedValue.*

See also:

array, boolean, integer, miNoMax, number, pointValue, pt, and *string.*

(pointDisplay *pointValue*
    { display }
)

PointDisplay is used for displaying point coordinates. The actual form that point coordinates have while being displayed is system–dependent and not specified by EDIF.

PointDisplay contains the data to be displayed, which must be a *pointValue,* and any number of *display* forms.

Example:

    (property Coordinates
       (point
          (pointDisplay (pt 50 105)
            (display text (origin (pt 20 30))))))

In the above example the *property* is in a coordinate space and its value, **(pt 50 105),** can be displayed at point **(20,30).** The receiving system may display the point coordinates in whatever form is appropriate for the system. For example the data may be displayed as: **"(50,105)"** (a string with parentheses and commas for delimiters) in one system, or **"50 150"** (a string with only spaces for delimiters) in another system.

Used in:

point.

See also:

booleanDisplay, display, integerDisplay, miNoMaxDisplay, numberDisplay, pt, and *stringDisplay.*

(pointList *{ pointValue }* **)**

PointList is used to specify an ordered list of points which usually represent a series of line segments within figure definitions. To describe a nontrivial figure it should contain at least two points in *path* and at least three in *polygon*.

Example:

```
(pointList
    (pt 0 1)
    (pt 1 4)
    (pt 0 3)
    (pt 0 1))
```

This is a simple point list.

Used in:

path, and *polygon.*

See also:

curve, and *figure.*

(pointSubtract *pointValue { pointValue }* **)**

pointSubtract

pointSubtract

PointSubtract is a point function that returns the vector difference between the first point and the *pointSum* of the remaining arguments. This is not available in Level 0 descriptions.

Points are subtracted as vectors; the resulting point has as x–coordinate the result of subtracting the individual x–coordinates, and as y–coordinate the result of subtracting the individual y–coordinates.

Example:

```
(pointSubtract
    (pt 13 25)
    (pt  4  8)
    (pt  2  6))
...
(pointSubtract
    (pt 13 25)
    (pointSum
        (pt  4  8)
        (pt  2  6)))
```

Both examples above return the point value **(pt 7 11).**

Used in:

pointValue.

See also:

point, pointSum, pointValue, xCoord, and *yCoord.*

(pointSum   *{ pointValue }*)

pointSum

pointSum

     PointSum is a point function which returns the vector sum of any number of points. It is not available in Level 0 descriptions.

     Coordinates are added separately to obtain the coordinates of the result.

     If no arguments are present, *pointSum* returns the value **(pt 0 0)**.

Example:

    (pointSum
       (pt 3 5)
       (pt 4 8))

The above example returns the point value **(pt 7 13)**.

Used in:

pointValue.

See also:

point, pointSubtract, xCoord, and *yCoord.*

	pointValue
pt	
	pointValue

PointValue describes the set of specifications of point values. The set includes only *pt* in Level 0 descriptions.

Example:

(dot (pt 10 100))

The above example specifies a dot located at **(10, 100).**

Used in:

arc, circle, curve, delta, dot, origin, point, pointDisplay, pointList, and *rectangle.*

See also:

edifLevel, and *pt.*

*pt	valueNameRef	pointSum	pointSubtract*	*pointValue* *pointValue*

PointValue describes the point value set. This is extended in Level 1 and Level 2 to include *pt* and functions that return EDIF point values. The value name reference must be of type *point*.

Example:

```
(pointSum
    (pt 1 2)
    (pt 3 4))
```

In this example *pointSum* is a point function which will return the value **(pt 4 6)**.

Used in:

arc, circle, curve, delta, dot, origin, point, pointDisplay, pointList, pointSubtract, pointSum, rectangle, xCoord, and *yCoord.*

See also:

booleanValue, edifLevel, integerValue, numberValue, and *stringValue.*

polygon

(**polygon** *pointList*
    { property }
)

polygon

A *polygon* represents a figure bounded by line segments joining consecutive points, including the line segment from the last point to the first point. If the first and last point are not the same, then the *polygon* contains the line segment between those two points. All polygons are closed by definition.

The *polygon* may not intersect itself, though it may have coincident segments.

Example:

```
(polygon
    (pointList
        (pt 0 1)
        (pt 1 4)
        (pt 0 3)))

(polygon
    (pointList
        (pt 0 1)
        (pt 1 4)
        (pt 0 3)
        (pt 0 1)))
```

This example shows two equivalent representations of the same triangle.

Used in:

figure.

See also:

rectangle, and *shape.*

```
(port  portNameDef
    { < direction > |                         direction of signal flow
      < unused > |                                port is unused
      < designator > |                     port (pin number) designator
      < dcFaninLoad > |                      load contributed as fan−in
      < dcFanoutLoad > |                    load contributed as fan−out
      < dcMaxFanin > |                     maximum allowed fan−in load
      < dcMaxFanout > |                   maximum allowed fan−out load
      < acLoad > |              small−signal contributed load (capacitive load)
      portDelay |                                  port delays
      property |
      comment |
      userData }
)
```

Port is the basic means of communicating signal information between cells and is the subject of all connectivity statements. An array of *ports* may be declared by using the *array* variant of *portNameDef*.

Port is used in the interface of a cell view of any type except **DOCUMENT** or **GRAPHIC** to define ports, arrayed ports, and bundle ports. Included with the definition are several attributes. *Direction* is included to specify the direction of the signal at that port. *DcMaxFanin, dcMaxFanout, dcFaninLoad,* and *dcFanoutLoad* are provided for description of load−checking rules required by certain technologies. *AcLoad* is used in calculation of signal delay. *Designator* is used to specify the designator name or number of a component port (pin number).

Example:

   (port IN (direction input))

This example declares an input port named **IN.**

Used in:

interface, and *listOfPorts.*

See also:

array, joined, offPageConnector, portBundle, portImplementation, and *viewType.*

portBackAnnotate

(portBackAnnotate *portRef*	*portBackAnnotate*
{ < designator > |	port (reference) designator
< dcFaninLoad > |	load contributed as fan−in
< dcFanoutLoad > |	load contributed as fan−out
< dcMaxFanin > |	maximum allowed fan−in load
< dcMaxFanout > |	maximum allowed fan−out load
< acLoad > |	small−signal contributed load (capacitive load)
portDelay |	port delays
property |	properties to be back annotated
comment }	user comments
)	

portBackAnnotate

PortBackAnnotate is used to back−annotate attributes and user properties which are associated with ports. The attributes for ports are: *designator, portDelay, dcFaninLoad, dcFanoutLoad, dcMaxFanin, dcMaxFanout,* and *acLoad.* User properties are back−annotated with the *property* construct. The attribute values or user property values override any values previously assigned within the original view or supply new properties.

Example:

```
(cell Foo ...
    (view V2 ...
        (interface ...
            (port P1 ...
                (property capacitance (number)
                    (unit CAPACITANCE)
                    (owner "EDIFCo"))))))
(cell Fer...
    (view V1 ...
        (interface ...
        (contents ...
            (instance I2 (viewRef V2 (cellRef Foo)) ...)))
        (viewMap
            (portBackAnnotate
                (portRef P1 (instanceRef I2 (viewRef V1)))
                (designator "2")
                (property capacitance (number (e 50 −12))
                    (unit CAPACITANCE) (owner "EDIFCo")))))
```

In the above example the pin−designator attribute *designator* and user−property **capacitance** owned by **"EDIFCo"** is back−annotated to the port instance **P1** of instance **I2** of view **V1** of cell **Fer.**

Used in:

viewMap.

See also:

designator, instanceBackAnnotate, netBackAnnotate, portInstance, portMap, and *property.*

(**portBundle** *portNameDef*
   listOfPorts
   { property |
   comment |
   userData }
)

PortBundle is used to collect ports, arrayed ports and other bundles of ports together into a group and give them a name. The port definitions included in the *listOfPorts* are ordered. The *portNameDef* of the *portBundle* may not be an *array*.

The port names created inside a *portBundle* are local to that bundle and could thus use the same names as other ports or port bundles without creating any conflict.

PortBundle may be used in the *interface* of any view type except **DOCUMENT** and **GRAPHIC**.

Example:

```
(portBundle pbExample
   (listOfPorts
      (port a)
      (port b)
      (port (array c 3))))
...

(portRef (member c 1) (portRef pbExample))
```

This example shows the definition of a port bundle with three components, one of which is an array, followed by a reference to the second element of that array.

Used in:

interface, and *listOfPorts.*

See also:

netBundle, permutable, port, portImplementation, portRef, and *viewType.*

(portDelay
    derivation
    delay | loadDelay
    { transition | becomes }
)

    PortDelay is an attribute of a port or port instance which is used to specify a delay and its derivation for the given set of transitions. If no *transition* or *becomes* is specified, then the default is any transition.

Example:

    (port P1
        (portDelay
            (derivation MEASURED)
            (loadDelay 25 2)
            (transition D U)))

The above example specifies a measured delay of **25** time units plus **2** time units per unit *acLoad* of load–dependent delay. This occurs on a transition from **D** to **U** of the port named **P1.**

Used in:

port, portBackAnnotate, and *portInstance.*

See also:

becomes, delay, derivation, loadDelay, netDelay, pathDelay, and *transition.*

(**portGroup** *{ portNameRef | portRef }*)

PortGroup is used to indicate a group of port references. The group is not an ordered list but a set. By grouping ports, a relationship between a group and a single port or another group can be established, for example, the relationship that four ports in one view taken together are the same as one port in another view. All ports referenced within *portGroup* must belong to the same view.

Example:

```
(portMap
  (portGroup
    (portRef port1 (viewRef V1))
    (portRef port2 (viewRef V1))
    (portRef port3 (viewRef V1))
    (portRef port4 (viewRef V1)))
  (portRef P1 (viewRef V2)))
```

The example above indicates that **port1, port2, port3,** and **port4** in view **V1,** taken together, correspond to port **P1** in view **V2.** There is no direct relationship implied between **port1, port2, port3,** and **port4.**

Used in:

event, and *portMap*.

See also:

netGroup, portRef, and *viewMap*.

---

	portImplementation
(portImplementation *portNameRef / portRef*	
{ < *connectLocation* > /	location for legal connection
figure /	geometry implementing the port
instance /	instance of **GRAPHIC** view
commentGraphics /	graphical annotation
propertyDisplay /	for displaying properties defined on ports
keywordDisplay /	for displaying attributes
property /	
comment /	
userData }	
)	
	portImplementation

PortImplementation may be used to implement ports, arrayed ports, members of arrayed ports, or port bundles. The construct may contain one *connectLocation* whose figures represent the area or point where it is valid to connect to the port for the purpose of establishing connectivity. The figures and **GRAPHIC** instances included in the *portImplementation* represent the port in any display of the cell. Comment text and graphics can be associated with the port and are included for annotation purposes only; they do not include port figures or names.

PropertyDisplay is used to display properties defined on the ports in the interface. *KeywordDisplay* is used to display attributes defined on the referenced port in the interface.

PortImplementation may also be applied within **SCHEMATIC** *pages* to *offPageConnectors*. The *viewType* restriction for *portImplementation* within *contents* is to **MASKLAYOUT, PCBLAYOUT, STRANGER,** and **SYMBOLIC** views. It may also occur within *symbol* or *protectionFrame*.

Example:

```
(port IN (direction input))
(port VDD)
(symbol
  (portImplementation IN
    (connectLocation
      (figure ports (dot (pt 10 10)))))
  (portImplementation VDD
    (connectLocation
      (figure Poly (dot (pt 100 50)))
      (figure Metal
        (rectangle (pt 50 50) (pt 100 55))))))
```

This example defines connect locations for ports **IN** and **VDD.**

Used in:

contents, page, protectionFrame, statement, and *symbol.*

See also:

connectLocation, offPageConnector, port, portBundle, and *viewType.*

(**portInstance** *portRef* | *portNameRef*
   { < *unused* > |
   < *designator* > |
   < *dcFaninLoad* > |
   < *dcFanoutLoad* > |
   < *dcMaxFanin* > |
   < *dcMaxFanout* > |
   < *acLoad* > |
   portDelay |
   property |
   comment |
   userData }
)

portInstance

if the port is unused
port (pin number) designator
load contributed as fan−in
load contributed as fan−out
maximum allowed fan−in load
maximum allowed fan−out load
small−signal contributed load (capacitive load)
port delays

portInstance

PortInstance is used to attach or modify properties and attributes of the occurrence of a port within an *instance*. *PortInstance* refers to the port instance and not the port in the cell view. The port instance inherits all properties and attributes of the port in the instantiated cell view. When the properties and attributes are inherited, the values may be overridden within the *portInstance* form for this particular instance or array of instances.

The *portRef* is used to access *ports* in *portBundles* and should not contain a nested *instanceRef* or *viewRef*.

Example:

    (cell LS04 (cellType generic)
      (view primary_symbol (viewType schematic)
        (interface
          (designator "UXXX")
          (port in (direction input) (designator "XX"))
          (port out (direction output) (designator "XX")))))

    (cell Top_level_schematic (cellType generic)
      (view schematic_sheet (viewType schematic)
        (interface ...)
        (contents
          (page single
            (instance &1
              (viewRef primary_symbol (cellRef LS04))
              (transform ...)
              (designator "U1")

(portInstance in (designator "1"))
(portInstance out (designator "2"))))))))

In this example, a generic component **LS04** will be instanced in every case as device "**UXXX**" with pins "**XX**" and "**XX**" unless these lower-level designators are overridden by higher-level designators such as these that appear in instance **1**. In this instance, and only this instance, the designators are specified to be "**U1**" with pins "**1**" and "**2**".

Used in:

instance.

See also:

port, and *portBackAnnotate.*

(**portList** { *portNameRef* | *portRef* })

PortList creates an ordered list of port references. It is used in a variety of constructs where such an ordered list is required.

Example:

```
(portBundle PB
    (listOfPorts (port PB1) (port PB2))
(port (array PA 2))
(port P1)
(port P2)
...
(joined
    (portRef PB) (portRef PA) (portList P1 P2))
```

In the example above an ordered list of port references, **P1, P2,** is created with the *portList* construct. **P1** is joined with **PB1** of bundle **PB** and (**member PA 0**), and **P2** is joined with **PB2** of bundle **PB** and (**member PA 1**).

Used in:

change, event, joined, logicInput, logicOutput, match, mustJoin, portListAlias, steady, and *weakJoined.*

See also:

logicList, member, portNameRef, and *portRef.*

(**portListAlias** *portNameDef*
     portList
)

PortListAlias provides an array-name alias for a list of ports. Any subsequent use of this name, as a whole or within the member construct, is equivalent to the use of the specified *portList.*

Array is not permitted in this construct.

Example:

    (**portListAlias allInputs**
        (**portList in1 in2 in3**))

This example defines **allInputs** as an alias for the three ports **in1,** **in2,** and **in3,** which should have been previously defined.

Used in:

simulate.

See also:

port, portBundle, and *portList.*

---

portMap

(portMap
    { portRef |
    portGroup |
    comment | user comments
    userData }   user-defined data
)

portMap

PortMap is used within *viewMap* to associate ports in different views which represent the same object. A *portMap* may be used to map several port objects of one view with one or more port objects of other views. Groups of ports are specified with the *portGroup* construct. A common use would be for mapping a port of a **SCHEMATIC** or **NETLIST** view to one or more ports within a **MASKLAYOUT** or **PCBLAYOUT** view.

The *portMap* cannot be used to establish netlist connectivity, and does not imply any inheritance of *properties* or attributes.

Example:

```
(portMap
   (portGroup
      (portRef port1a (viewRef pcb))
      (portRef port1b (viewRef pcb)))
   (portRef port1 (viewRef nets)))
```

The example above specifies explicitly that ports named **port1a** and **port1b** in the view named **pcb** represent the same object as the port named **port1** in the view named **nets.**

Used in:

viewMap.

See also:

instanceMap, instanceRef, netMap, portGroup, portRef, and *viewRef.*

	portNameDef
nameDef	*array*	*portNameDef*

PortNameDef is used to create a name for a *port* or *portBundle*. The scope of the name is to the end of the nearest enclosing *view*, *portBundle*, or *simulate* statement.

The use of *array* implies the creation of an array of ports. *Array* is not appropriate for names defined in *portBundle* or *portListAlias*.

Used in:

logicPort, offPageConnector, port, portBundle, and *portListAlias.*

See also:

array, and *portNameRef.*

---

nameRef | member   *portNameRef*

portNameRef

PortNameRef is used to reference a previously defined port name. If the corresponding *portNameDef* used an *array* then *member* may be used to reference a particular member of the array. A simple *nameRef* may be used to reference the entire array.

Member should not be used to access a *portBundle,* although it may be used to indicate a particular element of an array within such a bundle. *Member* is also inappropriate for use within *globalPortRef.*

Used in:

change, follow, globalPortRef, logicAssign, logicInput, logicOutput, maintain, match, portGroup, portImplementation, portInstance, portList, portRef, and *steady.*

See also:

portNameDef, and *member.*

(portRef *portNameRef*
    [portRef | instanceRef | viewRef]
)

PortRef is used to reference a port. It uses the name of the port and may also reference through the instance hierarchy and port hierarchy. *Member* is used to reference one port in an array of ports. Nested *portRef* constructs, e.g.

    (portRef ... (portRef ...))

are used to reference a port defined within a *portBundle*. Nested *instanceRef* constructs, e.g.

    (instanceRef ... (instanceRef ...))

are used to reference a port via the instance hierarchy. Nested instance reference should not be used in the context of a *portInstance*.

The first or outermost *portNameRef* in the syntax is the target port or port bundle; the nested constructs which follow define a reference path in a bottom–up manner. *InstanceRef* is used when the instance hierarchy is part of the reference path to the target port. Except in the context of *timing* or *viewMap,* the *instanceRef* must reference a simple, local instance. The *viewRef* is only semantically legal if the *portRef* originated from within the context of a *viewMap.*

Example:

    (portMap
        (portRef P1A
            (portRef P2A
                (viewRef V1A))) ...)

In the first example, a reference is made to a port named **P1A,** which is a port defined within a port bundle named **P2A** defined in the interface of the view name **V1A.**

    (portRef (member P1B 2)
        (instanceRef (member I2B 5)
            (viewRef V1B)))

In the second example, a member of a port array named **P1B** is referenced through the instance hierarchy via an instance array named **I2B,** which is specified in the contents of a view named **V1B**.

```
(portRef P1C
    (portRef P2C
        (instanceRef I1C
            (instanceRef I2C
                (viewRef V1C)))))
```

The last example references a port named **P1C,** which is a port defined within a port bundle named **P2C** referenced through the instance hierarchy via an instance named **I1C;   I1C** is referenced by an instance named **I2C** which is defined in the contents of the view named **V1C.**

Used in:

change, entry, event, follow, joined, logicAssign, logicInput, logicOutput, maintain, match, mustJoin, nonPermutable, permutable, portBackAnnotate, portGroup, portImplementation, portInstance, portList, portMap, portRef, steady, tableDefault, and *weakJoined.*

See also:

instance, instanceRef, member, page, port, portBundle, viewMap, and *viewRef.*

(**product** *{ numberValue }*)

Product is a number function which returns the product of the arguments. If there are no arguments, the result is 1. This is not available in Level 0 descriptions. In the special case where all arguments within *product* are *integerValues* the expression may also be used as an *integerValue*.

Example:

(**product 4 2**)

This example returns the number value **8.**

Used in:

integerValue, and *numberValue.*

See also:

abs, divide, max, min, mod, negate, subtract, and *sum.*

(program
    stringToken
    [version]
)

program

name of a program responsible for data creation
version of program responsible for data creation

program

The *program* statement identifies the software or program name which was responsible for creating the data, and optionally the version code of the program. Typically this information is of interest to the human writer when analyzing a problem.

Example:

    (written
        (timeStamp 1987 3 4 18 34 54)
        (program "EDIF_$Net" (Version "5.3")))

The above example specifies that the block of information was produced on **March 4, 1987** at **18:34:54 UTC** by the program **EDIF_$Net,** version **5.3.**

Used in:

written.

See also:

author, dataOrigin, status, timeStamp, and *version.*

(**property** *propertyNameDef*
   typedValue
   { < owner > |
   < unit > |
   property |
   comment }

to indicate system-specific property
for cross-library mapping of properties
properties may nest
user comment

Property is used to associate name value pairs with EDIF objects. The name of the property is defined by the *propertyNameDef*, and its type and value are specified by the *boolean, integer, miNoMax, number, point,* or *string* typed-value constructs. *Property* is not restricted by *viewType*.

The optional *owner* is used to indicate the owner or originator of the property type and its definition. The optional *unit* may be used to describe the units of the property so that the property values may be scaled. Properties can be nested to describe complex structures. Properties cannot be defined as arrays; therefore the *typedValue* should not be nested or contain multiple values.

Example:

   (**property xyz (integer 2) (owner "DianaCo") (unit CURRENT))**

The above example defines an integer property named **xyz** with a unit type of CURRENT and a value of **2.**

   (**property abc (boolean) (owner "XYZ Inc.")**
      (**property a (boolean (true)))**
      (**property b (integer 2))**
      (**property c (string "This is property abc")))**

In the above example the nested property **abc** is defined with three subproperties.

Used in:

cell, circle, commentGraphics, constraint, design, dot, figureGroup, figureGroupOverride, instance, instanceBackAnnotate, interface, logicPort, logicValue, net, netBackAnnotate, netBundle, offPageConnector, openShape, path, polygon, port, portBackAnnotate, portBundle, portImplementation, portInstance, property, protectionFrame, rectangle, shape, statement, symbol, view, and *written.*

See also:

boolean, integer, miNoMax, number, owner, point, propertyDisplay, string, typedValue, unit, and *userData.*

(**propertyDisplay** *propertyNameRef*
    { display }
)

propertyDisplay

PropertyDisplay is used to specify display locations and display attributes for the display of property values. It is used in the *interface* in the constructs which have a coordinate space associated with them, namely *portImplementation, protectionFrame,* and *symbol.* The value to display is referenced by a *propertyNameRef. PropertyDisplay* specified in the *protectionFrame* or *symbol* refers to a property defined in the interface of the view. *PropertyDisplay* when specified in the *portImplementation* refers to a property defined in a port. *PropertyDisplay* is not allowed directly within *interface* or *port.*

Example:

```
(interface
    (property IP (string "someValue"))
    (port in
        (property PP (string "portValue")))
    (symbol
        (propertyDisplay IP (display ...))
        (portImplementation in
            (propertyDisplay PP (display ...))))
    (protectionFrame
        (propertyDisplay IP (display ...))))
```

In the above example the value of the interface property named **IP** is to be displayed with the symbol and the protection frame. The value of the port property named **PP** is displayed with the port implementation of port **IN** of the symbol.

Used in:

portImplementation, protectionFrame, and *symbol.*

See also:

display, and *property.*

nameDef	*propertyNameDef*
	propertyNameDef

A *propertyNameDef* is a name used to identify a particular property attached to an object. No special meaning is associated with the choice of name in EDIF. Any external interpretation of a property which depends on the choice of name should only be expected with the prior agreement of both sender and receiver.

This name is local to the immediate context of the construct which contains the *property*.

Used in:

property.

See also:

propertyNameRef.

nameRef	*propertyNameRef*
	propertyNameRef

A *propertyNameRef* is used to identify a previously created property, for display purposes. The reference context is either the local *interface* or a *port* of the interface depending on the location of the enclosing *propertyDisplay*.

Used in:

propertyDisplay.

See also:

portImplementation, property, and *propertyNameDef.*

protectionFrame

(protectionFrame
    { portImplementation | terminal areas
    figure | figures used to implement the protection frame
    instance | instances of graphic views
    commentGraphics | graphical text for annotation
    < boundingBox > | bounding box of protection frame & terminals
    propertyDisplay | for displaying user properties from interface
    keywordDisplay | for displaying attributes and names from interface
    parameterDisplay | for displaying parameter values from interface
    property |
    comment |
    userData }

protectionFrame

ProtectionFrame provides an abstract representation of the cell view. For mask layout and symbolic layout views it would contain the protection frames covering the mask geometry of the *contents*. It also acts as a routing barrier within views that instantiate this view.

A *portImplementation* in the *protectionFrame* is used to represent a terminal area of the cell view. The *figure* is used to implement the protection frame. The implementation can also use instances of cell views of view type **GRAPHIC**. Comment graphics and text can be associated with the protection frame using the *commentGraphics* form. However, they are not part of the implementation. The *boundingBox* is used to specify the bounding box of a protection frame and describes the extent of the frame including the terminals but is not part of the frame.

PropertyDisplay is used to display user property values defined in the interface of the cell view. *KeywordDisplay* is used to display attribute values defined in the interface of the cell view. *Cell, designator* and *instance* are the only *keywordNameRefs* allowed within a *keywordDisplay* directly in a *protectionFrame*. *ParameterDisplay* is used to display parameter values. Such displays are described with respect to the coordinate space of the *protectionFrame*.

A *protectionFrame* may only be provided in the *interface* of views of type **MASKLAYOUT, PCBLAYOUT, STRANGER** and **SYMBOLIC.**

Example:

```
(interface
  (protectionFrame
    (figure P
       (rectangle (pt -4 -4) (pt 3 5)))
    (figure D
       (rectangle (pt  0 0) (pt 10 10)))
    (boundingBox
       (rectangle (pt -4 -4) (pt 10 10)))))
```

The above example describes a protection frame which contains figures on two figure groups, **P** and **D,** and the bounding box of the protection frame.

Used in:

interface.

See also:

boundingBox, figure, portImplementation, symbol, and *viewType.*

(pt *integerValue integerValue*)   *pt*

                                                                                        pt

---

A *pt* is used to specify the coordinates of all geometric data such as line drawings and filled areas. It is also used to specify locations when transforming objects such as instances and text. It is defined by the keyword *pt* followed by two *integerValues*. The first *integerValue* is the x–location, and the second *integerValue* is the y–location of the point.

Coordinates are scaled between *libraries* according to DISTANCE units.

Example:

   (pt 100 50)

This example specifies a point which is **100** units to the right of the coordinate origin and **50** units above it.

Used in:

pointValue.

See also:

arc, circle, curve, delta, dot, numberDefinition, origin, point, pointDisplay, pointList, and *rectangle.*

---

	range
*atLeast	atMost	between	exactly	greaterThan	lessThan*	
	range

Range represents one of the value range constructs. These are used to specify a number value or a range of number values in the context of physical design rules.

Example:

> **(lessThan 5)**
> **(greaterThan 10)**
> **(exactly 6)**
> **(between (atLeast (e 25 −1)) (atMost (e 35 −1)))**

The above range examples specify the range of real numbers which are: less than **5,** greater than **10,** exactly **6,** and between **2.5** and **3.5,** respectively.

Used in:

enclosureDistance,   figureArea,   figurePerimeter,   figureWidth, interFigureGroupSpacing, intraFigureGroupSpacing, notchSpacing, overhangDistance, overlapDistance, rangeVector, and *singleValueSet.*

See also:

atLeast,   atMost,   between,   exactly,   except,   greaterThan,   lessThan,   and multipleValueSet.

(rangeVector *{ range | singleValueSet })*

RangeVector is used to specify a vector of value ranges. A range vector is used when more than one value range is required in a physical design rule.

Example:

```
(rectangleSize   CONTACT_SIZE
    (figureGroupObject CONTACT)
    (rangeVector
        (exactly 3)
        (exactly 5)))
```

The *rectangleSize* rule requires a range vector of two value ranges. In the above example the rule named **CONTACT_SIZE** requires that rectilinear shapes within the figure group named **CONTACT** have a size of exactly **3** by **5.**

Used in:

multipleValueSet, and *rectangleSize.*

See also:

atLeast, atMost, between, exactly, greaterThan, lessThan, range, and *singleValueSet.*

(**rectangle** *pointValue pointValue { property }*)

Rectangle is a four−sided polygon with sides parallel to the axes. The specified points are the end points of either diagonal.

Example:

(**rectangle** (**pt 0 0**) (**pt 20 10**))

This rectangle has an area of **200** square units.

Used in:

boundingBox, figure, and *pageSize.*

See also:

circle, and *polygon.*

(**rectangleSize** *ruleNameDef*
   figureGroupObject
   rangeVector | multipleValueSet
   { comment |
   userData }
)

rectangleSize

rectangleSize

RectangleSize is used to specify the required size of adjacent edges within four–sided rectilinear figures. A single figure group is to be considered; four–sided rectilinear figures are to be selected. The lengths of any two adjacent edges must satisfy the specified value–range vector (a vector of two value ranges is required); the smaller edge length must satisfy one of the range vectors, and the larger edge length must satisfy the other range vector. The appropriate figures need not have been specified with the *rectangle* form. The equivalent geometry could, for example, be originally specified as a *polygon,* or created through a *figureOp.*

Example:

   (**rectangleSize Contact_Size**
      (**figureGroupObject Contact**)
      (**multipleValueSet**
         (**rangeVector** (**exactly 3**) (**exactly 5**))
         (**rangeVector** (**exactly 7**) (**exactly 8**))))

The above example rule requires that **Contact** size be **3** by **5**, or **7** by **8.**

Used in:

physicalDesignRule.

See also:

figureGroupObject, figureOp, multipleValueSet, polygon, rangeVector, rectangle, and *ruleNameDef.*

(rename
   identifier | name
   stringToken | stringDisplay
)

Rename may take the place of a simple name in name definition contexts. It provides a mechanism for recording previous spellings of certain identifiers. It is desirable that receiving systems replace the EDIF identifier with the original name if possible, as this may be more meaningful for human communication. However, their relationship in comparisons with other identifiers and rename strings should be verified as one that preserves the existing object–referencing structure: different identifiers should be renamed to distinct names.

Either the name or the string (or both) may be displayed. In later references, any *name* display should be interpreted as a request to display the chosen version of the name, which could be the string value or the literal identifier.

Example:

(port
   (rename portA "!port_A")
   (direction Input))

The above example defines a port named **portA,** which was called **!port_A** in the originating system.

Used in:

nameDef.

See also:

display, identifier, and *name.*

(resolves *{ logicNameRef }*)

      Resolves is used by *logicValue* in *simulationInfo* to define the current logic value as the outcome when the specified logic values are in contention on a net. When used to indicate the result of contention between two sources of the same value, this overrides the default condition of self–domination.

Example:

    (logicValue X
       (resolves T F))

In this example a net that has the logic values **T** and **F** applied to it will take on the logic value of **X.**

Used in:

logicValue.

See also:

dominates, simulationInfo, strong, and *weak.*

nameDef	*ruleNameDef*
	ruleNameDef

RuleNameDef is a name associated with each element within *physicalDesignRule*. It is intended to be used to identify design rule violations during geometric verification of a design. It must be different from any other rule name in the context of the same library.

Used in:

enclosureDistance,   *figureArea,*   *figurePerimeter,*   *figureWidth,* *interFigureGroupSpacing,*   *intraFigureGroupSpacing,*   *notAllowed,*   *notchSpacing,* *overhangDistance, overlapDistance,* and *rectangleSize.*

See also:

physicalDesignRule, and *simulateNameDef.*

(scale   *scale*
   numberValue   EDIF units
   numberValue   corresponding external units
   unit
)
                                                               scale

---

Scale is used to define the relationship between all EDIF numbers in a library and numbers outside of that library. The first number in scale represents an EDIF number. The second number is the equivalent number in the SI units such as meter, kilogram, and second – as described for *unit*.

Example:

    (library lib1
       (technology
          (numberDefinition
             (scale 1 (E 1 −6) (unit distance))
             (scale 2 (E 1 −3) (unit time)))) ...)

    (library lib2
       (technology
          (numberDefinition
             (scale 1 (e 254 −10) (unit distance)))) ...)

This states that all distances in library **lib1** are represented in microns, and time is represented in half−milliseconds.

In library **lib2,** the unit of distance is defined to be a micro−inch. If this library contains any time values, they should be interpreted in terms of seconds.

Used in:

numberDefinition.

See also:

gridMap, and *unit.*

---

	scaledInteger
*integerToken	e*	*scaledInteger*

An optional scale factor can be applied to an integer to represent fractional numbers or numbers too large to be expressed using an integer alone.

Only integer tokens are permitted directly or indirectly in this context, even within Level 1 expressions.

Example:

```
1234
(e    100  1)
(e     42  0)
(e      9 −1)
(e −12325 −3)
(e   −644  4)
```

The above examples represent the values **1234, 1000, 42, 0.9, −12.325,** and **−6440000** respectively.

Used in:

color, and *numberValue.*

See also:

e, integerValue, and *number.*

(scaleX *integerValue integerValue***)**

ScaleX is used to scale in the x direction a cell view upon instantiation. The first integer represents the numerator, and the second integer the denominator of the scale fraction. When not specified the scaling of the cell view is assumed to be 1, i.e. **(scaleX 1 1)** is the default. In all cases the fraction specified must be a positive value. It has the effect of multiplying all x−coordinates by the given fraction, before any rotation implied by any associated *orientation*.

Scaling occurs relative to the origin of the cell view. For example, given **(rectangle (pt −2 −2) (pt 2 2))** which is part of the cell view and given the x scaling **(scaleX 2 1)** the figure would be scaled before translation to **(rectangle (pt −4 −2) (pt 4 2))**.

When *orientation* is also involved, this scaling must be performed for the x−axis of the original view, whatever its final direction may be.

Example:

```
(instance Inst_1 (viewRef V1 (cellRef cell1))
    (transform
        (scaleX 2 1)
        (scaleY 4 1)))
```

This example scales the cell by **2** in the **x** direction.

Used in:

transform.

See also:

gridMap, scale, and *scaleY.*

(scaleY *integerValue integerValue*)

ScaleY is used to scale in the y direction a cell view upon instantiation. The first integer represents the numerator and the second integer the denominator of the scale fraction. When not specified the scaling of the cell view is assumed to be 1, that is **(scaleY 1 1)** is the default. In all cases the fraction specified must be a positive value. It has the effect of multiplying all y–coordinates by the given fraction, before any rotation implied by any associated *orientation.*

Scaling occurs relative to the origin of the cell view. For example, given **(rectangle (pt −2 −2) (pt 2 2))**, which is part of the cell view and given the y scaling **(scaleY 2 1)**, the figure would be scaled before translation to **(rectangle (pt −2 −4) (pt 2 4)).**

When *orientation* is also involved, this scaling must be performed for the y–axis of the original view, whatever its final direction may be.

Example:

```
(instance Inst_1 (viewRef V1 (cellRef cell1))
    (transform
        (scaleX 2 1)
        (scaleY 4 1)))
```

This example scales the cell by **4** in the **y** direction.

Used in:

transform.

See also:

gridMap, scale, and *scaleX.*

```
(section  stringValue                                    section
    { stringValue |                               section header name
    section |
    instance }
                                         of view type GRAPHIC or DOCUMENT only
)

                                                            section
```

Section is used to divide a document into sections. An EDIF string token is used to give a title to a section. If a section heading is not required, the null string (*""*) must be specified.

Sections may be nested with other sections. This nesting can be used by a document processor to give hierarchical number schemes to sections.

The body of the section is implemented using any number of EDIF string tokens. Instances of other **DOCUMENT** and **GRAPHIC** views may also be included in the section bodies, such as other documents and diagrams.

Only views of type **DOCUMENT** or **STRANGER** may contain this statement in their contents.

Example:

```
(section "Hierarchical Design"
    (section "Why it does not work"  "....")
    (section "An alternative: Matrix Design"
        "...."
        (section  "Each circuit has two functions"  "....")
        (section  "Early results"  "...."))
    (section "Summary"  "...."))
```

Used in:

contents, section, and *statement.*

See also:

stringValue, and *viewType.*

(**shape** *curve*
  { property }
)

Shape is similar to *polygon* except that it may include arcs in its perimeter. *Shape* is closed by definition. If the last point specified is not the same as the first point specified, a straight line is used to close the *shape*.

The *shape* must not intersect itself, although its edges may be coincident.

Example:

```
(shape
    (curve
        (pt 20 100)
        (arc
            (pt 40 100)
            (pt 60 110)
            (pt 40 120))
        (pt 20 120)))
```

This example consists of one arc from **(40, 100)** through **(60, 110)** to **(40, 120)** and three straight line segments – from **(40, 120)** to **(20, 120)**, from **(20, 120)** back to **(20, 100)**, and from **(20, 100)** to **(40, 100)**.

Used in:

figure.

See also:

arc, openShape, and *polygon.*

(simulate *simulateNameDef*
   { portListAlias |
   waveValue |
   apply |
   comment |
   userData }
)

Simulate is a named collection of simulation stimulus and response statements and is used in the *interface* and *contents* of views. Each *apply* statement is interpreted in the order in which it is recorded; the other constructs are declarative and are thus insensitive to order, except that any reference must be made after the corresponding definition. *Simulate* may be used in the *contents* of views of any type except **BEHAVIOR, DOCUMENT,** and **GRAPHIC.** It may also be used in the *interface* of any view type except **DOCUMENT** and **GRAPHIC.**

Example:

```
(simulate test1
    (portListAlias control
        (portList C1 C2 enable))
    (apply (cycle 2 (duration (e 5 −1)))
        (logicInput control
            (logicWaveform
                (logicList H H L)
                (logicList L H H)))
        (logicInput inBus
            (logicWaveform
                (logicList L L L L L)
                (logicList H L H H L)))
        (logicOutput Out
            (logicWaveform L H)))
    (apply (cycle 1 (duration 2))
        (logicInput  ... )
        (logicOutput ... )))
```

This example assumes that **C1, C2, enable,** and **Out** have been previously defined as ports and that **inBus** has been defined as an array of five ports. The first *apply* controls two cycles of activity, each lasting **0.5** time units; the second *apply* controls a single cycle lasting **2.0** time units. In all, this *simulate* involves **3.0** time units.

Used in:

contents, interface, and *statement.*

See also:

apply, logicInput, logicOutput, and *simulationInfo.*

April 27, 1987

nameDef	*simulateNameDef*
	simulateNameDef

A *simulateNameDef* is used to identify a *simulate* statement. It must be unique for each *simulate* in the context of the same *view*.

Used in:

simulate.

See also:

ruleNameDef, and *view.*

(simulationInfo
    { logicValue |
    comment |
    userData }

simulationInfo

All information about the logic values used within a library are collected in
simulationInfo, including relationships of ambiguity and wired functions. Mappings
between the logic values of different libraries can also be given, as well as the
electrical characteristics associated with each value.

Each logic value used within a *library* must be declared within the
corresponding *simulationInfo.* It is advisable to supply as much information as
possible in order to assist in mapping into external simulation values.

Example:

    (simulationInfo
        (logicValue T)
        (logicValue F))

This example shows a simple declaration of a pair of logic values with no further
information.

Used in:

technology.

See also:

booleanMap, currentMap, logicValue, and *voltageMap.*

(singleValueSet *{ range }*)

singleValueSet

singleValueSet

SingleValueSet is used to specify a set of value ranges. The use of more than one value range implies the union of the ranges; to satisfy the rule at least one value range must be satisfied.

Example:

```
(figureWidth polyWidth
    (figureGroupObject poly)
    (singleValueSet
        (exactly 5)
        (between (atLeast 3) (atMost 4))))
```

In the first example, the width of each figure on **poly** is legal only if it is equal to **5**, or greater than or equal to **3** and less than or equal to **4**. A more complicated constraining relationship can be specified when *singleValueSet* is used within a *rangeVector*.

```
(rectangleSize contact_size
    (figureGroupObject Contact)
    (rangeVector
        (singleValueSet (exactly 3) (exactly 7))
        (singleValueSet (exactly 5) (exactly 8))))
```

The second example **contact_size** rule requires that **Contact** size to be **3** by **5**, **3** by **8**, **7** by **5**, or **7** by **8**. The rule type requires a *rangeVector* of two value ranges. Two possibilities are specified for each value range, thus providing four constraining relationship combinations.

Used in:

enclosureDistance,   figureArea,   figurePerimeter,   figureWidth, interFigureGroupSpacing, intraFigureGroupSpacing, notchSpacing, overhangDistance, overlapDistance, and *rangeVector.*

See also:

multipleValueSet, physicalDesignRule, and *range.*

(site *viewRef [transform]*)

   Site is used to define the placement rules for a macrocell within a gate array. The *plug* defines a series of *socketSets* any of which can be used to correctly place this macrocell. Each *socketSet* in turn contains one or more *site* definitions which reference one site cell, and it identifies the combination of cells which must be used and the symmetry to be used. *Site* describes the class of placement sites which are legal for this cell.

   The *transform* indicates the required transformations which must occur for this site to be used. For a legal placement the net result of all plug and socket transforms together with the instance transform for the placement of the cell must produce the identity transform; that is they must result in no net change after all the operations are performed.

Example:

```
(cell M349
    (cellType Generic)
    (view Site_definition
        (viewType Symbolic)
        (interface
            (arrayRelatedInfo
                (arrayMacro
                    (plug
                        (socketSet (symmetry)
                            (site
                                (viewRef Site_definition
                                    (cellRef Site_cell)))
                            (site
                                (viewRef Site_definition
                                    (cellRef Site_cell))
                                (transform (orientation R90)))))))))))
```

This example specifies cell **M349**, which may be placed in any two instances of cell **site_cell** provided that one instance is normal rotation and the other is rotated **90** degrees. Since no symmetry statement is present in the *socketSet,* only the identity or **R0** symmetry is allowed; thus, no additional rotation or reflection is allowed during placement. The final orientation of the macro is the sum of the *plug, socket, socketSet,* and *site* instance transforms.

Used in:

socketSet.

See also:

arrayMacro, arrayRelatedInfo, plug, and *socket.*

(socket *[symmetry]***)**

Socket is used to define a site location in a gate array which may be satisfied by a macro cell placement during implementation of a gate array. A cell of this type consists of geometry which defines the underlying base pattern for the generic portion of a gate array.

Different *sites* may be defined for different classes of underlying circuitry or for different physical realizations of similar functions such as high–power and low–power sites. Any site cell may have several *sockets* to define a number of valid sets of symmetry for all instances of that site cell.

Example:

```
(Cell Site_cell
    (CellType Generic)
    (View Site_definition
        (ViewType Symbolic)
        (Interface
            (ArrayRelatedInfo
                (ArraySite
                    (Socket))))))
```

This example specifies cell **Site_cell,** which may be instanced in a base array to form as many sites for macro placement. In this case no symmetry is specified; so the identity transform of **R0** is assumed, and a macrocell may only be placed in this site if unrotated. When determining a valid placement, the total orientation is the sum of the *plug, socket,* and *site* instance used.

Used in:

arraySite.

See also:

arrayRelatedInfo, site, and *socketSet.*

(**socketSet** *symmetry* { *site* })

SocketSet is used to define the placement rules for a macrocell within a gate array. The *plug* defines a series of *socketSets,* any of which can be used to correctly place this macrocell. Each *socketSet* in turn contains one or more *site* definitions which reference one site cell, and the *socketSet* identifies the combination of cells which must be used and the *symmetry* to be used.

SocketSet is used to define the legal sites and the symmetry for legal placement of this *plug* cell in a base array site location. The *socketSet* must have all of its conditions satisfied in order to be used. The *plug* requires that any one of its *socketSets* be used for a valid placement.

Example:

```
(Cell M349  (CellType generic)
    (View Site_definition (ViewType Symbolic)
        (Interface
            (ArrayRelatedInfo
                (ArrayMacro
                    (Plug
                        (SocketSet
                            (symmetry
                                (Transform (orientation R0))
                                (Transform (orientation R90)))
                            (Site
                                (ViewRef Site_definition
                                    (CellRef Site_cell))))))))))
```

This example specifies cell **M349,** which may be placed in any single instance of cell **Site_cell** either at rotation **R0** or at rotation **R270.** The final orientation of the macro is the sum of the *plug, socket, socketSet,* and *site* instance transforms.

Used in:

plug.

See also:

arrayMacro, arrayRelatedInfo, and *site.*

---

specialCharacter

'!' | '#' | '$' | '&' | '"' | '(' | ')' | '*' | '+' | ',' |

'−' | '.' | '/' | ':' | ';' | '<' | '=' | '>' | '?' | '@' |

'[' | '\' | ']' | '^' | '_' | '`' | '{' | '|' | '}' | '~'

specialCharacter

These are the punctuation characters that are legal within string tokens.

The quote and percent characters are explicitly excluded from this list, as they have special significance within *stringTokens*. If required, such characters must be expressed with an *asciiCharacter* escape sequence.

Example:

"!#$&'()*+,−./:;<=>?@[\]^_`{|}~"

The above *stringToken* contains each of the *specialCharacters*.

Used in:

stringToken.

See also:

alpha, asciiCharacter, and *digit.*

---

statement

> *assign | block | comment | commentGraphics |*
> *constant | constraint | escape | figure | follow | if |*
> *instance | iterate | net | netBundle | logicPort | offPageConnector |*
> *portImplementation | property | section | simulate |*
> *timing | userData | variable | when | while*

statement

Statement construct is a grouping of Level 2 control constructs together with constructs normally found directly within *contents* or *page*.

Any restrictions associated with *viewType* and context apply to constructs included in *statement*.

Used in:

block, else, iterate, then, and *while.*

See also:

contents, page, and *viewType.*

(status
    { written |
    comment | user comments
    userData }   user−defined data
)

Status may appear in a variety of EDIF sections. Its primary purpose is to convey accounting and problem analysis information for the design information. *Status* provides the information needed to trace back to the source of each piece of data, the human author or organization which owns the data, the program name, and the software revision used for creation of specific parts of an EDIF file.

Status applies to the immediately enclosing form unless overridden by a lower−level *status* in an enclosed form. For example, a status within a given library applies to the whole of that library unless a cell within the library has a status, in which case the cell's status applies to that cell. Also, for example, if any *cell* in a *library* is modified, then that *library* should be considered to have changed.

Several *written* statements may be used to record a history of modifications.

Example:

```
(library L1
    (edifLevel 0)
    (technology ...)
    (status
        (written
            (timeStamp 1987 6 1 12 00 00)
            (program "EDIF_$Schem_out")))
    (cell C1 (cellType GENERIC)
        (status
            (written
                (timeStamp 1987 5 11 3 12 00)
                (program "EDIF_$IncrementalSchem_out"))) ...))
```

In the above example the information contained within the library **L1** was last modified on **June 1, 1987,** at **12:00:00 UTC** using the program **EDIF_$Schem_out.** The cell **C1** within the library **L1** was produced or modified on **May 11, 1987,** at **3:12:00 UTC,** using the program **EDIF_$IncrementalSchem_out.**

Used in:

cell, design, edif, external, library, and *view.*

See also:

author, dataOrigin, program, timeStamp, and *version.*

(steady
    portNameRef | portRef | portList
    duration
    [transition | becomes]

    Steady is used by *trigger* and *entry* for logic modeling to determine if the referenced port or ports have not changed in logic value for the specified amount of time. An optional *transition* or *becomes* may be specified to indicate the most recent change of logic value.

    Steady can be used with lists of port references and lists of logic values within its *transition*. When described with lists, the references must match one for one. The last to have changed needs to be steady for the prescribed time.

    In determining time of stability, only transitions at previous times should be considered. Thus a *table* may be used to determine how long a changing port was stable prior to that change.

Example:

    (when (trigger (steady D1 (duration 5)))
        (maintain ...)))

In this example the *trigger* will be satisfied when port **D1** has been steady for exactly **5** time units.

    (table
        (entry (steady D2 (duration 5)) (logicRef T) ...)
        (entry ...))

In the second example the *entry* will be effective if port **D2** has been steady for at least **5** time units.

    (when
        (trigger (steady D3 (duration 5) (becomes T)))
        (logicAssign ...))

In the third example the *trigger* will be satisfied when port **D3** has been at logic value **T** for exactly **5** time units.

```
(table
    (entry
        (steady D4 (duration 5) (transition F T))
        (logicRef T))
    (entry ... ))
```

In the last example the *entry* will be satisfied if the most recent transition on port **D4** was from logic value **F** to logic value **T,** and if this occurred at least **5** time units before the evaluation of the *table*.

Used in:

entry, and *trigger*.

See also:

change.

(strictlyIncreasing *numberValue { numberValue })*

strictlyIncreasing

StrictlyIncreasing is a Boolean function which returns *true* if the sequence of its arguments is strictly monotonically increasing (i.e. arg1 < arg2 < ... < argn); the function returns *false* otherwise. To be *true,* each value must be less than the next value. The degenerate case of a single value produces *true.*

Example:

   (strictlyIncreasing channelWidth 5)

In this example the function returns *true* if **channelWidth < 5.**

Used in:

booleanValue.

See also:

equal, and *increasing.*

(**string** *{ stringValue | stringDisplay | string }*)

String declares a *constant, parameter, property,* or *variable* value to be of type string. In strings any ASCII character can be specified including blanks. An optional *stringValue* can be specified, in which case the value serves as a default.

An array of string values can be defined by specifying multiple *stringValues* within a *string*. Nesting of the *string* construct is required to specify array values of two or more dimensions.

Example:

    (parameter sigName (string "VDD"))

In this example parameter **sigName** is declared to be of type *string*. A default string value of **"VDD"** is also specified.

    (constant (array TC 9)
       (string "Allan" "Hari" "Henry" "John"
          "Mike" "Paul" "Richard" "Sanjiv" "Susan"))
    (constant (array FAM 2 3)
       (string
          (string "D" "C" "E")
          (string "C" "G" "E")))

In the above example the constant **TC** is defined to be a one-dimensional string array with the following value assignments:

(member TC 0) = "Allan",
(member TC 1) = "Hari",
...,
(member TC 8) = "Susan".

FAM is defined to be a two-dimensional string array with the value assignments:

(member FAM 0 0) = "D", (member FAM 0 1) = "C", (member FAM 0 2) = "E",
(member FAM 1 0) = "C", (member FAM 1 1) = "G", (member FAM 1 2) = "E".

Used in:

string, and *typedValue.*

See also:

array, boolean, integer, miNoMax, number, point, and *stringValue.*

(stringDisplay   *stringValue*
   { display }

     StringDisplay is used for displaying string–valued design data. It is allowed in constructs that normally contain design data and which may exist in a coordinate space. Many constructs may exist both in places where there is a coordinate space as well as in places where there is no coordinate space.

     StringDisplay contains the data to be displayed, which must be a string value, and any number of *display* forms for multiple displays.

Example:

```
(instance I1 (viewRef V1 (cellRef C1))
    (designator
        (stringDisplay "U12"
            (display text
                (origin (pt 4 6)))))))
```

In the above example the *designator* attribute is in a coordinate space, and its value, **U12,** can be displayed at **(4,6).**

Used in:

annotate, designator, rename, and *string.*

See also:

display, integerDisplay, miNoMaxDisplay, and *numberDisplay.*

""   *stringToken*

   { alpha | asciiCharacter | digit | specialCharacter | whiteSpace }

""

                                               stringToken

This is a basic token type and is described as a sequence of printable characters surrounded by quotation marks. This is normally recognized by a lexical scanner.

A blank or tab character represents itself within string tokens; other white space characters (newline, and carriage return) are ignored. The quote and percent characters cannot be specified directly but may be represented using the *asciiCharacter* notation.

There is no limit to the length of a *stringToken*.

Example:

   "a string token"

   "quote% 34 %character"

   ""

This example illustrates three string tokens. The first is typical, the second contains an embedded description of quote character, and the third is a null string.

Used in:

author, comment, dataOrigin, form, literal, owner, program, rename, stringValue, userData, and *version.*

See also:

asciiCharacter, identifier, integerToken, and *specialCharacter.*

---

stringToken	*stringValue*
	stringValue

StringValue describes a primitive string value. In Level 0 the set includes only string tokens. This is extended in Level 1 to allow string expressions.

Example:

> "Hello world"
> "simulated by SPICE2 using the %34%CSIM%34% MOS model"

The second example is a string with the word **CSIM** embedded in quotes.

Used in:

annotate, designator, section, string, and *stringDisplay.*

See also:

asciiCharacter, integerValue, numberValue, and *stringToken.*

	stringValue
*stringToken	valueNameRef	concat*	
	stringValue

StringValue describes a string value. In Level 1 this includes string tokens, a value reference, and functions that return EDIF string values. The *valueNameRef* may refer to a *constant, parameter,* or *variable* definition of type *string.*

Example:

"Hello world"
...
(constant x (string "ABC"))
...
(concat x "XXX")

In the above example the **x** in the *concat* function is a constant value reference. The *concat* construct is a string function which returns the value "ABCXXX".

Used in:

annotate, concat, designator, section, string, and *stringDisplay.*

See also:

booleanValue, integerValue, numberValue, parameter, and *pointValue.*

(**strong** *logicNameRef*)

Strong is an attribute of a logic value which is used to indicate that the current logic value is stronger than the referenced logic value. *Strong* also implies that the present logic value *dominates* the referenced value.

Example:

```
(simulationInfo
    (logicValue F)
    (logicValue T
        (dominates F))
    ...
    (logicValue ST
        (strong T)))
```

The above example states that the logic value **ST** is stronger than the logic value **T**.

Used in:

logicValue.

See also:

dominates, resolves, simulationInfo, and *weak.*

---

	subtract
(**subtract** *numberValue { numberValue })*	*subtract*

Subtract is a number function which successively subtracts from the first argument the remaining arguments. If only one argument is present, it is the value of the expression.

In the special case where all arguments to *subtract* are *integerValues*, the expression may be used as an *integerValue*.

Example:

(**subtract** 13 6 5)
(**subtract** 13 (sum 6 5))

Both of the examples above returns the value **2**.

Used in:

integerValue, and *numberValue.*

See also:

abs, divide, max, min, mod, negate, product, and *sum.*

(**sum** *{ numberValue }*)

sum

sum

Sum is a number function which returns the sum of the arguments. If there are no arguments, the result is zero.

In the special case where all arguments to *sum* are *integerValues,* the expression may be used as an *integerValue.*

Example:

> **(constant a (integer 3))**
> **(constant b (integer 4))**
> **...**
> **(sum a b)**

The final expression in this example returns the value **7** by adding the value of **b** to the value of **a.**

Used in:

integerValue, and *numberValue.*

See also:

abs, divide, max, min, mod, negate, product, and *subtract.*

(symbol	
{ portImplementation /	ports of symbol
figure /	figures used to implement the symbol
annotate /	text as part of the symbol
instance /	instances of graphic views
commentGraphics /	text and figures for annotation
< pageSize > /	size of page containing graphics
< boundingBox > /	extent of symbol graphics
propertyDisplay /	to display properties from interface
keywordDisplay /	to display attributes and name from interface
parameterDisplay /	to display parameters from interface
property /	
comment /	
userData }	
)	

The *symbol* provides an abstract or schematic representation of a cell view. The symbol body can be implemented using figures or using instances of **GRAPHIC** views. Port implementations for symbols are described using *portImplementation*. Comment text and graphics can be associated with the symbol using *commentGraphics*. *Annotate* is used for textual display that should be preserved on instantiation of the symbol.

A single *boundingBox* can be included with the *symbol* to describe the extent of the symbol. The extent covers all of the symbol body, including the figures, port implementations, and the text translation points.

A *pageSize* can be included to be used by systems which require environmental information describing the size of the sheet the symbol is drawn on. A property value defined in the interface of the cell view can be displayed within the coordinate space of the symbol using the *propertyDisplay* form. Likewise, an attribute value defined in the interface of the cell view can be displayed within the coordinate space of the symbol using the *keywordDisplay* form. *Cell, designator* and *instance* are the only *keywordNameRefs* allowed within *keywordDisplay* in a symbol. In this context, where *designator* is used as a *keywordNameRef* within *keywordDisplay*, the *designator* is often referred to as a component reference designator. *ParameterDisplay* is provided to specify the display of a *parameter*.

A *symbol* may only be used in the *interface* of views of type **MASKLAYOUT, PCBLAYOUT, SCHEMATIC, STRANGER,** and **SYMBOLIC.**

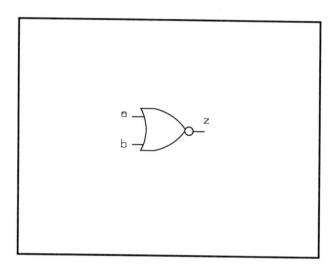

Figure 2-9 A typical symbol

Example:

```
(symbol
    (figure symbol_graphics
        (path (pointList (pt 1 0) (pt 1 2) (pt 3 1) (pt 1 0)))
        (path (pointList (pt 0 1) (pt 1 1)))
        (path (pointList (pt 3 1) (pt 4 1))))
    (portImplementation in
        (connectLocation (figure pin (dot (pt 0 1)))))
    (portImplementation out
        (connectLocation (figure pin (dot (pt 4 1)))))
    (boundingBox (rectangle (pt 0 0) (pt 4 2)))
    (pageSize (rectangle (pt −10 −10) (pt 10 10))))
```

The above example implements the symbol body and the ports **in** and **out.** The extent of the symbol is defined with the points **(0,0)** and **(4,2).** The size of the page the symbol is described within is defined with the two points **(−10,−10)** and **(10,10).**

Used in:

interface.

See also:

designator, portImplementation, and *protectionFrame.*

(**symmetry** *{ transform }*)

Symmetry is used to define the equivalent transformations which may be used for this cell without violating its physical constraints. Any one of the *transforms* defined in a *symmetry* may be used to define a valid match between *plug* and *socket*, generating a correct placement of the cell in a gate array.

Example:

```
(cell Site_cell (cellType generic)
    (view Site_definition (viewType symbolic)
        (interface
            (arrayRelatedInfo
                (arraySite
                    (socket
                        (symmetry
                            (transform (orientation R0)
                            (transform (orientation R90)
                            (transform (orientation R180)
                            (transform (orientation R270))))))))))
```

This specifies a cell **site_cell** which is symmetric for any of the four rotations but not for mirroring. This defines only the final orientation; a given system may achieve the required orientation by any combination of mirroring and rotation. When determining a valid placement, the total orientation is the sum of the *plug, socket, socketSet,* and the *site* instance used.

Used in:

socket, and *socketSet.*

See also:

arrayRelatedInfo, orientation, plug, and *transform.*

---

table

(table
  { entry | < tableDefault > }

table

Table is used within logic modeling to return a logic value selected from a table of values. The logic value returned is determined by the criterion in each *entry* of the table. An entry for all possible conditions should be specified. A *tableDefault* can be specified to catch any conditions not specified. The entries of the *table* should be checked in the order specified.

The *noChange* return within *entry* or *tableDefault* may be used to inhibit the action of a *table*.

Example:

```
(logicAssign OUT
    (table
        (entry (match IN T) (logicRef F))
        (entry (match IN F) (logicRef T))
        (tableDefault (logicRef X))))
```

The above example is part of a buffer using *logicAssign* and *table*. The table will return a logic value **F** to port **OUT** if the first entry condition is met. If the second entry condition is met, port **OUT** will take the logic value **T**. The *tableDefault* specifies that port **OUT** will take the logic value **X** if none of the other conditions are met.

Used in:

entry, follow, logicAssign, and *tableDefault.*

See also:

noChange.

(tableDefault
    logicRef | portRef | noChange | table
    [delay | loadDelay]
)

TableDefault is used within *table* to specify the result if no *entry* is satisfied.

Example:

(table
        (entry (match IN T) (logicRef T))
        (entry (match IN F) (logicRef F))
        (tableDefault (logicRef X)))

The above example describes the following statements: if the logic value of port **IN** is **T,** then return logic value **T** as the value of the table; if the logic value of port **IN** is **F,** then return the logic value of **F** as the value of the table; if neither of the two other conditions is met, then return the logic value **X** as the value of the table.

Used in:

table.

See also:

entry, and *noChange.*

---

technology

```
(technology  numberDefinition
    { figureGroup |
    fabricate |
    <simulationInfo > |
    < physicalDesignRule > |
    comment |
    userData }
)
```

technology

The *technology* construct contains the information related to the intended implementation of the library. The description applies to every component of the library. The *technology* block is required for every library. It includes scaling information, definitions of the figure groups and the default figure group attributes, and simulation information. *NumberDefinition* is required to ensure that scaling information is available before any values which may need to be scaled.

Example:

```
(library CMOS
    (edifLevel 0)
    (technology
        (numberDefinition
            (scale 1 (e 1 −6) (unit time))
            (scale 1 (e 1 −10) (unit distance)))
        (figureGroup Metal ... )
        (figureGroup Poly  ... )
        (fabricate L1 Metal)) ...)
```

In the above example the *technology* block defines the scales, figure group defaults and fabrication layers for the library named **CMOS**.

Used in:

external, and *library.*

See also:

fabricate, figureGroup, numberDefinition, physicalDesignRule, and *simulationInfo.*

(**technology** *numberDefinition*
    { figureGroup |
    fabricate |
    < simulationInfo > |
    < physicalDesignRule > |
    constant |
    constraint |
    comment |
    userData }

Technology for Level 1 libraries is the same as *technology* for Level 0 with the addition of *constant* and *constraint*. Such *constants* may be referred to in any subsequent expression within the library.

Example:

(**technology**
    (**numberDefinition** (**scale 25** (**e 1 −6**) (**unit distance**)))
    (**constant lambda** (**integer 25**)) **...**)

This example illustrates the use of *constant* within a Level 1 *technology*.

Used in:

external, and *library*.

See also:

constant, constraint, and *edifLevel*.

---

technology

```
(technology  numberDefinition
    { figureGroup |
    fabricate |
    < simulationInfo > |
    < physicalDesignRule > |
    constant |
    constraint |
    block |
    if |
    iterate |
    while |
    comment |
    userData }
)
```

technology

Technology is the same as for Level 1 with the addition of *block, if, iterate,* and *while* constructs. In this context, *statement* is restricted to *block, comment, constraint, escape, if, iterate, userData,* and *while.*

Used in:

external, and *library.*

See also:

if, iterate, and *while.*

(textHeight *integerValue*)

TextHeight is used to express the height of text in a figure group. The integer value is expressed in distance units.

TextHeight may be specified within *figureGroup* in the technology block of a library. In this case the text height is the default character height value to be used for text in the figure group. *TextHeight* may also be specified in the *figureGroupOverride* within a *display*. In this case the text height value is used to override the default text height value of a single display.

Example:

    (numberDefinition
        (scale 1 (e 1 −3) (unit distance)))
        (figureGroup TextDisplay
            (textHeight 8) ...))

The first example in a *technology* construct defines a default text height of **8 mm.**

    (display
        (figureGroupOverride TextDisplay
            (textHeight 15) ...))

The second example overrides the default text height with a value of **15 mm** for this display.

Used in:

figureGroup, and *figureGroupOverride.*

See also:

display, and *justify.*

(then *{ statement }* **)**

    Then   is a flow-of-control construct which is used in conjunction with the *if* and *else* forms to achieve conditional invocation of EDIF statements. The *if* construct takes a Boolean test expression. If the Boolean value evaluates to *true,* then the statements within the *then* form are executed; if the Boolean value evaluates to *false* and there is an *else* statement, the statements within the *else* are executed. Otherwise, no statements are executed.

Example:

```
(if (strictlyIncreasing n 5)
    (then
        (assign m (integer 1)))
    (else
        (assign m (integer (sum n 1)))))
```

In this example if **n** < **5** then **m** will be assigned the value **1.** If **n** is **5** or higher, **m** will be assigned the value **n+1.**

Used in:

if.

See also:

else and *statement.*

(timeInterval
    event | offsetEvent
    event | offsetEvent | duration
)

TimeInterval is used to describe an interval between two times. Times can be described by events or offset events. The first construct gives the beginning of the time interval; the second construct gives the end of the time interval, or its duration.

A *duration* can be used instead of the second event, to explicitly specify the length of the interval.

Example:

    (timeInterval
        (event (portRef A) (transition I O))
        (duration 17))

In the first example the time interval described is from the time when port **A** changes from **I** to **O,** to the time **17** time units after the event. Both the event time and the point **17** time units after are included in the window.

    (timeInterval
        (event (portRef ENA) (transition H L))
        (offsetEvent
            (event (portRef P1) (becomes Z))
            (e 14 −1)))

In the second example the time interval is from the time when port **ENA** changes from **H** to **L,** to **1.4** time units after the port **P1** next becomes **Z.**

Used in:

forbiddenEvent.

See also:

duration, event, and *offsetEvent.*

(timeStamp	*timeStamp*
integerToken	year
integerToken	month
integerToken	day
integerToken	hour
integerToken	minute
integerToken	second
)	
	timeStamp

The *timeStamp* identifies the time in Universal Time Coordinated when the data was created or last modified. The year includes the century. If part of a file is created and then modified, a new *written* with a new *timeStamp* may be inserted to indicate this. *TimeStamp* is required in *written*.

The integer tokens are interpreted, in order, as the year, month, day, hour, minute, and second respectively. All values must be specified.

Example:

    (status
        (written
            (timeStamp 1986 12 31 23 59 59)))

The above *status* indicates that the associated data was created or modified on **December 31st, 1986** at **23:59:59 UTC.**

Used in:

written.

See also:

status.

(timing *derivation*
    { pathDelay |
    forbiddenEvent |
    comment |
    userData }
)

Timing is used to provide a set of path delays or timing constraints (forbidden events). The derivation of the values is also given. This may be used in the *interface* of views of any type except **DOCUMENT** or **GRAPHIC**, and the *contents* of views of any type except **BEHAVIOR**, **DOCUMENT**, or **GRAPHIC**.

Example:

    (timing
        (derivation required)
        (pathDelay
            (delay (mnm (e 18 −1) (e 37 −1) (e 84 −1)))
            (event (portRef CK) (transition L H))
            (event (portRef Q) (transition L H)))
        (forbiddenEvent
            (timeInterval
                (offsetEvent (event (portRef CK) (transition H L)) (e −48 −1))
                (duration (e 72 −1)))
            (event (portRef D))))

This example describes a required path delay from port **CK** to port **Q.** The delay required has a minimum value of **1.8** time units, a nominal value of **3.7** time units, and a maximum value of **8.4** time units. The *forbiddenEvent* statement requires that port **D** is stable for at least **4.8** time units before a falling (**H** to **L**) transition of **CK** and remains stable for at least **2.4** time units after the **CK** transition, giving a stability requirement of **7.2** time units.

Used in:

contents, instance, instanceBackAnnotate, interface, and *statement.*

See also:

derivation, forbiddenEvent, netDelay, pathDelay, portDelay, and *viewType.*

(**transform**	*transform*
[*scaleX*]	default: 1/1
[*scaleY*]	default: 1/1
[*delta*]	default: {(**pt 0 0**)}
[*orientation*]	default: **R0**
[*origin*]	default: (**pt 0 0**)
)	
	transform

Transform is used to locate an instance or array of instances in a view of a cell. *ScaleX* and *scaleY* are used to indicate scale factors for the instance. *Delta* may be used when *transform* occurs within *instance*. In this context it is used for arrays of instances, with each point corresponding to a dimension in the *array*. *Orientation* is used to describe one of eight possible instance orientations. *Origin* is used to describe the translation point of an instance or of the first element of an instance array.

Each operation within *transform* is applied in the specified order.

Example:

```
(instance inst_1
   (viewRef V1 (cellRef cell1))
   (transform
      (scaleX 2 1)
      (scaleY 3 1)
      (orientation R90)
      (origin (pt 10 70)))))
```

In the above example the instance is scaled by **2** in the **x** direction and by **3** in the **y** direction. The instance is then rotated **90** degrees and placed at **(10,70)**.

A typical point such as **(100,500)** in **V1** would map to **(-1490,270)**.

Used in:

instance, site, and *symmetry.*

See also:

delta, gridMap, orientation, origin, scale, scaleX, and *scaleY.*

---

	transition
(transition	
logicNameRef | *logicList* | *logicOneOf*	previous value
logicNameRef | *logicList* | *logicOneOf*	present value
)	
	transition

Transition is used to describe a logic state transition from the first specified logic value to the last specified value.

LogicList is used in conjunction with lists or arrays of ports. When used the size of the logic list must match the size of the port list.

In the case of a *transition* which contains a *logicList,* the transition occurs as soon as the following conditions are met. At some previous time each associated port had a logic value equal to the corresponding value of the first *logicList;* each port has a logic value equal to the corresponding value of the second *logicList;* each individual port has had at most one logic transition between these times.

LogicOneOf is used to provide a choice of logic values or logic lists. Any match in the *logicOneOf* is considered a match for the *transition* statement.

Example:

(transition L H)

The first example specifies the transition from the logic value **L** to the logic value **H.**

(transition Z (logicOneOf H L))

The second example specifies the transition from the logic value **Z** to the logic value **H** or the transition from the logic value **Z** to the logic value **L.**

Used in:

change, event, netDelay, portDelay, and *steady.*

See also:

becomes, logicList, logicOneOf, and *pathDelay.*

(trigger
    { *change* **|**
    steady **|**
    initial **}**
)

Trigger is used with the *when* construct in logic modeling to specify the conditions which should cause the actions of the enclosing *when* statement to be performed. If more than one argument is present the *trigger* is activated when any of them becomes satisfied.

Example:

```
(when
    (trigger (initial))
    (logicAssign OUT (logicRef X)))
(when
    (trigger (steady IN (duration 5)))
    (logicAssign OUT (portRef IN)))
(when
    (trigger (change IN (becomes (logicOneOf Z X))))
    (logicAssign OUT (logicRef X) (delay 5)))
```

The above example describes a four-state buffer using *when* and *trigger*. The first *trigger* is used to initialize the simulation model. The second *trigger* states that whenever port **IN** has been steady for exactly **5** time units, the logic value of port **IN** is assigned to the port **OUT**. The third *trigger* states that when port **IN** changes to either logic value **Z** or logic value **X,** the logic value **X** should be assigned to port **OUT** after a delay of **5** time units.

Used in:

when.

See also:

change, follow, initial, logicAssign, and *steady.*

(true)   *true*

                                                                          true

---

    True is an EDIF Boolean value. It is expressed as a keyword to avoid clashes with value names in higher-level descriptions.

Example:

    (property LLL
        (boolean
            (true)))

The above example defines a property named **LLL** which has the value **true.**

Used in:

booleanValue.

See also:

false.

---

boolean | integer | miNoMax | number | point | string

typedValue

typedValue

TypedValue is used to declare the type and value of a *constant, parameter, property,* or *variable.*

An array of typed values can be defined by specifying multiple values within a *typedValue.* Nesting of the *typedValue* constructs is required to specify array values of two or more dimensions. The number of items directly within *typedValue* corresponds to the first dimension of an array; the structure of such nested typed values is determined by the remaining array dimensions.

Example:

    (parameter wordWidth (integer 16))

In this example the parameter **wordWidth** is declared to be of type *integer* and has a default typed value of **16.**

    (constant (array BA1 2) (boolean (false) (true)))
    (constant (array IA2 2 3)
       (integer
          (integer 2 7 45)
          (integer 1 0 22)))

In the above example the constant **BA1** is defined to be a one–dimensional Boolean array with the value assignments **(member BA1 0) = (false), (member BA1 1) = (true).** **IA2** is defined to be a two–dimensional integer array with the following value assignments:

(member IA2 0 0) = 2, (member IA2 0 1) = 7, (member IA2 0 2) = 45,
(member IA2 1 0) = 1, (member IA2 1 1) = 0, (member IA2 1 2) = 22.

Used in:

assign, constant, parameter, parameterAssign, property, and *variable.*

See also:

array, boolean, integer, miNoMax, number, point, and *string.*

(unconstrained)

Unconstrained is a special value used only within *mnm* to indicate the absence of a bound.

Example:

```
(mnm
    5
    15
    (unconstrained))
```

This example indicates a minimal value of **5,** a nominal value of **15,** and no maximal value.

Used in:

mnm.

See also:

undefined.

(undefined)

undefined

undefined

Undefined is a special value to indicate the lack of any defined value. In many cases this may be interpreted as an error condition. It can only be used within *mnm*.

Example:

(mnm
    5
    (undefined)
    10)

This example indicates that the nominal value is not defined.

Used in:

mnm.

See also:

unconstrained.

---

union

(union
    figureGroupRef | figureOp
    { figureGroupRef | figureOp }
)

union

Union describes the union of figure group objects. A location is contained within the *union* if it is contained within any of the given figure group objects.

Example:

(union
    (figureGroupRef Poly)
    (figureGroupRef Transistor))

This specifies a new set of figure–group objects which are formed by the union of **Poly** and **Transistor.**

Used in:

figureOp.

See also:

figureGroupRef, and *intersection.*

---

unit

(unit

    ANGLE | CAPACITANCE | CONDUCTANCE | CHARGE | CURRENT |
    DISTANCE | ENERGY | FLUX | FREQUENCY | INDUCTANCE | MASS |
    POWER | RESISTANCE | TEMPERATURE | TIME | VOLTAGE

)

unit

Unit documents the type of units being used for an associated property or parameter. The unit type is necessary when referencing or importing data from a different *library*. The appropriate scaling is applied whenever a data value is exported from or imported into a library; it is determined by the type of the receiving parameter.

The *unit* is used to determine which *scale* statement should be used to map *parameters* and *properties* between libraries. The *scale* statements relate:

- **ANGLE** to radians,

- **CAPACITANCE** to farads,

- **CONDUCTANCE** to siemens (inverse ohms),

- **CHARGE** to coulombs,

- **CURRENT** to amperes,

- **DISTANCE** to meters,

- **ENERGY** to joules,

- **FLUX** to webers,

- **FREQUENCY** to hertz (cycles per second),

- **INDUCTANCE** to henrys,

- **MASS** to kilograms,

- **POWER** to watts,

- **RESISTANCE** to ohms,

- **TEMPERATURE** to degrees kelvin,

- TIME to seconds, and

- VOLTAGE to volts.

Example:

**(technology
      (numberDefinition
            (scale 10 1 (unit TIME))) ...)**

The first example declares that one EDIF time unit is one–tenth of a second, within this *library*.

**(property CellWidth (integer 20)
      (unit DISTANCE))**

The next example indicates that the value of property **CellWidth** is **20** DISTANCE units.

**(parameter Drive (integer 10)
      (unit CURRENT))**

The final example indicates that the value parameter **Drive** is **10** CURRENT units.

Used in:

parameter, property, and *scale.*

See also:

numberDefinition, and *technology.*

(unused)   *unused*

unused

     Unused ia an attribute of ports, port instances, and off–page connectors. When this is embedded in a *port* in the *interface* of a *view,* it indicates that this particular port is not being used by the view and hence the external environment may use it for any purpose without influencing the operation of the cell in any way. When used in an *offPageConnector* it indicates that the particular off–page connector will not be used for doing any interpage connectivity. When used in the *portInstance* in an *instance* in the *contents* of a *view,* it indicates that the port of an instantiated view will not be used by the instantiating view; that is, it is not connected to any *net* in that view.

Example:

    (interface
       (port A (unused)) ...)

In the first example, the port named **A** is not used for internal connections and so is free for use by the external environment.

    (contents
       (instance AND2_3
          (viewRef ...)
          (portInstance B (unused))))

Within the *instance* this indicates that port **B** of the view referred to by *viewRef* in this instance is not used for connectivity of the local view.

Used in:

offPageConnector, port, and *portInstance.*

See also:

contents, interface, joined, and *net.*

(**userData** *identifier*
    { integerToken | stringToken | identifier | form }
)

UserData is provided as a means to add local user extensions. It is intended that this be used for experimenting with constructs that could potentially be included as official constructs in later releases of EDIF. The meaning contained in this construct is entirely controlled by prior agreement of both sender and receiver and, as such, is not to be considered as transportable in any general sense. It is not subject to any *viewType* restrictions.

The sender of unexpected *userData* should be warned that the reader may ignore important information or may object to such a file. The receiver of unexpected *userData* should beware simply ignoring such information since it may be considered important by the sender. However, it should be considered reasonable for the receiver to communicate further regarding this information.

UserData must conform to all EDIF syntax and semantic rules, and any constructs within *userData* must retain the same syntax and semantics as defined in the EDIF specification. Each *userData* defines a single construct with user–defined semantics. If special semantic interpretation is required for some object within the *userData* then another *userData* must be defined. For example, the keyword *cell* must always mean an EDIF cell even within a *userData*. If some altered form of *cell* is required, then another *userData* must be used with its own identifier and its own special semantics. In addition, the fact that the context is *userData* cannot be used to restructure or redefine the overall EDIF structure. For example a *cell* must still be in a *library,* and all referenced names must be defined.

UserData should be thought of as an escape hatch for data which cannot be currently expressed in EDIF and is to be used with great care (as an emergency procedure) when engineering needs dictate an immediate solution. Any extensive use of this construct indicates EDIF may need enhancement, and hence the use should be brought to the attention of the EDIF Committee.

Continued or persistent use of this form is strongly discouraged.

Example:

```
(design ALU_32
   (cellRef ALU_CMOS (libraryRef CMOS2M))
   (userData ABCprivate
      (userData use (viewRef ALU_PHYSICAL) PLOT)
      (userData use (viewRef ALU_DOC) PRINT)))
```

This example shows reference to views to be used for various purposes without using standard EDIF constructs.

```
(library example
   (userData strangeness
      (cell normal_cell
         (cellType generic)
         (view some_view (viewType ...)
            (interface ...)
            (contents ...))
      (userData cell_like_form unique_cell
         (contents ...)))))
```

This *userData* defines a construct similar to *cell*, but without a view or interface. The nested *contents* construct must obey the normal syntax for that keyword. Even though the cell named **normal_cell** is defined in a standard *cell* construct, it should not be expected to be accepted or treated in the desired way unless specific instructions have been exchanged regarding **strangeness.**

Used in:

after, apply, arrayRelatedInfo, cell, commentGraphics, contents, design, edif, enclosureDistance, external, figure, figureArea, figureGroup, figureGroupOverride, figurePerimeter, figureWidth, instance, instanceMap, interface, interFigureGroupSpacing, intraFigureGroupSpacing, library, logicPort, logicValue, net, netBundle, netMap, notAllowed, notchSpacing, offPageConnector, overhangDistance, overlapDistance, page, physicalDesignRule, port, portBundle, portImplementation, portInstance, portMap, protectionFrame, rectangleSize, simulate, simulationInfo, statement, status, symbol, technology, timing, view, viewMap, when, and *written.*

See also:

comment, and *property.*

	valueNameDef
nameDef | *array*	*valueNameDef*

   ValueNameDef is used to name values of types *boolean, integer, miNoMax, number, point,* or *string.* *Array* may be used to define an array of values.

   The scope of a value name extends from the end of its defining form to the smallest enclosing *block, external, library, page,* or *view.*

Example:

   (constant n (integer 3))

This declares an *integer* value named **n.**

Used in:

constant, parameter, and *variable.*

See also:

array, block, interface, page, technology, and *valueNameRef.*

---

nameRef | member

valueNameRef

valueNameRef

A *valueNameRef* is used to reference a previously defined value. In the case of Level 0, the definition of the value can only be a parameter defined in the interface of a view of a cell in an external library or previously defined library at Level 1 or Level 2. The value type must be appropriate to its use, as must its array structure.

An *integer* value may be referenced in place of a *number* value, and a *number* value may be referenced in place of a *miNoMax* value.

Example:

   (sum n 1)

The identifier **n** must be a previously defined value name.

Used in:

assign, booleanValue, integerValue, numberValue, parameterAssign, parameterDisplay, pointValue, and *stringValue.*

See also:

array, member, miNoMaxValue, and *valueNameDef.*

variable

variable

(**variable** *valueNameDef typedValue*)

Variable is used to define variables which may then be referenced within Level 1 expressions, Level 2 flow-of-control statements, expressions, assignment statements, or constructs which allow a *valueNameRef* and are within the scope of the variable definition. Variables defined in the interface of a view are available to the entire view; variables defined in the contents of a view are available only within the contents of the view. The scope of local variables is from the end of their declaration to the end of the smallest enclosing *block* statement, *page,* or *view,* and temporarily overrides any value of the same name defined in a larger scope.

The type and initial value of a variable is specified with a *boolean, integer, miNoMax, number, point,* or *string* typed value. Variable arrays are specified with an *array* name.

Variable is not subject to any *viewType* restrictions.

Example:

```
(variable w (integer))
(variable x (integer 12))
(variable y (number (divide (sum x 4) x)))
(variable (array NA 8) (number))
(variable (array IA 8) (integer 1 2 3 4 5 6 7 8))
(variable (array BA 2 3)
    (boolean (boolean (true) (false) (true)) (boolean (false) (true) (false))))
```

In the above example the following variables are defined: an integer **w** with no initial value; an integer **x** with an initial value of **12,** a number **y** with an initial value of **0.75;** a one-dimensional number array **NA** with no defined initial value; a one-dimensional integer array **IA** with an initial value for (**member IA 0**) of **1,** (**member IA 1**) of **2,** ..., (**member IA 7**) of **8;** a two-dimensional Boolean array **BA** with an initial value for (**member BA 0 0**) of (**true**), (**member BA 0 1**) of (**false**) (**member BA 0 2**) of (**true**), ..., (**member BA 1 2**) of (**false**).

Used in:

contents, interface, page, and *statement.*

See also:

array, assign, block, boolean, constant, else, integer, iterate, miNoMax, number, point, string, then, typedValue, valueNameDef, valueNameRef, and *while.*

(**version** *stringToken*)

Version is used to provide a revision code (defined by the EDIF writer) which can be used to keep track of the origin and creator of the written EDIF data. If problems occur the version information may be used to help analyze them. Any interpretation of the revision code must be external to the EDIF file.

Example:

    (dataOrigin "EDIFCo, Atlantic Division"
        (version "D10−37"))
    (program "NetLister"
        (version "3.72"))

In the above example, version strings are specified for the data from which the EDIF information was created and for the program which created the EDIF data. The format for the version strings was determined by the writer.

Used in:

dataOrigin, and *program.*

See also:

status, stringToken, and *written.*

(view *viewNameDef*
    viewType   a required view type
    interface   a required interface
    { < status > | status of view
    < contents > | implementation of cell view
    comment | user comments
    property | properties of the view
    userData }
)

View is used to specify a data representation, or perspective of a *cell*. The representation is classified by the *viewType*. The valid view types are specified under *viewType*.

View has a required *interface* to define the interaction of the cell with its external environment, an optional *status* construct, an optional *contents* section describing the internal details of the view, and an arbitrary number of *comment*, *property,* and *userData* statements.

No *view* contains direct references to another *view* of the same *cell*. The various components of different views may be related within a *viewMap*. All names defined within a view are local to that view. View names in a cell share the same name space and are required to be distinct for distinct views.

Example:

```
(cell Foo
    (cellType generic)
    (view IC_Layout_Representation
        (viewType MASKLAYOUT)
        (interface ... )
        (status ... )
        (contents ... ))
    (view PCB_Layout_Representation
        (viewType PCBLAYOUT)
        (interface ... )
        (status ... )
        (contents ... ))
    (view Netlist_Representation
        (viewType NETLIST)
        (interface ... )
        (status ... )
```

        (contents ...)
      (viewMap ....))

In the above example three different representations or views of the cell name **Foo** are specified: the view named **IC_Layout_Representation** where the data for a mask layout of the cell can be found, the view named **PCB_Layout_Representation** where the data for a PCB layout of the cell can be found, and the view named **Netlist_Representation** where the data for a netlist of the cell can be found.

Used in:

cell.

See also:

contents, instance, interface, site, status, viewList, viewMap, viewNameDef, viewNameRef, viewRef, and *viewType.*

(viewList *{ viewRef / viewList }* **)**

　　ViewList is an ordered list of view references. It is used to describe an arrayed instance which references multiple views.

　　When used, the number of referenced views must match the size of the corresponding instance array. If all view references are identical, this may be replaced by a single view reference.

Example:

```
(instance (array inst_array 3 2)
   (viewList
      (viewList
         (viewRef abc (cellRef cellA1))
         (viewRef abc (cellRef cellA2)))
      (viewList
         (viewRef abc (cellRef cellB1))
         (viewRef abc (cellRef cellB2)))
      (viewList
         (viewRef abc (cellRef cellC1))
         (viewRef abc (cellRef cellC2)))))
```

In the above example a **3** by **2** two-dimensional instance array named **inst_array** is created. **(member inst_array 0 0)** references view **abc** of cell **cellA1;**　**(member inst_array 0 1)** references view **abc** of cell **cellA2;**　... and **(member inst_array 2 1)** references view **abc** of cell **cellC2.**

Used in:

instance, and *viewList.*

See also:

array, viewNameRef, and *viewRef.*

(viewMap
  { portMap |
  portBackAnnotate |
  instanceMap |
  instanceBackAnnotate |
  netMap |
  netBackAnnotate |
  comment |
  userData }
)

ViewMap allows mappings between objects of the same type in different views; it also allows back annotation to be expressed. *Cells* may have many different views which contain different representations of the cell. Since each view is a description of the same cell, the views are related in certain ways.

ViewMap is used within a cell to express relationships between objects of the same type in different views. It is also used to back–annotate EDIF attribute values and user–property values to objects defined or referenced within the context of a view. Three types of objects can be specified in the *viewMap:* ports, nets, and instances.

The *viewMap* must come after any *view* that is referenced, and may not directly reference any other *cell*.

Example:

```
(view V1 (viewType Schematic)
    (interface
        (port A (designator "")))  ...)
(view V2 (viewType Symbolic)
    (interface (port A)) ...)
(viewMap
    (portMap
        (portRef A (viewRef V1))
        (portRef A (viewRef V2)))
    (portBackAnnotate
        (portRef A (viewRef V1))
        (designator "23")))
```

In the above example a relationship is specified between the port named **A** in the view named **V1** and the port named **A** in the view named **V2**. This relationship implies that the two ports are the same data object defined in two different representations or views. Also the pin–name designator of the port named **A** of the view named **V1** is back annotated to the string value of **23.**

The fact that both port representations have the local name **A** within their respective views has no significance.

Used in:

cell.

See also:

instanceBackAnnotate, instanceMap, netBackAnnotate, netMap, portBackAnnotate, and *portMap.*

nameDef	

A *viewNameDef* is used to name each view of a cell. This will be used in the context of *viewMap* and *instance* statements.

The scope for view names is provided by the enclosing *cell* definition. Different views within the same cell must have different names, even if they have different *viewTypes*.

It should not be assumed that the choice of names for *views* has any effect on their interpretation.

Example:

```
(cell C ...
    (view V ...))
```

In this example **V** is used as a view name definition.

Used in:

view.

See also:

cell, viewNameRef, and *viewRef.*

---

nameRef   *viewNameRef*

viewNameRef

ViewNameRef identifies a previously defined *view*. This is needed in the context of *instance* statements and *viewRefs*.

Example:

(instance I
    (viewRef V (cellRef C))

In this example, **V** is a reference to a view defined within a cell named **C**.

Used in:

viewRef.

See also:

view, and *viewNameDef.*

(viewRef *viewNameRef [cellRef]***)**

ViewRef is part of the generic name referencing mechanism in EDIF that provides indirect referencing and extends the range of accessibility to an object from beyond its immediate range. The first or outermost *viewNameRef* in the syntax is the target view, where the nested constructs which follow define a reference path in a bottom–up manner. The *viewRef* construct is used to reference a view by *viewNameRef* and optionally qualify it by a *cellRef,* which in turn can be optionally qualified by a *libraryRef.* The *viewRef* construct is used at any place where there is a need to reference a view. If the view being referenced belongs to a cell which is defined in a different library, then *viewRef* is required to have a nested *cellRef* form with a *libraryRef* form specified within it.

Within the *instance* and *site* constructs, the *cellRef* is always required in the *viewRef.*

The *viewRef* is required to be the top of the referencing path in all name referencing constructs used in the context of *viewMap,* and should never contain a nested *cellRef* in this context.

Example:

> (instance I_ALU_32
>   (viewRef V1
>   (cellRef ALU_32
>   (libraryRef CMOS2M))) ...)

In this example, the instance named **I_ALU_32** references the view named **V1** of the cell named **ALU_32** which is defined in the library named **CMOS2M**. *CellRef* is required within *viewRef* in the context of *instance.*

> (portMap
>   (portRef P1
>   (instanceRef I1
>   (viewRef V1))) ...)

In the second example the *viewRef* is required to be the top of the referencing path, and thus *cellRef* is not allowed to be nested in this *viewRef.* Here a port named **P1** is referenced through the instance hierarchy via the instance named **I1** which is previously defined in the *contents* of the view named **V1** in the current cell.

Used in:

instance, instanceRef, netRef, portRef, site, and *viewList.*

See also:

cellRef, instanceBackAnnotate, instanceGroup, instanceMap, netBackAnnotate, netGroup, netMap, portBackAnnotate, portGroup, portMap, and *viewNameRef.*

(viewType
   **BEHAVIOR | DOCUMENT | GRAPHIC | LOGICMODEL | MASKLAYOUT |
   NETLIST | PCBLAYOUT | SCHEMATIC | STRANGER | SYMBOLIC**

ViewType is used to specify the type of a view. The *viewType* indicates the intended use of the view. It also places restrictions on the statements appropriate within the *contents* of such a view in the same way that the *edifLevel* restricts the choice of statements.

The possible view types are:

- **BEHAVIOR** to describe the behavior of a cell,

- **DOCUMENT** to describe the documentation of a cell,

- **GRAPHIC** to describe a "dumb" graphics and text representation of displayable or printable information,

- **LOGICMODEL** to describe the logic-simulation model of the cell,

- **MASKLAYOUT** to describe an integrated circuit layout,

- **NETLIST** to describe a netlist,

- **PCBLAYOUT** to describe a printed circuit board layout,

- **SCHEMATIC** to describe the schematic representation and connectivity of a cell,

- **STRANGER** to describe an as yet unknown representation of a cell, and

- **SYMBOLIC** to describe a symbolic layout.

A cell may contain more than one *view* of the same type. **STRANGER** views are not generally transportable and may use any of the constructs in the syntax of *contents* or *interface*.

ViewType imposes a restriction on the constructs that may be used within the *interface* or *contents* of a view, or as nested *statements* in Level 2. *Comment* and *userData* are always available; *constant*, *constraint*, and *variable* may be used at Level 1 or higher; *assign*, *block*, *if*, *iterate*, and *while* may be used at Level 2, in addition to nested *escape* statements.

The *interface* of any view may include *properties*. *Parameters* may be declared in any *interface* except in the context of a Level 0 *library*. An *external* library may not use contents statements in any view.

Specific *viewType* restrictions for *interface* are imposed as follows. **DOCUMENT** and **GRAPHIC** views may not use any further *interface* constructs. Other view types may use *designator, joined, mustJoin, permutable, port, portBundle, simulate, timing,* and *weakJoined.* In addition, a **SCHEMATIC** interface may include a *symbol;* a **MASKLAYOUT, PCBLAYOUT** or **SYMBOLIC** interface may include *arrayRelatedInfo, protectionFrame,* or *symbol.* *Figure* is only available within the *protectionFrame* or *symbol* of an *interface.*

The *contents* of a view also has semantic restrictions on the available statements. **BEHAVIOR** views may not use any further constructs. **DOCUMENT** contents may include *sections* and *instances* of views of type **DOCUMENT** or **GRAPHIC**; **GRAPHIC** contents may use *boundingBox, commentGraphics, figure,* or *instances* of views of type **GRAPHIC**. **LOGICMODEL** contents may use *follow, instance, logicPort, simulate, timing,* or *when* statements.

The *contents* of **MASKLAYOUT, PCBLAYOUT** and **SYMBOLIC** views and the *pages* of **SCHEMATIC** views may include *boundingBox, commentGraphics, instance, net, netBundle, portImplementation, simulate,* or *timing.* **MASKLAYOUT** and **PCBLAYOUT** contents may use *figure* directly. **SYMBOLIC** contents and **SCHEMATIC** pages may only use *figure* within *commentGraphics, net, netBundle,* or *portImplementation.*

NETLIST contents may use *instance, net, netBundle, simulate,* and *timing.* A **NETLIST** view may not use *figure,* even within the context of a *net* or *netBundle.* The contents of **SCHEMATIC** views may include *offPageConnector, page, simulate,* and *timing,* but no *instance.*

There are no *viewType* restrictions on the statements available within a **STRANGER** view.

Example:

```
(cell test_cell
   (cellType generic)
   (view spiceInput
      (viewType netlist)...)
   (view logicSim
      (viewType netlist) ...)
   (view maskset3
      (viewType maskLayout) ...)
   (view schematic
      (viewType schematic) ...))
```

This example shows four distinct views of a cell: two of *viewType* **NETLIST,** and one each of *viewType* **SCHEMATIC** and **MASKLAYOUT**. Semantic information is conveyed only by the view type: the view name is purely an identifier, and the spelling of a view name (e.g. **spiceInput** or **schematic**) bears no semantic weight, except to identify different views by name.

Used in:

view.

See also:

cell, cellType, contents, display, instance, and *page.*

visible

visible

(**visible** *booleanValue*)

Visible is an attribute of *figureGroups* which is used to enable or inhibit graphical display. It may be specified within *figureGroup* to provide a default value throughout a library, or modified within *figureGroupOverride*. If not specified in either location, a visibility of *true* is assumed.

Example:

```
(display
    (figureGroupOverride redText
        (visible (false)))
    (origin (pt 125 300)))
```

This example illustrates a *display* specification at point **(125,300)** which should normally be invisible.

Used in:

figureGroup, and *figureGroupOverride.*

See also:

color, display, and *textHeight.*

(voltageMap *miNoMaxValue*)

VoltageMap is an attribute of a logic value used to specify its electrical characteristics. *VoltageMap* gives a value or range of values to specify the accepted voltage values for the defined logic value. This is scaled according to **VOLTAGE** units.

Example:

```
(technology
    (numberDefinition
        (scale 1 (e 1 −1) (unit voltage)))
    (simulationInfo
        (logicValue T
            (voltageMap (mnm 25 48 50)))))
```

In the above example, the logic value **T** has an accepted range of values of **2.5** to **5.0** volts and a nominal value of **4.8** volts.

Used in:

logicValue.

See also:

currentMap, miNoMaxValue, simulationInfo, and *unit.*

waveValue

(waveValue *logicNameDef*
    numberValue
    logicWaveform
)

waveValue

WaveValue is used to assign a name to a waveform fragment, specified in a *logicWaveform* construct. It is a name that can then be used in place of a logic name in the context of subsequent *logicInput, logicOutput,* and *waveValue* statements. It is found only within *simulate* in the *interface* or *contents* of views. It specifies a delta time between the values contained in the given *logicWaveform*. In this context, *logicWaveform* should not contain a *logicList*.

In use, the value may need to be extended or truncated to fit a specified cycle time. Any extension is to be interpreted as a repetition of the last specified logic value in the *logicWaveform* of the *waveValue*.

Example:

    (waveValue CLK 2
        (logicWaveform L H H H H L L))

    (waveValue XX 1
        (logicWaveform (ignore)))

This shows the definition of wave value **CLK** as a low–high–low clock pulse and **XX** as an ignore value.

Used in:

simulate.

See also:

cycle, ignore, logicInput, logicOutput, logicValue, and *logicWaveform.*

(**weak** *logicNameRef*)

Weak is an attribute of a logic value which indicates that the current logic value is weaker than the referenced logic value. This also implies that the referenced value *dominates* the present value.

Example:

>   (**logicValue WT**
>   (**weak T**))

The above example states that the logic value **WT** is weaker than the logic value **T**.

Used in:

logicValue.

See also:

simulationInfo, strong, and *dominates.*

---

weakJoined

(weakJoined
    { portRef |
    portList |
    joined }
)

weakJoined

WeakJoined is used to indicate that external connections may be made to any of the referenced *ports* and that corresponding ports may not be used as feed-throughs. This statement is similar to *joined* when used in the *interface* of a view. The interpretation of nested *portLists* is the same as for *joined*. Only ports defined in the local *interface* may be referenced within *weakJoined*.

WeakJoined may contain nested *joined* statements and may be nested within *mustJoin*, thus forming a tree structure. Within the interface, a port may be referenced at most once in *joined, mustJoin* and *weakJoined*.

Example:

    (weakJoined
        (portRef gateTop)
        (portRef gateBottom))

This example declares that connections may be made to either **gateTop** or to **gateBottom** with the same effect, but the connection **gateTop** to **gateBottom** may not be used as a feed-through.

Used in:

interface, and *mustJoin.*

See also:

joined.

(**when** *trigger*
    { after |
    follow |
    logicAssign |
    maintain |
    comment |
    userData }

when

When is used to describe event-driven behavior for logic modeling. *When* contains a group of actions which should to take place whenever the specified trigger is activated. Actions are the *after, follow, logicAssign,* and *maintain* constructs.

This statement may only be used within views of type **LOGICMODEL** or **STRANGER.** The order in which *when* statements are specified within *contents* is not significant.

Example:

(**when**
    (**trigger (initial)**)
    (**logicAssign OUT (portRef IN)**))
(**when**
    (**trigger (steady IN (duration 5))**)
    (**logicAssign OUT (portRef IN)**))
(**when**
    (**trigger (change IN (becomes (logicOneOf Z X))**))
    (**logicAssign OUT (logicRef X) (delay 5)**))

The above example describes a four-state buffer using *when* and *trigger*.

Used in:

contents, and *statement.*

See also:

after, follow, logicAssign, maintain, trigger, and *viewType.*

(while *booleanValue*
    { statement }
)

While is a flow–of–control form used for conditional iteration in Level 2 descriptions. Looping continues until the Boolean condition is *false* at the start of a loop. Testing of the Boolean condition occurs at the beginning of each iteration.

This *statement* has no effect if the *booleanValue* evaluates to *false* on entry. If it evaluates to *true,* then each of the enclosed statements is executed in the given order. If there has not been an escape from the *while* loop, the compound statement is re–executed as soon as each of the enclosed statements have been processed, including the re–evaluation of the controlling Boolean value.

The *while* loop is terminated either by an enclosed *escape* or when the control value evaluates to *false* at the start of an iteration.

While is not subject to *viewType* restrictions, although the nested *statements* are.

Example:

    (assign n (integer 8))
    (assign v (integer −1))
    (while (strictlyIncreasing n 10)
       (assign v (integer (product v n)))
       (assign n (integer (sum n 1))))

In the above example the value of **v** after executing the while loop will be **−72.** The value of **n** will be **10.**

Used in:

contents, interface, page, statement, and *technology.*

See also:

block, edifLevel, escape, if, and *iterate.*

---

whiteSpace

whiteSpace

A *whiteSpace* character is either a horizontal tab, line feed, carriage return, or blank. These have ASCII codes of 9, 10, 13 and 32 respectively. Any token *(identifier, integerToken, stringToken)* not preceding a parenthesis '(' or ')' or percent sign '%' within *asciiCharacter* must be followed by one or more *whiteSpace* characters.

The only situation where *whiteSpace* is significant (except for separating tokens) is the blank or tab characters within a *stringToken*. At least one *whiteSpace* character or parenthesis must occur between any tokens, and further *whiteSpace* may be added in such locations without causing any change of interpretation.

Although not explicitly stated elsewhere, *whiteSpace* may also be added next to left or right parentheses (outside string tokens) without effect.

The first character after a sequence of *whiteSpace* characters not within a *stringToken* fully determines the type of token. A quote '"' begins a *stringToken;* ampersand '&' or *alpha* begins an *identifier;* a plus '+', minus '−', or *digit* begins an *integerToken;* a left parenthesis '(' indicates the start of a *form,* and a right parenthesis ')' indicates the end of a corresponding *form.* Parentheses may be considered to be single-character tokens.

Example:

(portList a b)

The white-space between port names **a** and **b** is required to avoid misinterpreting this as a single name **ab.**

Used in:

stringToken.

See also:

$goal, alpha, asciiCharacter, digit, identifier, integerToken, and *specialCharacter.*

```
(written  timeStamp                                    written
    { < author > |              name of person who created data
    < program > |       program name and version that created data
    < dataOrigin > |      location where created and version of data
    property |
    comment |
    userData }
)
                                                       written
```

Written includes information relating to the writer of the EDIF file. It must include a *timeStamp* and may include program identification, human or organization identification, or location information to help the reader trace the origin of a particular part of an EDIF file.

Example:

```
(written
    (timeStamp 1986 11 30 22 7 29)
    (author "J. Knecht")
    (dataOrigin "Castalia")
    (program "Glasperlenspiel"))
```

This example shows a typical *written* statement. In this case, the EDIF data was created or modified on **November 30, 1986.** The person **"J. Knecht"** was involved in the process which occurred at location **"Castalia"**. The program that created the new or modified data was called **"Glasperlenspiel"**, and no version number was specified.

Used in:

status.

See also:

author, dataOrigin, program, and *timeStamp.*

	xCoord
(xCoord *pointValue*)	*xCoord*

XCoord is an integer function that returns the x-coordinate of its point argument. The value returned is treated as a simple integer in expressions.

Example:

   (xCoord
      (pt 3 0))

This example returns the integer value **3**. A more realistic use of the function would be to apply it to a point variable or to a parameter reference of type *point.*

Used in:

integerValue, and *numberValue.*

See also:

pointSubtract, pointSum, pt, and *yCoord.*

(**xor** *{ booleanValue }*)   *xor*

                                                                                 xor

---

   Xor returns the exclusive or of its arguments. The value *true* is returned if an odd number of the statements evaluates to *true*. If an even number of statements evaluate to *true* the function returns *false*. This includes the case where no argument evaluates to *true* or the trivial case in which no arguments are present, in which case the function returns *false*.

Example:

```
(xor
    (equal x y)
    (equal x z))
```

The above example will return the Boolean value *true* if **x** equals **y** or **x** equals **z**, but **x, y** and **z** are not all equal.

Used in:

booleanValue.

See also:

and, equal, not, and *or.*

(yCoord *pointValue***)**

YCoord is an integer function that returns the y–coordinate of its point argument. The value returned is treated as a simple integer value within expressions.

Example:

(yCoord
    (pt 3 7))

The above example returns the integer value **7**.

Used in:

integerValue, and *numberValue.*

See also:

pointSubtract, pointSum, pt, and *xCoord.*

EDIF GRAMMAR

Introduction

In the following description, it is assumed that implementors have gained knowledge of the semantics from earlier sections of this document and are prepared to use it within the syntactic and semantic processes of their particular EDIF translators.

The syntax for keyword definition (*keywordMap*) is given for each of the keyword levels; however, the use of defined keywords is not explicitly incorporated into all the following productions. Such use is legal when expansion of the keyword is legal.

Delimiters are space, tab, newline, and carriage–return. They are optional immediately before and immediately after a left or right parenthesis. However, they are required to separate tokens. This is described in more detail on the *whiteSpace* reference page.

Notations

All terminals of the grammar are enclosed by apostrophes. Since EDIF does not distinguish cases, the keywords need not appear in the same case as shown. An implementation should treat 'SCALE', 'Scale', and 'scale' as the same identifier.

The vertical bar "|" separates alternatives. For example, A | B | C represents exactly one occurrence of A or B or C.

Parentheses "( )" show syntactic association. For example, A (B | C) denotes A B or A C. The parentheses used for syntactic association should not be confused with the terminals '(' and ')'.

Braces "{ }", indicate zero or more occurrences of the enclosed syntactic construct. For example, { A | B } represents the empty sequence, as well as A B, and A B B B, B B A B A, and so on.

Brackets "[ ]" indicate an optional construct.

Angled brackets "< >" signify a construct that may occur at most once within the immediately enclosing syntactic grouping structure. For example, { A | < B > } represents all sequences of zero or more A's that contain at most one B; that is, A, A A, B, A A B A, B A A A A, and the empty sequence are all valid sequences.

The terminals of EDIF are the string token, integer token, and identifier token. They are defined on the corresponding reference pages.

Level 0

```
$goal ::= edif

acLoad ::= '(' 'acLoad'
        ( miNoMaxValue | miNoMaxDisplay )
        ')'

after ::= '(' 'after'
        miNoMaxValue
        { logicAssign | follow | maintain | comment | userData }
        ')'

annotate ::= '(' 'annotate'
        ( stringValue | stringDisplay )
        ')'

apply ::= '(' 'apply'
        cycle
        { logicInput | logicOutput | comment | userData }
        ')'

arc ::= '(' 'arc'
        pointValue
        pointValue
        pointValue
        ')'

array ::= '(' 'array'
        nameDef
        integerValue
        { integerValue }
        ')'

arrayMacro ::= '(' 'arrayMacro'
        plug
        ')'

arrayRelatedInfo ::= '(' 'arrayRelatedInfo'
        ( arrayMacro | arraySite | baseArray )
        { comment | userData }
        ')'

arraySite ::= '(' 'arraySite'
        socket
        ')'
```

```
atLeast ::= '(' 'atLeast'
        numberValue
        ')'

atMost ::= '(' 'atMost'
        numberValue
        ')'

author ::= '(' 'author'
        stringToken
        ')'

baseArray ::= '(' 'baseArray'
        ')'

becomes ::= '(' 'becomes'
        ( logicNameRef | logicList | logicOneOf )
        ')'

between ::= '(' 'between'
        ( atLeast | greaterThan )
        ( atMost | lessThan )
        ')'

boolean ::= '(' 'boolean'
        { booleanValue | booleanDisplay | boolean }
        ')'

booleanDisplay ::= '(' 'booleanDisplay'
        booleanValue
        { display }
        ')'

booleanMap ::= '(' 'booleanMap'
        booleanValue
        ')'

booleanValue ::=
        false | true

borderPattern ::= '(' 'borderPattern'
        integerValue
        integerValue
        boolean
        ')'
```

borderWidth ::= '(' 'borderWidth'
        integerValue
        ')'

boundingBox ::= '(' 'boundingBox'
        rectangle
        ')'

cell ::= '(' 'cell'
        cellNameDef
        cellType
        { < status > | view | < viewMap > | property | comment | userData }
        ')'

cellNameDef ::=
        nameDef

cellNameRef ::=
        nameRef

cellRef ::= '(' 'cellRef'
        cellNameRef
        [libraryRef]
        ')'

cellType ::= '(' 'cellType'
        ('GENERIC' | 'TIE' | 'RIPPER')
        ')'

change ::= '(' 'change'
        (portNameRef | portRef | portList)
        [transition | becomes]
        ')'

circle ::= '(' 'circle'
        pointValue
        pointValue
        { property }
        ')'

color ::= '(' 'color'
        scaledInteger
        scaledInteger
        scaledInteger
        ')'

```
comment ::= '(' 'comment'
        { stringToken }
        ')'

commentGraphics ::= '(' 'commentGraphics'
        { annotate | figure | instance | < boundingBox > | property
        | comment | userData }
        ')'

compound ::= '(' 'compound'
        { logicNameRef }
        ')'

connectLocation ::= '(' 'connectLocation'
        { figure }
        ')'

contents ::= '(' 'contents'
        { instance | offPageConnector | figure | section | net
        | netBundle | page | commentGraphics | portImplementation | timing
        | simulate | when | follow | logicPort | < boundingBox > | comment
        | userData }
        ')'

cornerType ::= '(' 'cornerType'
        ( 'EXTEND' | 'ROUND' | 'TRUNCATE' )
        ')'

criticality ::= '(' 'criticality'
        ( integerValue | integerDisplay )
        ')'

currentMap ::= '(' 'currentMap'
        miNoMaxValue
        ')'

curve ::= '(' 'curve'
        { arc | pointValue }
        ')'

cycle ::= '(' 'cycle'
        integerValue
        [ duration ]
        ')'
```

```
dataOrigin ::= '(' 'dataOrigin'
        stringToken
        [ version ]
        ')'

dcFaninLoad ::= '(' 'dcFaninLoad'
        ( numberValue | numberDisplay )
        ')'

dcFanoutLoad ::= '(' 'dcFanoutLoad'
        ( numberValue | numberDisplay )
        ')'

dcMaxFanin ::= '(' 'dcMaxFanin'
        ( numberValue | numberDisplay )
        ')'

dcMaxFanout ::= '(' 'dcMaxFanout'
        ( numberValue | numberDisplay )
        ')'

delay ::= '(' 'delay'
        ( miNoMaxValue | miNoMaxDisplay )
        ')'

delta ::= '(' 'delta'
        { pointValue }
        ')'

derivation ::= '(' 'derivation'
        ( 'CALCULATED' | 'MEASURED' | 'REQUIRED' )
        ')'

design ::= '(' 'design'
        designNameDef
        cellRef
        { < status > | property | comment | userData }
        ')'

designator ::= '(' 'designator'
        ( stringValue | stringDisplay )
        ')'

designNameDef ::=
        nameDef
```

```
difference ::= '(' 'difference'
        ( figureGroupRef | figureOp )
        { figureGroupRef | figureOp }
        ')'

direction ::= '(' 'direction'
        ( 'INOUT' | 'INPUT' | 'OUTPUT' )
        ')'

display ::= '(' 'display'
        ( figureGroupNameRef | figureGroupOverride )
        [ justify ]
        [ orientation ]
        [ origin ]
        ')'

dominates ::= '(' 'dominates'
        { logicNameRef }
        ')'

dot ::= '(' 'dot'
        pointValue
        { property }
        ')'

duration ::= '(' 'duration'
        numberValue
        ')'

e ::= '(' 'e'
        integerToken
        integerToken
        ')'

edif ::= '(' 'edif'
        edifFileNameDef
        edifVersion
        edifLevel
        keywordMap
        { < status > | external | library | design | comment | userData }
        ')'

edifFileNameDef ::=
        nameDef

edifLevel ::= '(' 'edifLevel'
        integerToken
        ')'
```

```
edifVersion ::= '(' 'edifVersion'
        integerToken
        integerToken
        integerToken
        ')'

enclosureDistance ::= '(' 'enclosureDistance'
        ruleNameDef
        figureGroupObject
        figureGroupObject
        ( range | singleValueSet )
        { comment | userData }
        ')'

endType ::= '(' 'endType'
        ( 'EXTEND' | 'ROUND' | 'TRUNCATE' )
        ')'

entry ::= '(' 'entry'
        ( match | change | steady )
        ( logicRef | portRef | noChange | table )
        [ delay | loadDelay ]
        ')'

event ::= '(' 'event'
        ( portRef | portList | portGroup | netRef | netGroup )
        { transition | becomes }
        ')'

exactly ::= '(' 'exactly'
        numberValue
        ')'

external ::= '(' 'external'
        libraryNameDef
        edifLevel
        technology
        { < status > | cell | comment | userData }
        ')'

fabricate ::= '(' 'fabricate'
        layerNameDef
        figureGroupNameRef
        ')'

false ::= '(' 'false'
        ')'
```

figure ::= '(' 'figure'
        (figureGroupNameRef | figureGroupOverride)
        { circle | dot | openShape | path | polygon | rectangle | shape
        | comment | userData }
        ')'

figureArea ::= '(' 'figureArea'
        ruleNameDef
        figureGroupObject
        (range | singleValueSet)
        { comment | userData }
        ')'

figureGroup ::= '(' 'figureGroup'
        figureGroupNameDef
        { < cornerType > | < endType > | < pathWidth > | < borderWidth >
        | < color > | < fillPattern > | < borderPattern > | < textHeight >
        | < visible > | includeFigureGroup | property | comment | userData }
        ')'

figureGroupNameDef ::=
        nameDef

figureGroupNameRef ::=
        nameRef

figureGroupObject ::= '(' 'figureGroupObject'
        (figureGroupNameRef | figureGroupRef | figureOp)
        ')'

figureGroupOverride ::= '(' 'figureGroupOverride'
        figureGroupNameRef
        { < cornerType > | < endType > | < pathWidth > | < borderWidth >
        | < color > | < fillPattern > | < borderPattern > | < textHeight >
        | < visible > | property | comment | userData }
        ')'

figureGroupRef ::= '(' 'figureGroupRef'
        figureGroupNameRef
        [libraryRef]
        ')'

figureOp ::=
        difference | intersection | inverse | oversize | union

figurePerimeter ::= '(' 'figurePerimeter'
            ruleNameDef
            figureGroupObject
            (range | singleValueSet)
            { comment | userData }
            ')'

figureWidth ::= '(' 'figureWidth'
            ruleNameDef
            figureGroupObject
            (range | singleValueSet)
            { comment | userData }
            ')'

fillPattern ::= '(' 'fillPattern'
            integerValue
            integerValue
            boolean
            ')'

follow ::= '(' 'follow'
            (portNameRef | portRef)
            (portRef | table)
            [delay | loadDelay]
            ')'

forbiddenEvent ::= '(' 'forbiddenEvent'
            timeInterval
            { event }
            ')'

form ::= '(' keywordNameRef
            { integerToken | stringToken | identifier | form }
            ')'

globalPortRef ::= '(' 'globalPortRef'
            portNameRef
            ')'

greaterThan ::= '(' 'greaterThan'
            numberValue
            ')'

gridMap ::= '(' 'gridMap'
            numberValue
            numberValue
            ')'

```
ignore ::= '(' 'ignore'
       ')'

includeFigureGroup ::= '(' 'includeFigureGroup'
       ( figureGroupRef | figureOp )
       ')'

initial ::= '(' 'initial'
       ')'

instance ::= '(' 'instance'
       instanceNameDef
       ( viewRef | viewList )
       { < transform > | parameterAssign | portInstance
       | < designator > | timing | property | comment | userData }
       ')'

instanceBackAnnotate ::= '(' 'instanceBackAnnotate'
       instanceRef
       { < designator > | timing | property | comment }
       ')'

instanceGroup ::= '(' 'instanceGroup'
       { instanceRef }
       ')'

instanceMap ::= '(' 'instanceMap'
       { instanceRef | instanceGroup | comment | userData }
       ')'

instanceNameDef ::=
       nameDef | array

instanceNameRef ::=
       nameRef | member

instanceRef ::= '(' 'instanceRef'
       instanceNameRef
       [ instanceRef | viewRef ]
       ')'

integer ::= '(' 'integer'
       { integerValue | integerDisplay | integer }
       ')'
```

integerDisplay ::= '(' 'integerDisplay'
        integerValue
        { display }
        ')'

integerValue ::=
        integerToken

interface ::= '(' 'interface'
        { port | portBundle | < symbol > | < protectionFrame >
        | < arrayRelatedInfo > | parameter | joined | mustJoin
        | weakJoined | permutable | timing | simulate | < designator >
        | property | comment | userData }
        ')'

interFigureGroupSpacing ::= '(' 'interFigureGroupSpacing'
        ruleNameDef
        figureGroupObject
        figureGroupObject
        (range | singleValueSet)
        { comment | userData }
        ')'

intersection ::= '(' 'intersection'
        (figureGroupRef | figureOp)
        { figureGroupRef | figureOp }
        ')'

intraFigureGroupSpacing ::= '(' 'intraFigureGroupSpacing'
        ruleNameDef
        figureGroupObject
        (range | singleValueSet)
        { comment | userData }
        ')'

inverse ::= '(' 'inverse'
        (figureGroupRef | figureOp)
        ')'

isolated ::= '(' 'isolated'
        ')'

joined ::= '(' 'joined'
        { portRef | portList | globalPortRef }
        ')'

justify ::= '(' 'justify'
    ('UPPERLEFT' | 'UPPERCENTER' | 'UPPERRIGHT' | 'CENTERLEFT'
    | 'CENTERCENTER' | 'CENTERRIGHT' | 'LOWERLEFT' | 'LOWERCENTER'
    | 'LOWERRIGHT')
    ')'

keywordDisplay ::= '(' 'keywordDisplay'
    keywordNameRef
    { display }
    ')'

keywordLevel ::= '(' 'keywordLevel'
    integerToken
    ')'

keywordMap ::= '(' 'keywordMap'
    keywordLevel
    { comment }
    ')'

keywordNameRef ::=
    identifier

layerNameDef ::=
    nameDef

lessThan ::= '(' 'lessThan'
    numberValue
    ')'

library ::= '(' 'library'
    libraryNameDef
    edifLevel
    technology
    { < status > | cell | comment | userData }
    ')'

libraryNameDef ::=
    nameDef

libraryNameRef ::=
    nameRef

libraryRef ::= '(' 'libraryRef'
    libraryNameRef
    ')'

```
listOfNets ::= '(' 'listOfNets'
        { net }
        ')'

listOfPorts ::= '(' 'listOfPorts'
        { port | portBundle }
        ')'

loadDelay ::= '(' 'loadDelay'
        ( miNoMaxValue | miNoMaxDisplay )
        ( miNoMaxValue | miNoMaxDisplay )
        ')'

logicAssign ::= '(' 'logicAssign'
        ( portNameRef | portRef )
        ( portRef | logicRef | table )
        [ delay | loadDelay ]
        ')'

logicInput ::= '(' 'logicInput'
        ( portNameRef | portRef | portList )
        logicWaveform
        ')'

logicList ::= '(' 'logicList'
        { logicNameRef | logicOneOf | ignore }
        ')'

logicMapInput ::= '(' 'logicMapInput'
        { logicRef }
        ')'

logicMapOutput ::= '(' 'logicMapOutput'
        { logicRef }
        ')'

logicNameDef ::=
        nameDef

logicNameRef ::=
        nameRef

logicOneOf ::= '(' 'logicOneOf'
        { logicNameRef | logicList }
        ')'
```

```
logicOutput ::= '(' 'logicOutput'
        ( portNameRef | portRef | portList )
        logicWaveform
        ')'

logicPort ::= '(' 'logicPort'
        portNameDef
        { property | comment | userData }
        ')'

logicRef ::= '(' 'logicRef'
        logicNameRef
        [ libraryRef ]
        ')'

logicValue ::= '(' 'logicValue'
        logicNameDef
        { < voltageMap > | < currentMap > | < booleanMap > | < compound >
        | < weak > | < strong > | < dominates > | < logicMapOutput >
        | < logicMapInput > | < isolated > | resolves | property | comment
        | userData }
        ')'

logicWaveform ::= '(' 'logicWaveform'
        { logicNameRef | logicList | logicOneOf | ignore }
        ')'

maintain ::= '(' 'maintain'
        ( portNameRef | portRef )
        [ delay | loadDelay ]
        ')'

match ::= '(' 'match'
        ( portNameRef | portRef | portList )
        ( logicNameRef | logicList | logicOneOf )
        ')'

member ::= '(' 'member'
        nameRef
        integerValue
        { integerValue }
        ')'

miNoMax ::= '(' 'miNoMax'
        { miNoMaxValue | miNoMaxDisplay | miNoMax }
        ')'
```

```
miNoMaxDisplay ::= '(' 'miNoMaxDisplay'
       miNoMaxValue
       { display }
       ')'

miNoMaxValue ::=
       numberValue | mnm

mnm ::= '(' 'mnm'
       ( numberValue | undefined | unconstrained )
       ( numberValue | undefined | unconstrained )
       ( numberValue | undefined | unconstrained )
       ')'

multipleValueSet ::= '(' 'multipleValueSet'
       { rangeVector }
       ')'

mustJoin ::= '(' 'mustJoin'
       { portRef | portList | weakJoined | joined }
       ')'

name ::= '(' 'name'
       identifier
       { display }
       ')'

nameDef ::=
       identifier | name | rename

nameRef ::=
       identifier | name

net ::= '(' 'net'
       netNameDef
       joined
       { < criticality > | netDelay | figure | net | instance
       | commentGraphics | property | comment | userData }
       ')'

netBackAnnotate ::= '(' 'netBackAnnotate'
       netRef
       { netDelay | < criticality > | property | comment }
       ')'
```

netBundle ::= '(' 'netBundle'
      netNameDef
      listOfNets
      { figure | commentGraphics | property | comment | userData }
      ')'

netDelay ::= '(' 'netDelay'
      derivation
      delay
      { transition | becomes }
      ')'

netGroup ::= '(' 'netGroup'
      { netNameRef | netRef }
      ')'

netMap ::= '(' 'netMap'
      { netRef | netGroup | comment | userData }
      ')'

netNameDef ::=
      nameDef | array

netNameRef ::=
      nameRef | member

netRef ::= '(' 'netRef'
      netNameRef
      [netRef | instanceRef | viewRef]
      ')'

noChange ::= '(' 'noChange'
      ')'

nonPermutable ::= '(' 'nonPermutable'
      { portRef | permutable }
      ')'

notAllowed ::= '(' 'notAllowed'
      ruleNameDef
      figureGroupObject
      { comment | userData }
      ')'

```
notchSpacing ::= '(' 'notchSpacing'
        ruleNameDef
        figureGroupObject
        ( range | singleValueSet )
        { comment | userData }
        ')'

number ::= '(' 'number'
        { numberValue | numberDisplay | number }
        ')'

numberDefinition ::= '(' 'numberDefinition'
        { scale | < gridMap > | comment }
        ')'

numberDisplay ::= '(' 'numberDisplay'
        numberValue
        { display }
        ')'

numberValue ::=
        scaledInteger

offPageConnector ::= '(' 'offPageConnector'
        portNameDef
        { < unused > | property | comment | userData }
        ')'

offsetEvent ::= '(' 'offsetEvent'
        event
        numberValue
        ')'

openShape ::= '(' 'openShape'
        curve
        { property }
        ')'

orientation ::= '(' 'orientation'
        ( 'R0' | 'R90' | 'R180' | 'R270' | 'MX' | 'MY' | 'MYR90' | 'MXR90' )
        ')'

origin ::= '(' 'origin'
        pointValue
        ')'
```

```
overhangDistance ::= '(' 'overhangDistance'
        ruleNameDef
        figureGroupObject
        figureGroupObject
        ( range | singleValueSet )
        { comment | userData }
        ')'

overlapDistance ::= '(' 'overlapDistance'
        ruleNameDef
        figureGroupObject
        figureGroupObject
        ( range | singleValueSet )
        { comment | userData }
        ')'

oversize ::= '(' 'oversize'
        integerValue
        ( figureGroupRef | figureOp )
        cornerType
        ')'

owner ::= '(' 'owner'
        stringToken
        ')'

page ::= '(' 'page'
        instanceNameDef
        { instance | net | netBundle | commentGraphics | portImplementation
        | < pageSize > | < boundingBox > | comment | userData }
        ')'

pageSize ::= '(' 'pageSize'
        rectangle
        ')'

parameter ::= '(' 'parameter'
        valueNameDef
        typedValue
        [ unit ]
        ')'

parameterAssign ::= '(' 'parameterAssign'
        valueNameRef
        typedValue
        ')'
```

parameterDisplay ::= '(' 'parameterDisplay'
    valueNameRef
    { display }
    ')'

path ::= '(' 'path'
    pointList
    { property }
    ')'

pathDelay ::= '(' 'pathDelay'
    delay
    { event }
    ')'

pathWidth ::= '(' 'pathWidth'
    integerValue
    ')'

permutable ::= '(' 'permutable'
    { portRef | permutable | nonPermutable }
    ')'

physicalDesignRule ::= '(' 'physicalDesignRule'
    { figureWidth | figureArea | rectangleSize | figurePerimeter
    | overlapDistance | overhangDistance | enclosureDistance
    | interFigureGroupSpacing | intraFigureGroupSpacing | notchSpacing
    | notAllowed | figureGroup | comment | userData }
    ')'

plug ::= '(' 'plug'
    { socketSet }
    ')'

point ::= '(' 'point'
    { pointValue | pointDisplay | point }
    ')'

pointDisplay ::= '(' 'pointDisplay'
    pointValue
    { display }
    ')'

pointList ::= '(' 'pointList'
    { pointValue }
    ')'

```
pointValue ::=
      pt

polygon ::= '(' 'polygon'
      pointList
      { property }
      ')'

port ::= '(' 'port'
      portNameDef
      { < direction > | < unused > | < designator > | < dcFaninLoad >
      | < dcFanoutLoad > | < dcMaxFanin > | < dcMaxFanout >
      | < acLoad > | portDelay | property | comment | userData }
      ')'

portBackAnnotate ::= '(' 'portBackAnnotate'
      portRef
      { < designator > | < dcFaninLoad > | < dcFanoutLoad >
      | < dcMaxFanin > | < dcMaxFanout > | < acLoad > | portDelay
      | property | comment }
      ')'

portBundle ::= '(' 'portBundle'
      portNameDef
      listOfPorts
      { property | comment | userData }
      ')'

portDelay ::= '(' 'portDelay'
      derivation
      ( delay | loadDelay )
      { transition | becomes }
      ')'

portGroup ::= '(' 'portGroup'
      { portNameRef | portRef }
      ')'

portImplementation ::= '(' 'portImplementation'
      ( portNameRef | portRef )
      { < connectLocation > | figure | instance | commentGraphics
      | propertyDisplay | keywordDisplay | property | comment | userData }
      ')'
```

portInstance ::= '(' 'portInstance'
  (portNameRef | portRef)
  { < unused > | < designator > | < dcFaninLoad > | < dcFanoutLoad >
  | < dcMaxFanin > | < dcMaxFanout > | < acLoad > | portDelay
  | property | comment | userData }
  ')'

portList ::= '(' 'portList'
  { portNameRef | portRef }
  ')'

portListAlias ::= '(' 'portListAlias'
  portNameDef
  portList
  ')'

portMap ::= '(' 'portMap'
  { portRef | portGroup | comment | userData }
  ')'

portNameDef ::=
  nameDef | array

portNameRef ::=
  nameRef | member

portRef ::= '(' 'portRef'
  portNameRef
  [portRef | instanceRef | viewRef]
  ')'

program ::= '(' 'program'
  stringToken
  [version]
  ')'

property ::= '(' 'property'
  propertyNameDef
  typedValue
  { < owner > | < unit > | property | comment }
  ')'

propertyDisplay ::= '(' 'propertyDisplay'
  propertyNameRef
  { display }
  ')'

propertyNameDef ::=
        nameDef

propertyNameRef ::=
        nameRef

protectionFrame ::= '(' 'protectionFrame'
        { portImplementation | figure | instance | commentGraphics
        | < boundingBox > | propertyDisplay | keywordDisplay
        | parameterDisplay | property | comment | userData }
        ')'

pt ::= '(' 'pt'
        integerValue
        integerValue
        ')'

range ::=
        atLeast | atMost | between | exactly | greaterThan | lessThan

rangeVector ::= '(' 'rangeVector'
        { range | singleValueSet }
        ')'

rectangle ::= '(' 'rectangle'
        pointValue
        pointValue
        { property }
        ')'

rectangleSize ::= '(' 'rectangleSize'
        ruleNameDef
        figureGroupObject
        (rangeVector | multipleValueSet)
        { comment | userData }
        ')'

rename ::= '(' 'rename'
        (identifier | name)
        (stringToken | stringDisplay)
        ')'

resolves ::= '(' 'resolves'
        { logicNameRef }
        ')'

ruleNameDef ::=
        nameDef

```
scale ::= '(' 'scale'
        numberValue
        numberValue
        unit
        ')'

scaledInteger ::=
        integerToken | e

scaleX ::= '(' 'scaleX'
        integerValue
        integerValue
        ')'

scaleY ::= '(' 'scaleY'
        integerValue
        integerValue
        ')'

section ::= '(' 'section'
        stringValue
        { stringValue | section | instance }
        ')'

shape ::= '(' 'shape'
        curve
        { property }
        ')'

simulate ::= '(' 'simulate'
        simulateNameDef
        { portListAlias | waveValue | apply | comment | userData }
        ')'

simulateNameDef ::=
        nameDef

simulationInfo ::= '(' 'simulationInfo'
        { logicValue | comment | userData }
        ')'

singleValueSet ::= '(' 'singleValueSet'
        { range }
        ')'
```

```
site ::= '(' 'site'
         viewRef
         [ transform ]
         ')'

socket ::= '(' 'socket'
           [ symmetry ]
           ')'

socketSet ::= '(' 'socketSet'
              symmetry
              { site }
              ')'

status ::= '(' 'status'
           { written | comment | userData }
           ')'

steady ::= '(' 'steady'
           ( portNameRef | portRef | portList )
           duration
           [ transition | becomes ]
           ')'

string ::= '(' 'string'
           { stringValue | stringDisplay | string }
           ')'

stringDisplay ::= '(' 'stringDisplay'
                  stringValue
                  { display }
                  ')'

stringValue ::=
           stringToken

strong ::= '(' 'strong'
           logicNameRef
           ')'

symbol ::= '(' 'symbol'
           { portImplementation | figure | annotate | instance | commentGraphics
           | < pageSize > | < boundingBox > | propertyDisplay
           | keywordDisplay | parameterDisplay | property | comment
           | userData }
           ')'
```

```
symmetry ::= '(' 'symmetry'
        { transform }
        ')'

table ::= '(' 'table'
        { entry | < tableDefault > }
        ')'

tableDefault ::= '(' 'tableDefault'
        ( logicRef | portRef | noChange | table )
        [ delay | loadDelay ]
        ')'

technology ::= '(' 'technology'
        numberDefinition
        { figureGroup | fabricate | < simulationInfo >
        | < physicalDesignRule > | comment | userData }
        ')'

textHeight ::= '(' 'textHeight'
        integerValue
        ')'

timeInterval ::= '(' 'timeInterval'
        ( event | offsetEvent )
        ( event | offsetEvent | duration )
        ')'

timeStamp ::= '(' 'timeStamp'
        integerToken
        integerToken
        integerToken
        integerToken
        integerToken
        integerToken
        ')'

timing ::= '(' 'timing'
        derivation
        { pathDelay | forbiddenEvent | comment | userData }
        ')'
```

transform ::= '(' 'transform'
        [scaleX]
        [scaleY]
        [delta]
        [orientation]
        [origin]
        ')'

transition ::= '(' 'transition'
        (logicNameRef | logicList | logicOneOf)
        (logicNameRef | logicList | logicOneOf)
        ')'

trigger ::= '(' 'trigger'
        { change | steady | initial }
        ')'

true ::= '(' 'true'
        ')'

typedValue ::=
        boolean | integer | miNoMax | number | point | string

unconstrained ::= '(' 'unconstrained'
        ')'

undefined ::= '(' 'undefined'
        ')'

union ::= '(' 'union'
        (figureGroupRef | figureOp)
        { figureGroupRef | figureOp }
        ')'

unit ::= '(' 'unit'
        ('ANGLE' | 'CAPACITANCE' | 'CONDUCTANCE' | 'CHARGE' | 'CURRENT'
        | 'DISTANCE' | 'ENERGY' | 'FLUX' | 'FREQUENCY' | 'INDUCTANCE' | 'MASS'
        | 'POWER' | 'RESISTANCE' | 'TEMPERATURE' | 'TIME' | 'VOLTAGE')
        ')'

unused ::= '(' 'unused'
        ')'

userData ::= '(' 'userData'
        identifier
        { integerToken | stringToken | identifier | form }
        ')'

valueNameDef ::=
          nameDef | array

valueNameRef ::=
          nameRef | member

version ::= '(' 'version'
          stringToken
          ')'

view ::= '(' 'view'
          viewNameDef
          viewType
          interface
          { < status > | < contents > | comment | property | userData }
          ')'

viewList ::= '(' 'viewList'
          { viewRef | viewList }
          ')'

viewMap ::= '(' 'viewMap'
          { portMap | portBackAnnotate | instanceMap | instanceBackAnnotate
          | netMap | netBackAnnotate | comment | userData }
          ')'

viewNameDef ::=
          nameDef

viewNameRef ::=
          nameRef

viewRef ::= '(' 'viewRef'
          viewNameRef
          [cellRef]
          ')'

viewType ::= '(' 'viewType'
          ('BEHAVIOR' | 'DOCUMENT' | 'GRAPHIC' | 'LOGICMODEL' | 'MASKLAYOUT'
          | 'NETLIST' | 'PCBLAYOUT' | 'SCHEMATIC' | 'STRANGER' | 'SYMBOLIC')
          ')'

visible ::= '(' 'visible'
          booleanValue
          ')'

```
voltageMap ::= '(' 'voltageMap'
        miNoMaxValue
        ')'

waveValue ::= '(' 'waveValue'
        logicNameDef
        numberValue
        logicWaveform
        ')'

weak ::= '(' 'weak'
        logicNameRef
        ')'

weakJoined ::= '(' 'weakJoined'
        { portRef | portList | joined }
        ')'

when ::= '(' 'when'
        trigger
        { after | follow | logicAssign | maintain | comment | userData }
        ')'

written ::= '(' 'written'
        timeStamp
        { < author > | < program > | < dataOrigin > | property | comment
        | userData }
        ')'
```

April 27, 1987

Level 1

```
abs ::= '(' 'abs'
        numberValue
        ')'

and ::= '(' 'and'
        { booleanValue }
        ')'

booleanValue ::=
        false | true | valueNameRef | and | or | not | xor | equal
        | increasing | strictlyIncreasing

ceiling ::= '(' 'ceiling'
        numberValue
        ')'

concat ::= '(' 'concat'
        { stringValue }
        ')'

constant ::= '(' 'constant'
        valueNameDef
        typedValue
        ')'

constraint ::= '(' 'constraint'
        booleanValue
        { property }
        ')'

contents ::= '(' 'contents'
        { instance | offPageConnector | figure | section | net
        | netBundle | page | commentGraphics | portImplementation | timing
        | simulate | when | follow | logicPort | < boundingBox >
        | constant | constraint | variable | comment | userData }
        ')'

divide ::= '(' 'divide'
        numberValue
        { numberValue }
        ')'
```

equal ::= '(' 'equal'
        numberValue
        { numberValue }
        ')'

fix ::= '(' 'fix'
        numberValue
        ')'

floor ::= '(' 'floor'
        numberValue
        ')'

increasing ::= '(' 'increasing'
        numberValue
        { numberValue }
        ')'

integerValue ::=
        integerToken | valueNameRef | floor | ceiling | fix
        | mod | xCoord | yCoord | abs | max | min | negate
        | product | subtract | sum

interface ::= '(' 'interface'
        { port | portBundle | < symbol > | < protectionFrame >
        | < arrayRelatedInfo > | parameter | joined | mustJoin
        | weakJoined | permutable | timing | simulate | < designator >
        | constant | constraint | variable | property | comment | userData }
        ')'

max ::= '(' 'max'
        numberValue
        { numberValue }
        ')'

min ::= '(' 'min'
        numberValue
        { numberValue }
        ')'

miNoMaxValue ::=
        numberValue | mnm

mod ::= '(' 'mod'
        integerValue
        integerValue
        ')'

negate ::= '(' 'negate'
      numberValue
      ')'

not ::= '(' 'not'
      booleanValue
      ')'

numberValue ::=
      scaledInteger | valueNameRef | floor | ceiling | fix
       | mod | xCoord | yCoord | divide | abs | max | min
       | negate | product | subtract | sum

or ::= '(' 'or'
      { booleanValue }
      ')'

page ::= '(' 'page'
      instanceNameDef
      { instance | net | netBundle | commentGraphics | portImplementation
      | < pageSize > | < boundingBox > | constant | constraint | variable
      comment | userData }
      ')'

pointSubtract ::= '(' 'pointSubtract'
      pointValue
      { pointValue }
      ')'

pointSum ::= '(' 'pointSum'
      { pointValue }
      ')'

pointValue ::=
      pt | valueNameRef | pointSum | pointSubtract

product ::= '(' 'product'
      { numberValue }
      ')'

strictlyIncreasing ::= '(' 'strictlyIncreasing'
      numberValue
      { numberValue }
      ')'

stringValue ::=
      stringToken | valueNameRef | concat

subtract ::= '(' 'subtract'
       numberValue
       { numberValue }
       ')'

sum ::= '(' 'sum'
       { numberValue }
       ')'

technology ::= '(' 'technology'
       numberDefinition
       { figureGroup | fabricate | < simulationInfo >
       | < physicalDesignRule > | constant | constraint | comment
       | userData }
       ')'

variable ::= '(' 'variable'
       valueNameDef
       typedValue
       ')'

xCoord ::= '(' 'xCoord'
       pointValue
       ')'

xor ::= '(' 'xor'
       { booleanValue }
       ')'

yCoord ::= '(' 'yCoord'
       pointValue
       ')'

Level 2

```
assign ::= '(' 'assign'
        valueNameRef
        typedValue
        ')'

block ::= '(' 'block'
        { statement }
        ')'

contents ::= '(' 'contents'
        { instance | offPageConnector | figure | section | net
        | netBundle | page | commentGraphics | portImplementation | timing
        | simulate | when | follow | logicPort | < boundingBox >
        | constant | constraint | variable | assign | block | if | iterate
        | while | comment | userData }
        ')'

else ::= '(' 'else'
        { statement }
        ')'

escape ::= '(' 'escape'
        ')'

if ::= '(' 'if'
        booleanValue
        then
        [ else ]
        ')'

interface ::= '(' 'interface'
        { port | portBundle | < symbol > | < protectionFrame >
        | < arrayRelatedInfo > | parameter | joined | mustJoin
        | weakJoined | permutable | timing | simulate | < designator >
        | constant | constraint | variable | assign | block | if
        | iterate | while | property | comment | userData }
        ')'

iterate ::= '(' 'iterate'
        { statement }
        ')'
```

page ::= '(' 'page'
      instanceNameDef
      { instance | net | netBundle | commentGraphics | portImplementation
      | < pageSize > | < boundingBox > | constant | constraint | variable
      | assign | block | if | iterate | while | comment | userData }
      ')'

statement ::=
      assign | block | comment | commentGraphics
      | constant | constraint | escape | figure | follow | if
      | instance | iterate | net | netBundle | logicPort
      | offPageConnector | portImplementation | property | section
      | simulate | timing | userData | variable | when | while

technology ::= '(' 'technology'
      numberDefinition
      { figureGroup | fabricate | < simulationInfo >
      | < physicalDesignRule > | constant | constraint | block | if
      | iterate | while | comment | userData }
      ')'

then ::= '(' 'then'
      { statement }
      ')'

while ::= '(' 'while'
      booleanValue
      { statement }
      ')'

Keyword Level 1

keywordAlias ::= '(' 'keywordAlias'
      keywordNameDef
      keywordNameRef
      ')'

keywordMap ::= '(' 'keywordMap'
      keywordLevel
      { keywordAlias | comment }
      ')'

keywordNameDef ::=
      identifier

Keyword Level 2

actual ::= '(' 'actual'
        formalNameRef
        ')'

build ::= '(' 'build'
        keywordNameRef
        { literal | actual | build | comment }
        ')'

formal ::= '(' 'formal'
        formalNameDef
        [optional]
        ')'

formalNameDef ::=
        identifier

formalNameRef ::=
        identifier

generate ::= '(' 'generate'
        { literal | actual | build | comment }
        ')'

keywordDefine ::= '(' 'keywordDefine'
        keywordNameDef
        keywordParameters
        generate
        ')'

keywordMap ::= '(' 'keywordMap'
        keywordLevel
        { keywordAlias | keywordDefine | comment }
        ')'

keywordParameters ::= '(' 'keywordParameters'
        { formal }
        ')'

literal ::= '(' 'literal'
        { integerToken | stringToken | identifier | form }
        ')'

optional ::= '(' 'optional'
      (literal | actual | build)
      ')'

Keyword Level 3

build ::= '(' 'build'
      keywordNameRef
      { literal | actual | build | forEach | comment }
      ')'

collector ::= '(' 'collector'
      ')'

forEach ::= '(' 'forEach'
      (formalNameRef | formalList)
      { build | actual | literal | forEach | comment }
      ')'

formal ::= '(' 'formal'
      formalNameDef
      [optional | collector]
      ')'

formalList ::= '(' 'formalList'
      { formalNameRef }
      ')'

generate ::= '(' 'generate'
      { literal | actual | build | forEach | comment }
      ')'

CHARACTER LIST

Code:	Char.:	Used in:	Comments
0	NUL		
1	SOH		
2	STX		
3	ETX		
4	EOT		
5	ENQ		
6	ACK		
7	BEL		bell
8	BS		back space
9	HT	*whiteSpace*	horizontal tab
10	LF	*whiteSpace*	line feed
11	VT		vertical tab
12	FF		form feed
13	CR	*whiteSpace*	carriage return
14	SO		
15	SI		
16	DLE		
17	DC1		
18	DC2		
19	DC3		
20	DC4		
21	NAK		
22	SYN		
23	ETB		
24	CAN		
25	EM		
26	SUB		
27	ESC		
28	FS		
29	GS		
30	RS		
31	US		

Code:	Char.:	Used in:	Comments
32	SPA	*whiteSpace*	blank space
33	'!'	*specialCharacter*	
34	'"'	*stringToken*	quote
35	'#'	*specialCharacter*	
36	'$'	*specialCharacter*	
37	'%'	*asciiCharacter*	percent
38	'&'	*identifier* and *specialCharacter*	ampersand
39	'''	*specialCharacter*	
40	'('	*form* and *specialCharacter*	left parenthesis
41	')'	*form* and *specialCharacter*	right parenthesis
42	'*'	*specialCharacter*	
43	'+'	*integerToken* and *specialCharacter*	plus sign
44	','	*specialCharacter*	
45	'−'	*integerToken* and *specialCharacter*	minus sign
46	'.'	*specialCharacter*	
47	'/'	*specialCharacter*	
48	'0'	*digit*	
49	'1'	*digit*	
50	'2'	*digit*	
51	'3'	*digit*	
52	'4'	*digit*	
53	'5'	*digit*	
54	'6'	*digit*	
55	'7'	*digit*	
56	'8'	*digit*	
57	'9'	*digit*	
58	':'	*specialCharacter*	
59	';'	*specialCharacter*	
60	'<'	*specialCharacter*	
61	'='	*specialCharacter*	
62	'>'	*specialCharacter*	
63	'?'	*specialCharacter*	

Code:	Char.:	Used in:	Comments
64	'@'	*specialCharacter*	
65	'A'	*alpha*	
66	'B'	*alpha*	
67	'C'	*alpha*	
68	'D'	*alpha*	
69	'E'	*alpha*	
70	'F'	*alpha*	
71	'G'	*alpha*	
72	'H'	*alpha*	
73	'I'	*alpha*	
74	'J'	*alpha*	
75	'K'	*alpha*	
76	'L'	*alpha*	
77	'M'	*alpha*	
78	'N'	*alpha*	
79	'O'	*alpha*	
80	'P'	*alpha*	
81	'Q'	*alpha*	
82	'R'	*alpha*	
83	'S'	*alpha*	
84	'T'	*alpha*	
85	'U'	*alpha*	
86	'V'	*alpha*	
87	'W'	*alpha*	
88	'X'	*alpha*	
89	'Y'	*alpha*	
90	'Z'	*alpha*	
91	'['	*specialCharacter*	
92	'\'	*specialCharacter*	
93	']'	*specialCharacter*	
94	'^'	*specialCharacter*	
95	'_'	*identifier* and *specialCharacter*	underscore

Code:	Char.:	Used in:	Comments
96	'`'	*specialCharacter*	
97	'a'	*alpha*	
98	'b'	*alpha*	
99	'c'	*alpha*	
100	'd'	*alpha*	
101	'e'	*alpha*	
102	'f'	*alpha*	
103	'g'	*alpha*	
104	'h'	*alpha*	
105	'i'	*alpha*	
106	'j'	*alpha*	
107	'k'	*alpha*	
108	'l'	*alpha*	
109	'm'	*alpha*	
110	'n'	*alpha*	
111	'o'	*alpha*	
112	'p'	*alpha*	
113	'q'	*alpha*	
114	'r'	*alpha*	
115	's'	*alpha*	
116	't'	*alpha*	
117	'u'	*alpha*	
118	'v'	*alpha*	
119	'w'	*alpha*	
120	'x'	*alpha*	
121	'y'	*alpha*	
122	'z'	*alpha*	
123	'{'	*specialCharacter*	
124	'|'	*specialCharacter*	
125	'}'	*specialCharacter*	
126	'~'	*specialCharacter*	
127	**DEL**		

SYMBOLIC CONSTANTS

Symbolic constant:	Used in:
ANGLE	*unit*
BEHAVIOR	*viewType*
CALCULATED	*derivation*
CAPACITANCE	*unit*
CENTERCENTER	*justify*
CENTERLEFT	*justify*
CENTERRIGHT	*justify*
CHARGE	*unit*
CONDUCTANCE	*unit*
CURRENT	*unit*
DISTANCE	*unit*
DOCUMENT	*viewType*
ENERGY	*unit*
EXTEND	*cornerType* and *endType*
FLUX	*unit*
FREQUENCY	*unit*
GENERIC	*cellType*
GRAPHIC	*viewType*
INDUCTANCE	*unit*
INOUT	*direction*
INPUT	*direction*
LOGICMODEL	*viewType*
LOWERCENTER	*justify*
LOWERLEFT	*justify*
LOWERRIGHT	*justify*
MASKLAYOUT	*viewType*
MASS	*unit*
MEASURED	*derivation*

Symbolic constant:	**Used in:**
MX	*orientation*
MXR90	*orientation*
MY	*orientation*
MYR90	*orientation*
NETLIST	*viewType*
OUTPUT	*direction*
PCBLAYOUT	*viewType*
POWER	*unit*
R0	*orientation*
R180	*orientation*
R270	*orientation*
R90	*orientation*
REQUIRED	*derivation*
RESISTANCE	*unit*
RIPPER	*cellType*
ROUND	*cornerType* and *endType*
SCHEMATIC	*viewType*
STRANGER	*viewType*
SYMBOLIC	*viewType*
TEMPERATURE	*unit*
TIE	*cellType*
TIME	*unit*
TRUNCATE	*cornerType* and *endType*
UPPERCENTER	*justify*
UPPERLEFT	*justify*
UPPERRIGHT	*justify*
VOLTAGE	*unit*

ViewType Matrices

The following chart lists the constructs that are directly permissible in the *interface* section for each EDIF *viewType*.

INTERFACE	BEHAVIOR	DOCUMENT	GRAPHIC	LOGICMODEL	MASKLAYOUT	NETLIST	PCBLAYOUT	SCHEMATIC	STRANGER	SYMBOLIC
port	*			*	*	*	*	*	*	*
portBundle	*			*	*	*	*	*	*	*
symbol			*				*		*	*
protectionFrame			*				*		*	*
arrayRelatedInfo			*				*		*	*
parameter	*	*	*	*	*	*	*	*	*	*
joined	*			*	*	*	*	*	*	*
mustJoin	*			*	*	*	*	*	*	*
weakJoined	*			*	*	*	*	*	*	*
permutable	*			*	*	*	*	*	*	*
timing	*			*	*	*	*	*	*	*
simulate	*			*	*	*	*	*	*	*
designator	*			*	*	*	*	*	*	*
constant	*	*	*	*	*	*	*	*	*	*
constraint	*	*	*	*	*	*	*	*	*	*
variable	*	*	*	*	*	*	*	*	*	*
assign	*	*	*	*	*	*	*	*	*	*
block	*	*	*	*	*	*	*	*	*	*
if	*	*	*	*	*	*	*	*	*	*
iterate	*	*	*	*	*	*	*	*	*	*
while	*	*	*	*	*	*	*	*	*	*
property	*	*	*	*	*	*	*	*	*	*
comment	*	*	*	*	*	*	*	*	*	*
userData	*	*	*	*	*	*	*	*	*	*

The following chart lists the constructs that are directly permissible in the *contents* section for each EDIF *viewType*.

CONTENTS	BEHAVIOR	DOCUMENT	GRAPHIC	LOGICMODEL	MASKLAYOUT	NETLIST	PCBLAYOUT	SCHEMATIC	STRANGER	SYMBOLIC	SCHEM PAGE
instance		*	*	*	*	*	*	*	*	*	
offPageconnector							*	*			
figure			*		*		*	*			
section		*						*			
net					*	*	*	*		*	*
netBundle					*	*	*	*		*	*
page							*	*			
commentGraphics			*		*		*	*	*		*
portImplementation					*		*	*	*		*
timing				*	*	*	*	*	*		
simulate				*	*	*	*	*	*		
when				*				*			
follow				*				*			
logicPort				*				*			
boundingBox			*		*		*	*		*	*
pageSize											*
constant	*	*	*	*	*	*	*	*	*	*	*
constraint	*	*	*	*	*	*	*	*	*	*	*
assign	*	*	*	*	*	*	*	*	*	*	*
block	*	*	*	*	*	*	*	*	*	*	*
if	*	*	*	*	*	*	*	*	*	*	*
iterate	*	*	*	*	*	*	*	*	*	*	*
variable	*	*	*	*	*	*	*	*	*	*	*
while	*	*	*	*	*	*	*	*	*	*	*
comment	*	*	*	*	*	*	*	*	*	*	*
userData	*	*	*	*	*	*	*	*	*	*	*